Managing vocational training systems

Copyright © International Labour Organization 2000
First published 2000

Publications of the International Labour Office enjoy copyright under Protocol 2 of the Universal Copyright Convention. Nevertheless, short excerpts from them may be reproduced without authorization, on condition that the source is indicated. For rights of reproduction or translation, application should be made to the Publications Bureau (Rights and Permissions), International Labour Office, CH-1211 Geneva 22, Switzerland. The International Labour Office welcomes such applications.

Libraries, institutions and other users registered in the United Kingdom with the Copyright Licensing Agency, 90 Tottenham Court Road, London W1P OLP (Fax: +44 207 631 5500), in the United States with the Copyright Clearance Center, 222 Rosewood Drive, Danvers, MA 01923 (Fax: +1 978 750 4470), or in other countries with associated Reproduction Rights Organizations, may make photocopies in accordance with the licences issued to them for this purpose.

Gasskov, Vladimir
Managing vocational training systems: A handbook for senior administrators
International Labour Office, Geneva, 2000
/management development guide/, /training management/, /vocational education/, /vocational training/, developed country/, /developing country/. 06.02
ISBN 92-2-110867-8

ILO Cataloguing in Publication Data

The designations employed in ILO publications, which are in conformity with United Nations practice, and the presentation of material therein do not imply the expression of any opinion whatsoever on the part of the International Labour Office concerning the legal status of any country, area or territory or of its authorities, or concerning the delimitation of its frontiers.

The responsibility for opinions expressed in signed articles, studies and other contributions rests solely with their authors, and publication does not constitute an endorsement by the Intenational Labour Office of the opinions expressed in them.

Reference to names of firms and commercial products and processes does not imply their endorsement by the International Labour Office, and any failure to mention a particular firm, commercial product or process is not a sign of disapproval.

ILO publications can be obtained through major booksellers or ILO local offices in many countries, or direct from ILO Publications, International Labour Office, CH-1211 Geneva 22, Switzerland. Catalogues or lists of new publications are available free of charge from the above address.

Printed and bound in Great Britain by Biddles Ltd, www.Biddles.co.uk

Managing vocational training systems

A handbook for senior administrators

Vladimir Gasskov

INTERNATIONAL LABOUR OFFICE • GENEVA

CONTENTS

Introduction 1

Module 1. Managing the government role in vocational education and training (VET) 5
  Unit 1. The government role in VET 5
    1.1 The function of VET 5
    1.2 Arguments for state involvement in VET 7
      1.2.1 The efficiency argument 7
      1.2.2 The equity argument 8
    1.3 Types of government intervention 9
    1.4 National VET policy framework 13

Module 2. The management concept of VET 19
  Unit 1. Manageability in training systems 19
    1.1 Principal types of VET systems and training modes 19
      1.1.1 Types of VET systems 19
      1.1.2 Training modes 21
    1.2 Manageability of VET systems and constraints 24
      1.2.1 The management concept 24
      1.2.2 Factors in manageability 26
      1.2.3 Manageability of VET systems 27
      1.2.4 Decision-making criteria 31
    1.3 Strategic management 32
      1.3.1 The strategic management concept 32
      1.3.2 Strategic management of national training systems 35
      1.3.3 Management strategies applied by national VET systems 37

Unit 2. Improving the accountability of VET administrators 38
    2.1 Management in government 38
        2.1.1 Policy making 38
        2.1.2 New concept of public management 40
    2.2 Improving the accountability of government departments
        and agencies 41
        2.2.1 Accountability of government departments 41
        2.2.2 Accountability of government agencies 42
        2.2.3 Monitoring management contracts 46
        2.2.4 New legal patterns of VET organizations 50

Unit 3. Developing internal management policies 53
    3.1 Effective management policies in VET systems 53
    3.2 Performance measurement as a management tool 60
        3.2.1 Performance indicators and criteria 60
        3.2.2 Performance indicators and criteria in the
            VET sector 61

Module 3. VET management and organizational structures 65
Unit 1. Configuration of organizational and management structures 65
    1.1 Management structures 65
    1.2 Organizational structures 66
        1.2.1 Organizational configuration 66
        1.2.2 Principles of organization design 67
        1.2.3 Types of organizational structure 69
    1.3 Trends in organizing VET systems 72
    1.4 Decentralizing vocational education and training 75
        1.4.1 Advantages and disadvantages 75
        1.4.2 Patterns of decentralization 76

Unit 2. Organizational structures in vocational education 78
    2.1 Government-administered vocational education 78
        2.1.1 Direct administration by central government 79
        2.1.2 Vocational education structures divided between
            government levels 81
        2.1.3 Delegation to lower-level government 81
        2.1.4 Full delegation to local level 84
    2.2 Administration through management intermediaries 86
    2.3 Delegating power to independent schools 86
    2.4 Guiding the dual training system 90

Unit 3. Organizational structures in labour market training 92
   3.1 Types of labour market training structure 92
   3.2 Government-administered training systems 93
      3.2.1 Direct administration of training by government departments 93
      3.2.2 Coordinating the training operations of various government ministries 95
      3.2.3 Programme-based organization structures 97
   3.3 Training administered by national training agencies 100
      3.3.1 Managing training as part of labour market administration 100
      3.3.2 Coordinating separate employment and training structures 100
      3.3.3 Incorporated labour market training agencies 105
   3.4. Administering training through management intermediaries 106

Unit 4. Industry-based organization of training 107
   4.1 Types of industry training organization 107
   4.2 Industry training agencies 108
   4.3 Sector-based management and training support structures . . 112
      4.3.1 Industry Training Organizations in the United Kingdom 113
      4.3.2 Sectoral Training Committees in Denmark 113
      4.3.3 Sectoral training bodies in the Netherlands 114

Unit 5. Management and organization of VET technical support 115
   5.1 Configuration of support structures 115
   5.2 Managing national VET qualifications 116
   5.3 Developing national curricula 121
   5.4 Managing skills assessment and certification in the United Kingdom 123
   5.5 Developing vocational instructors in the United Kingdom . . 126

Module 4. VET target setting and planning 127
Unit 1. VET planning concepts 127
   1.1 The need for planning 127
   1.2 Planning VET programmes 128
   1.3 Planning driven by individual demand 129
   1.4 Planning based on market signals 132
   1.5 Strategic national planning 133

Unit 2. Planning based on labour market signals 134
    2.1 Collecting labour market information 134
        2.1.1 Factors affecting planning 134
        2.1.2 Organization of labour market analysis 135
    2.2 Identifying labour market signals 138
        2.2.1 Industry signals 138
        2.2.2 Demand from young people 141
        2.2.3 Demand from special needs groups 143
    2.3 Reacting to labour market signals 143
    2.4 Planning cycle based on market signals 143

Unit 3. Strategic VET planning 144
    3.1 Systemic strategic planning 144
        3.1.1 Evaluating future demand for VET services 144
        3.1.2 Setting VET objectives 152
    3.2 Strategic planning involving rate-of-return analysis 155
    3.3 Strategic planning involving policy considerations and
        international comparisons 156
    3.4 Common problems in strategic planning 160
    3.5 An example of systemic strategic planning: Australia 164
        3.5.1 Strategic planning at federal level 164
        3.5.2 Victoria's State Training Profile 167
        3.5.3 Funding VET plans 176

Unit 4. Analytical instruments 177
    4.1 Measuring programme effectiveness 177
    4.2 Measuring programme cost-effectiveness 178
    4.3 Tracer studies 180
    4.4 Reverse tracer studies 184
    4.5 Rate-of-return analysis 185

Module 5. Financing VET 193
    Unit 1. Concept of VET financing 193
        1.1 Who should finance training? 193
            1.1.1 Government financing 193
            1.1.2 Private financing 196
        1.2 Public financing schemes 198
            1.2.1 Financing as a management technique 198
            1.2.2 Structure of financing schemes 199
            1.2.3 Allocation formulas for financing schools 200

    1.3 Funding problems and solutions 201
    1.4 Risks of decentralized and market-based financing
        schemes 203
    1.5 Requirements for VET funding mechanisms 204

Unit 2. Financing vocational education 205
    2.1 Types of funding scheme in vocational education 205
    2.2 Multi-level funding led by central government 206
    2.3 Multi-level funding led by local government 207
    2.4 Funding schemes that involve training taxes 208
    2.5 Funding schemes that involve market forces 209
        2.5.1 Performance-related financing 209
        2.5.2 Financing through vouchers 213
        2.5.3 Cost recovery 215
    2.6 Financing the dual system 217

Unit 3. Financing labour market training 218
    3.1 Types of funding scheme in labour market training 218
    3.2 Funding national training agencies 219
        3.2.1 Direct funding 219
        3.2.2 Contract funding 220
    3.3 Funding through national programmes 222
    3.4 Funding through management intermediaries 223
    3.5 Sources of funding in countries in transition 224
    3.6 Career development loans 225

Unit 4. Financing enterprise training 226
    4.1 Government-employer financing arrangements 226
    4.2 Sectoral training development funds 228
    4.3 Government incentives for enterprise training 231
    4.4 Revenue-generating levies 232
        4.4.1 Payroll taxes 232
        4.4.2 Taxes on the value of work contracts and exports 235
        4.4.3 Taxes on expatriates 236
    4.5 Levy-exemption schemes 236
    4.6 Levy-grant schemes 240
    4.7 Paid education and training leave 242
    4.8 Advantages and disadvantages of levy-based schemes 244

Module 6. Guiding training providers 247
   Unit 1. Government administration of training providers 247
       1.1 Direct administration versus independent operators 247
       1.2 Government guidance and control 248
          1.2.1 School management structure 248
          1.2.2 Management by rules 250
          1.2.3 Central curriculum 250
          1.2.4 Instructor development 250
          1.2.5 Planning, budgeting and financing 251
       1.3 Administering lycées in France 251
          1.3.1 The role of central government 251
          1.3.2 The role of the regions 252
          1.3.3 Self-management of lycées 253
          1.3.4 Staffing and financing 253
          1.3.5 GRETAs as a solution for lycée flexibility 255
          1.3.6 Steering institutions 256

   Unit 2. Providers as independent operators 258
       2.1 Self-management of providers 258
       2.2 Organizational structures and staffing 259
       2.3 Programming and planning 260
       2.4 Budgeting and financing 261
       2.5 Technical guidance and quality control 262
       2.6 Controlling and reporting 263
       2.7 Guiding British Colleges of Further Education 265
          2.7.1 Organizational and management structure
              of colleges 266
          2.7.2 Management of operations 268
          2.7.3 Monitoring systems 269

Bibliography 273

Tables

2.1	Training modes utilized by different VET systems	25
2.2	Traditional and new management concepts in public VET administration	41
3.1	Sector-based training agencies in Brazil (1995)	109
4.1	Local sectoral labour market information	141
4.2	Local labour market information on young people	142
4.3	Labour market information on the unemployed	144
4.4	Labour market signals and responses	146
4.5	FEFC requirements for strategic planning (3-year rolling programme)	149
4.6	Planning engineer/technician level programmes in Malaysia (1985-95)	159
4.7	Government training resource allocation to Victorian industries for 1995 and 1996	173
4.8	Achieving VET system development objectives	173
4.9	Training provision to industries for 1996–1997	175
4.10	Summary of tracer study findings	183
4.11	Comparative effectiveness of training programmes	183
4.12	Comparative public cost-effectiveness of training programmes	185
4.13	Comparative social rates of return by programme	190
5.1	Grants for school-teaching expenses in Denmark	211
6.1	Comparative features of guidance patterns	249
6.2	Evaluation indicators in French lycées	257

Figures

2.1	Principal VET systems	21
3.1	Functional organization of a ministerial training department	70
3.2	Product-based structure of a training agency	70
3.3	Client-focused structure of a training agency	70
3.4	Geographical organization of a national training agency	71
3.5	Programme organization of a ministerial training department	71
3.6	Structural components of the vocational education system	73
3.7	Patterns of decentralization in vocational education and training	77
3.8	Institution-based structure of vocational education (Republic of Korea, 1995)	79

3.9	Field-of-study-based organizational structure of education (Flemish Community of Belgium, 1996)	80
3.10	Vocational education structures divided between government levels (Brazil, 1995)	81
3.11	Vocational education structures at the local level (United States, 1996)	84
3.12	Coordination structure in the dual training system (Germany, 1995)	91
3.13	Integrated VET administration (Canada, 1996)	93
3.14	Government-administered training system (Pakistan, 1995)	95
3.15	Administration of the federal labour market training programme (United States, 1995).	98
3.16	Regional labour market administration (Denmark, 1995)	100
3.17	The National Labour Market Authority (Denmark, 1995)	101
3.18	Decentralized coordination of employment and training operations (France, 1996)	103
3.19	Organization of SENAI National Department (Brazil, 1995)	110
3.20	Organization of SENAI Regional Department (Brazil, 1995)	111
4.1	Labour market information needed for local VET planning	145
4.2	Stages of national strategic VET planning	151
4.3	Questionnaire: Survey of graduates of training institutions	181
4.4	Questionnaire for reverse tracer study	186

Boxes

1.1	Vocational qualification for all in the Netherlands	7
1.2	Features of perfect training markets	11
1.3	Government regulation of training markets in France	14
1.4	Examples of alternative policy options	15
1.5	Continuing training policy in France	17
2.1	Flexible training programmes in the Netherlands	30
2.2	Approaches for improving the manageability of VET systems	31
2.3	Contractual arrangements in New Zealand	43
2.4	Government-training agency management contract in Belgium	47
2.5	Management contracts in France	48
2.6	Monitoring agency contracts in the United Kingdom	49
2.7	VET organizations as companies limited by guarantee in the United Kingdom	51
2.8	Freedom of educational choice in the Netherlands	52
2.9	Planning and budgeting in the VET sector of New Zealand	56
2.10	Budgeting for results in the Government of the United States	57

3.1	Management of vocational education in the Republic of Korea	80
3.2	Organization of technical education in Brazil	82
3.3	Delegation of power in vocational education in France	83
3.4	Management of vocational education in the United States	85
3.5	Administering colleges through the United Kingdom Further Education Funding Council	87
3.6	Flat management structure in Denmark	88
3.7	Independent schools in the Netherlands	89
3.8	Administration and coordination in the German-type dual system	90
3.9	Integrated administration of education and training in Canada	93
3.10	The training system in Pakistan	96
3.11	The need to coordinate training programmes in the Philippines	97
3.12	Programme-based management structures in the United States	98
3.13	Labour market training agency in Denmark	102
3.14	Coordination of employment and training operations in France	103
3.15	Incorporated labour market training in Sweden	105
3.16	Administering labour market training through intermediate agencies in the United Kingdom	106
3.17	Central management of vocational education awards in France	117
3.18	Industry contributions to VET qualifications in Denmark	118
3.19	Competence-based national vocational qualifications in the United Kingdom	119
3.20	Curriculum development in vocational education in Denmark	122
4.1	VET programming in the United States	131
4.2	Organization of labour market analysis and VET planning in France	136
4.3	Organization of labour market analysis in the Netherlands	138
4.4	Strategic and operational VET planning in the United Kingdom	148
4.5	Client-driven management in Fox Valley Technical College, Wisconsin (United States)	150
4.6	Questions to ask in assessing future demand for VET services	153
4.7	Checklist for formulating objectives	156
4.8	Setting strategic objectives in Indonesia	157
4.9	Planning education and training programmes with long lead times in Malaysia	158
4.10	National VET targets in Denmark	160
4.11	National VET targets in the United Kingdom	161
4.12	Decentralized planning in Italy	163

5.1	Pros and cons of investment in training	195
5.2	Principal types of government-employer financing arrangement	227
5.3	Features of sectoral training development funds	229
5.4	Government incentives for enterprise training	232
5.5	Features of revenue-generating levies	234
5.6	Features of levy-exemption schemes	238
5.7	The levy-exemption scheme in France	238
5.8	Features of levy-grant mechanisms	241
5.9	Conclusions on levy-based funding schemes.	245

INTRODUCTION

Effective public management has been a key issue for many years in all countries. First, most public service systems operate in the difficult conditions of ever-growing demand and diminishing financial allocations. This means that they will probably never be able to meet the demand for services in full. Another important challenge is the demand for equitable access to services; due to insufficient government resources, this is always very difficult to achieve.

Second, public management aims at maximizing the social good, which is difficult to measure. As a result, criteria for assessing the performance of public services are sometimes vague and subjective. Establishing priorities for responding to needs is extremely difficult, and some administrators may turn to political rather than management criteria when deciding what services to deliver. By contrast, private sector managers' ultimate target is profit, which is easier to measure. Administering public services effectively is thought to be much more difficult than achieving managerial success in private enterprise (Kubr, 1982).

Third, in the era of the market, efficiency in public service systems is vital as they have to compete with private and other non-government providers of services which are often very flexible and efficient. This environment pressures public administrators to use professional management techniques and to develop and upgrade their managerial competence on a continuous basis.

Fourth, most approaches to improving public management require great freedom – the freedom of organizations to change and the freedom of managers to implement decisions. However, most public service systems and organizations, particularly in developing countries, do not possess an essential flexibility in setting targets, budgeting, staffing and allocating resources. This severely constrains public management's ability to respond with flexibility to the demand for services. The organizational structure of government can be one major reason for this. Highly centralized systems of administration in which most decisions are made at the top often leave little freedom to managers. Another reason might be a rigid national budgeting process, which provides little flexibility and few incentives for true management of the supply of services.

Fifth, public services, by their nature, need long-term strategic management. Public management derives its goals from broad economic and social environments and has to define and implement basic choices regarding the purpose of services, long-term goals and development aims, target sectors and populations, means of action and resource allocation.

Public vocational education and training (VET) systems as a public service currently face a multiplicity of challenges. These include weak industry demand for new labour and increased need for upgrading existing employees; increasing demand of young people for training; increasing need to manage the access of disadvantaged groups to training and income-generating activities. In many countries, public VET systems fail to utilize their capacity efficiently because of inadequate organization and management skills (see Middleton et al., 1993; United Nations Department for Development Support and Management Services, 1993). Many VET systems lack the necessary institutional capacity, infrastructure and training legislation, and they tend to create parallel and overcentralized organizational structures. VET administrators often lack the skills to determine priorities adequately, to apply strategic management concepts to national education and training systems and to use modern planning, budgeting and funding techniques.

Some industrialized countries have recently undergone essential management reforms, which have affected public services and VET systems. Major changes include the creation of administrative and advisory bodies involving the government, social partners and other parties; introduction of strategic VET planning on a national scale; increased accountability of administrators through the introduction of market mechanisms into public services and through the institution of performance measurement; delegation of management responsibilities and funds to service providers; and conversion of traditional government VET organizations into public companies. New efforts have been made to improve the equitable access of social groups to education, training and income-generating activities, as well as to manage the gap between training supply and labour market demand for VET services.

The goals of this book are (1) to provide state-of-the-art materials relating to the management and organization of public VET systems and (2) to suggest a framework for developing the management competence of senior administrators and to encourage them to move towards professional excellence.

This book targets senior administrators, defined as officials in charge of VET departments of national education and labour ministries, or related departments of lower-level government administration; managers of national training agencies and institutions providing technical support; and members of management and advisory councils and boards. The concept of professional public administration assumes that administrative or managerial issues should not be replaced by political issues. Senior public administrators should, therefore, be distinguished from government "top executives" who formulate and supervise the implementation of VET policies (Oman et al., 1992).

VET administrators increasingly need professional management skills as well as a technical understanding of their field. Although they are sometimes trained in general management, they may be unable to apply this knowledge fully. Just as the aims of public service can be distinguished from those of private enterprise, the management competence needed in public service systems differs from that required for managing private business. Moreover, management of education and training differs from management of, for instance, public health systems. Consequently, senior administrators should possess a general management qualification which reflects their ability to organize a national VET system; identify national education and training needs; establish strategic priorities and targets; participate in the government budgeting process; and develop internal management policies for staffing and related issues, planning and allocating resources, and measuring performance. This book seeks to address such needs.

The book is organized by areas of management function and consists of six modules with 19 learning units. It is assumed, therefore, that senior managers are able to identify their areas of weakness and will consult the relevant modules.

Module 1, "Managing the government role in VET", reviews approaches to deciding the degree of government involvement in the provision of vocational education and training. It also provides guidelines for a national training policy and suggests a means of developing national training markets.

Module 2, "The management concept of VET", reviews recent trends involving a division of responsibility between policy makers, advisors and administrators as well as the role of contractual management arrangements. It also describes the application of performance measurement to VET systems and reviews internal management policy on staffing, planning, budgeting and monitoring.

Module 3, "VET management and organizational structures", looks at patterns of organization and management structures in vocational education and labour market training systems. It also reviews industry training organizations which have recently emerged and become increasingly involved in standard setting, training needs analysis and planning, technical assistance to training schools and assessment of trainees.

Module 4, "VET target setting and planning", describes approaches to setting national objectives; it also addresses strategic and operational planning. It distinguishes between national strategic planning, planning based on labour market signals and individual demand-driven planning. It reviews the principles of setting objectives on a rate-of-return basis and the use of tracer studies in the comparative assessment of training programmes. It describes the techniques applied by training providers for interpreting labour market signals and responding to them through operational planning.

Module 5, "Financing VET", suggests a structure for funding mechanisms and reviews schemes for financing vocational education, labour market training and government-regulated financing of training in enterprises. It distinguishes between funding as budgeting and fund disbursement, financing as an investment, and financing as a management technique. This module describes the advantages and risks of performance-based funding schemes and decentralized schemes.

Module 6, "Guiding training providers", describes the framework that needs to be established by governments to ensure the productive operation of public VET providers. It summarizes government policies on decentralizing management and technical powers to providers; their guidance and supervision; resource allocation and incentives; local planning and the interaction between VET providers, local governments and the social partners. Two major alternatives are described: providers functioning in a centralized administration and funding paradigm and autonomous providers operating in the market within the national legal, planning and funding framework.

Each training module includes illustrations of VET management practice in both industrialized and developing countries. Current trends and best practice in the administration of national VET systems are reviewed in ten countries – Australia, Belgium, Brazil, Canada, Denmark, France, the Republic of Korea, Pakistan, the United Kingdom and the United States. The descriptions, which have been provided by national experts to whom we express our sincere gratitude, define the situation between 1995 and 1997. The variety of management practices reflects different national traditions of public administration and conditions in which VET systems operate. Where possible, the strengths and weaknesses of various practices and the conditions necessary for realizing possible benefits have been specified.

MANAGING THE GOVERNMENT ROLE IN VOCATIONAL EDUCATION AND TRAINING (VET)

Module 1

Unit 1. The government role in VET

Learning objectives

This unit is designed to provide a better knowledge of:

1. The broad mandate of vocational education and training
2. The efficiency and equity arguments for government involvement in VET
3. The role of private training markets and measures for promoting them
4. National VET policy frameworks

1.1 The function of VET

The mandate of vocational education and training is manifold. First, the vocational education and training system should deliver both foundation and specialist skills to private individuals, enabling them to find employment or launch their own business, to work productively and adapt to different technologies, tasks and conditions. The ultimate economic objective of education and training is improved personal and social productivity (the efficiency argument).

Second, skill training is often an instrument for structural change. Large numbers of workers may have to leave jobs that are no longer in demand, move to new jobs that will be created or learn to perform old jobs in new ways with different technologies. Training systems, along with other agencies that provide a safety net and assistance in finding new employment, play an important role in retraining redundant workers and help reduce the social cost of change. Education and training systems are also increasingly involved in continuing retraining and upgrading programmes for employees at all levels from engineer to semi-skilled worker.

Third, there is always a need to equalize the opportunities that people have to earn their living through the acquisition of skills (the equity argument). Education and training appear to be important factors in earning disparities. Although investing in training cannot, in itself, equalize income distribution, a more equal distribution of state-funded education and training tends to affect income distribution. However, equal opportunity and equal outcome are not synonymous, and the outcome of training may still remain unequal. One technique for estimating equality of training opportunities is to compare public spending on VET per individual in various groups, such as urban and rural residents, male and female workers, or younger and older workers (Carnoy, 1993).

Fourth, education and training can be viewed as a tool for achieving national economic and social objectives, such as encouraging regional development and supporting priority industrial sectors, expanding exports, attracting foreign investment and raising wages. This policy aims to change the economic and social situation through training, with other means used as leverage for this change.

Fifth, in addition to the economic benefits, education and training can generate massive social benefits (externalities), such as crime reduction, health improvement and better social cohesion, which accrue to society as a whole rather than to individuals. Although these broad externalities are very difficult to quantify, they are thought to be significant. In this regard, it is becoming increasingly common, particularly in wealthier countries, to see VET as an important avenue for the socialization of young people. The rationale is that young people need vocational knowledge and skills as well as general education. There is a recognized need for a minimum vocational qualification level for each adult, including early school leavers, to enable them to function adequately in the labour market and in society (see box 1.1). Under such policies, the government training offer may be linked to the job market only to a limited extent. Public VET provision becomes both student demand-driven and labour market-driven, which means that the government may offer courses to all who wish to enrol. Instead of training students for a certain number of available or forthcoming jobs, the government may set targets for a certain rate of participation.

Sixth, training can have benefits not directly connected with employment. Vocational skills and knowledge enable people to provide services, such as medical care or car and house maintenance, to their families and neighbours, and to reduce their expenditure on such services. Programmes offering such useful qualifications, which reduce the cost of living, are very popular in many countries. For many occupations, such as nursing or automobile maintenance, the number of trainees may considerably exceed the number of existing and forthcoming jobs with the relevant skill profile.

> **Box 1.1 Vocational qualification for all in the Netherlands**
>
> In the Netherlands, the starting-level *vocational qualification for all* is defined as a qualification equal to that of an entry-level skilled worker; practically, it is equivalent to the certificate of an initial apprenticeship course. This starting qualification level is seen as a basis for continuing training and is set for school leavers, job seekers and those already employed. The Government accepts full responsibility for training people up to 27 years of age.
>
> A 1992 regulation encouraged people in employment to obtain a qualification that would enable them to pursue continuing training. For employees, the cost of the starting training level is shared equally between the Government and the relevant industrial sector. For the unemployed with no starting qualification, training at this level is the responsibility of the Central Employment Office.
>
> Source: Hövels and Meijer, 1994.

1.2 Arguments for state involvement in VET

1.2.1 The efficiency argument

The so-called *efficiency argument* assumes that skill development will generate positive private and social benefits (externalities). Educated and trained workers produce and earn more than those who are less educated and trained. As a result, society benefits from higher national productivity and national income, while individuals enjoy a higher personal income.

While education and training benefit trainees, VET can also yield benefits for other members of society. The social benefits associated with skills acquisition are, however, speculative and extremely difficult to assess. Primary education has been found to produce more social benefits than other kinds of education and training, since it develops the basic knowledge necessary for work, socializes the population and reduces the risks associated with the behaviour of non-socialized individuals (Psacharopoulos and Woodhall, 1985). Abundant skills may induce a shift toward skill-intensive production on a national scale and determine the path of national economic growth. A high national skill level may also attract foreign investment and promote export manufacturing and growth. The measure of social benefits that can emerge from training depends on the country's internal and external conditions. For example, the rapid development of regional export markets may create the necessary conditions for social benefits and become an argument for increasing public investment in skills development.

However, in many countries national training investment is thought to be insufficient to support economic growth and social development. There are several reasons for low levels of investment. First, markets often fail to provide sufficient incentives for individuals and enterprises to allocate adequate funds to skill training. The major weakness in the link between market pressure and employer investment in training is that training usually affects productivity and profits very indirectly. Training is one of many factors involved in manufacturing; its capacity to produce tangible results cannot be separated from other inputs. The efficiency of training ultimately depends on management's ability to combine various inputs effectively. A correlation between firms' economic results and their training expenditure can be demonstrated because the competence of employees affects labour productivity, perhaps to the same extent as physical capital. However, the amount spent on training is not the only significant factor, and a greater training investment does not necessarily produce better results.

Second, both employers and employees may be reluctant to pay for training. Most employers prefer to operate in the short-term mode and attempt to save on labour costs as well as on physical capital. In addition, employers are often reluctant to invest in basic training because workers trained in a broad range of skills can easily move to other employers (poaching argument). Private individuals may not perceive incentives and thus may also under-invest in their own skill development.

Third, especially in the poorer countries, limited family savings and underdeveloped financial markets may reduce the opportunity to borrow privately for education and training. Furthermore, human capital is perishable and, unlike physical capital, does not provide collateral before or after it has accumulated.

Fourth, information on labour and training markets may be insufficient, outdated or misdirected, while individuals, enterprises and providers may be unable or unprepared to utilize this information for practical decisions. This failure may result in poor choices regarding investment in training. The degree of inefficiency may be high, since neither individuals nor enterprises can estimate future market demand for goods and services and the related demand for skills.

The above factors may reduce the level of market-provided VET below the socially desirable (optimal) level that would affect national productivity; they may also reduce the social and private benefits from education and training.

1.2.2 *The equity argument*

The so-called *equity argument* relates to government interest in maintaining equitable access to vocational education and training services. Although equal access to education and training contributes to reducing income disparities, the equalizing role of training in terms of income should not be overestimated. Vocational training has been found to produce far less impact on income differentials than general academic education. Moreover, it is the prior general education which determines access to training. An approach to equalization which is confined solely to training will therefore produce only marginal improvements in the situation of disadvantaged groups. Investment in training of disadvantaged groups, without sufficient investment in basic education, can make only a limited impact on their income (Psacharopoulos, 1994; Middleton et al., 1993).

Equity in access to VET has several dimensions, including equal access to financing, to information on labour- and training markets, and to training facilities. Individuals and enterprises cannot finance training on the same terms. Disparities in income and savings between individuals, on the one hand, and enterprises on the other hand, as well as the absence of national mechanisms to provide loans and grants, are among the financial issues relating to equity of access. Another point is that populations of some regions, particularly rural areas, often do not have equal access to training institutions and programmes, or information about them, in comparison with other, usually urban, populations. Equal access to information and to VET programmes is scarcely secured when the information function is left to market forces.

As market forces acting alone tend to under-provide skill training, thereby reducing individual and national productivity and the corresponding private and social benefits, the need arises for government involvement in VET. Governments commonly intervene to ensure the social and private benefits from education and training by maintaining national skill acquisition at a certain level. To achieve this aim, governments encourage private training markets and establish state VET systems which offer free programmes. National systems also attempt to contribute to equitable access to training, mainly by building institutions across the country and sometimes by providing funds and fellowships to groups which are under-represented in training and employment; they can also supply information on labour and training markets to consumers.

1.3 Types of government intervention

Training regulated by market forces. A great deal of education and training is successfully carried out by private training markets. In some countries, private individuals undertake vocational education and training on their own with relatively little funding from the government. This situation may be found, for instance, where VET programmes are not publicly funded and where, at the same time, the private benefits arising from training investments appear attractive. The individuals who finance their own education and training are assumed to aim at maximizing their lifelong income or satisfying educational needs. They may also be assumed to have the necessary information on labour and training markets as well as the ability to understand and compare benefits from educational investment with returns from other investments. If this process is efficient, then government authorities are not expected to answer the question of how many skilled people a country needs now or will need in the future. Nor is the government expected to intervene in the skills acquisition process except for training groups who are unable to pay for courses or have no access to training providers. Developed VET markets that provide services to those who demand and can afford them are much more cost-efficient than government provision. However, the number of countries in which developed training markets have been observed is limited.

The market demand for skills is usually expressed through enterprise demand for skilled labour, internal retraining and skill upgrading of employees. Additional demand for training is generated by private individuals and may be only very indirectly linked to the true market demand for skills. The market forces-based mechanism assumes that if there are too many skilled people in a certain occupation, their earnings will be too low to keep them in that occupation. If there are too few, the market will create incentives for importing skilled labour from other enterprises, regions or countries, or the work will have to be done by non-professionals. This model of skills acquisition may be appropriate in the conditions of perfect labour markets which are transparent and provide incentives to enterprises and individuals to invest in training. Such markets are expected to be highly flexible in order to adjust to fluctuations in demand for skilled labour (Richards and Amjad, 1994). The German-type dual training system is an example of such a self-regulated market model. In theory, the number of training places offered each year directly reflects employer demand for new workers. However, since this mechanism is based on enterprise demand alone and ignores student demand for VET, it regulates only part of the national training activities. Government intervention is required to accommdate excess demand for training through direct provision of school-based training as well as through fiscal incentives to expand employer training places.

As long as there are enough buyers and providers of training services the market may be considered as established. In perfect markets, the supply of services normally follows the development of demand. If all those who wanted training were able to buy as much as they need, the basis for the government role in VET would be eliminated. However, this never happens since certain groups of people either cannot afford to buy education and training or have no direct access to training providers or programmes. Moreover, the conditions of perfect training markets never materialize (see box 1.2). In many economies, training markets have not emerged or are weak.

> **Box 1.2 Features of perfect training markets**
>
> As with any other markets, perfect training markets require the following conditions:
>
> - enough buyers and sellers to create a basis for competition;
> - prices established through competition which reflect service scarcity and quality;
> - freedom for consumers to choose training providers;
> - availability to consumers of sufficient information on the quality and relevance of training offered by individual providers; and
> - access of all potential consumers to financing and training providers.

Training markets are driven by specific motives and are not concerned with many public VET functions, such as ensuring social equity and achieving national development targets. Private providers seek profit rather than equitable territorial distribution of training opportunities and, for whatever reason, may not wish to offer courses in some regions and skill areas. The need then arises for government involvement. Countries vary considerably in the level of development of their labour and training markets and in the role that their governments have and wish to play in VET.

Encouraging training markets. The major types of government intervention are:

- offering incentives to private training providers;
- introducing compulsory measures;
- encouraging market forces in public training; and
- improving information on labour and training markets.

In order to strengthen private training markets, governments can offer loans to enterprises enabling them to build training centres. Enterprise training expenditure can be deducted from tax bills, and their training programmes can be co-financed from public sources. Employer involvement in training can also be expanded through public campaigns and technical assistance to firms. Governments can generate positive publicity for employers who expand their involvement in human resources development. Individuals can also be offered government-backed training loans which would encourage them to take upgrading programmes. As long as there is sufficient demand for private services, the role of proprietary providers can be encouraged. Government subsidies offered to such providers may be a cost-efficient way to provide quality education and training, although the regulation of private training suppliers may need to be reviewed in order to ensure quality and maintain reasonable training fees. Governments, for instance, may set a ceiling on profit margins; this kind of regulation seems to work better than fixing the rate of fees. When profits accumulate but cannot be fully distributed between owners, there is a greater chance of maintaining expenditure on training equipment at a reasonably high level. (In the Philippines, the level of distributable profits is set at 10 per cent. From the residual profits, some private colleges use 60 per cent to increase wages and channel 30 per cent to training equipment.) When a ceiling is imposed on student fees, private institutions may find profit margins too low or they may offer under-financed and low quality programmes.

Training demand may also be generated through compulsory measures. Governments can introduce fiscal and administrative policies requiring enterprises to maintain socially desirable levels of training expenditure or provision. In practice, the appropriate level can be estimated on the basis of the training expenditure of successful firms. Of course, such estimates are sector-specific and reflect different technological levels and skill structures. Compulsory measures result in expanded private demand for training and in a stronger supply of services.

Another common way to encourage training activities involving private sources is to establish national employment funds and introduce unemployment insurance systems. Employment funds have been introduced in many countries and have raised funds from enterprises, employees and public budgets for retraining the unemployed and upgrading the workforce.

A variety of measures have been introduced to create quasi-markets in state education and training. In some countries, governments require public providers to earn part of their budgets by selling services in the market. Funds can also be allocated to end users rather than to public providers, enabling trainees to buy services from any provider. Direct public provision of VET may be replaced with contracting out programmes on the basis of bidding. As a result, the government becomes the major procurer and funder rather than the provider of training. Performance-based financing of training providers has also been implemented. State institutions may be encouraged to compete with private training providers on an equal footing.

The government can also help the various actors involved to make informed decisions regarding labour- and training markets. Information should be freely available to the public on wages and employment, wage regulations, minimum wage and wage ranges, links between wages and qualifications, labour mobility, and related topics. Employers may also need to be informed about the availability, quality and cost of training. Market information may be supplied to trainees, job-seekers and firms by labour exchanges and training authorities. Labour market observatories may be established for the purpose of collecting and interpreting data on local employment opportunities and training outcomes and for disseminating findings to all providers and users. Ideally, market observation would be built into the activities of training providers.

In some industrialized countries which have encouraged market forces in vocational training, it has become necessary to ensure that free provision of training services by the government, as well as subsidized training provided by public centres on a commercial basis, do not distort training markets. Low training fees charged by public centres may undercut private sector providers and push them out of the market. Such interventions also encourage the price of training to deviate from market rates (see box 1.3).

1.4 National VET policy framework

The creation of a public vocational education and training system is a major intervention. While state systems can be found in all countries, their incidence varies greatly depending on the form of government and its policies regarding the relative role of public and private institutions. In some countries, there is strong political resistance to utilizing market forces in the provision and financing of VET, as education and training are traditionally perceived as a desirable element of public services. In other countries, the major role of public VET is limited to the provision of pre-employment training for young people, while government support to industry is considered economically and politically unjustified. There are also countries where the training role of industry is equal to or greater than that of the government.

The established priorities for government involvement provide the basis for a national *VET policy framework* which includes a set of principal assumptions and decisions regarding the role of the state, as agreed by the government, the social partners, training professionals and other groups. Most policy decisions are confirmed and strengthened through national educational and labour legislation, while others may change from time to time. Government departments dealing with VET and national councils or boards usually lead the policy development process and balance the interests of all parties concerned. Strategic and operational decisions that are assigned to training administrators should be based on the national policy framework.

There are many other issues relating to the *administration* of the government system, including organization and decentralization, budgeting and financing, planning, monitoring and staffing. Although these issues relate to a VET system, they are not really *training* policy issues, but rather matters connected with the provision of public services, regardless of the area of service. A separation between VET policy and administration provides a basis for assigning

> **Box 1.3 Government regulation of training markets in France**
>
> In France, the courses directly purchased by consumers only account for 1.5 per cent of the total value of training services provided (worth FF35 billion a year). Most services are purchased by contractors on behalf of consumers. For instance, companies purchase on behalf of their employees and public authorities on behalf of job seekers.
>
> The Government has established the consumers' right to training. It regulates the training market by imposing obligations on training agencies regarding advertising, the provision of information on curricula and the organization of placement periods for trainees. Agencies are obliged to establish contracts with trainees in order to fix the rights and obligations of the parties. Training agencies which offer courses funded by the State are to be accredited. In addition to the legislation regarding consumers' rights, training operations are governed by regulations set out in the Labour Code, which fix the obligations of training firms in terms of accounting and management and their obligations vis-à-vis the trainees. More obligations are imposed on private organizations than on public ones.
>
> However, the recent involvement of public agencies in commercial training has revealed whole areas where these regulations are inadequate. The Vocational Training Federation (FFP) has issued a report highlighting the shortcomings. The FFP recently protested against the entrance of the national labour market training agency (AFPA) into the training market while maintaining the benefits it enjoys as a public agency. A lawsuit for unfair competition was filed by a private training organization, which reflects the need to clarify public training organizations' commercial operations. The involvement of state educational establishments in the training market raises similar issues. Public VET providers charge fees while their wage-related and operating costs are supported by the State. These public establishments, whose operations account for 20 per cent of the training market, provide courses at prices that no private organization could possibly afford. Such practices are criticized by private companies as unfair competition.
>
> Source: Willems, 1994.

responsibilities to the right bodies, administrative levels and professionals. Responsibility for management decisions on decentralizing training systems, measuring the performance of training institutions or strategic planning should be given to people who are qualified in both public administration and education/training. Governments are increasingly making an effort to develop professionals able to deal with these matters.

Module 1. Managing the government role in VET

The following may be considered as national VET policy issues:

- the system's mission (what is vocational education and training for?);
- citizens' rights to public VET services;
- governments' and social partners' responsibility for VET;
- distribution of public training services (eligibility and conditions);
- national priorities for training provision (including target groups) and system development;
- education and training avenues and teaching principles;
- types of provider and status of instructors;
- skill standards and vocational qualifications;
- national curriculum for training institutions and vocational curriculum for general education;
- skills assessment and certification; and
- national textbooks.

Each policy issue may have a number of options (Fluitman, 1997). Some of these are presented in box 1.4, which illustrates the structure of issues to be reflected in VET policy frameworks (the statements themselves are merely examples). See also box 1.5 for an example of a continuing training policy.

Box 1.4 Examples of alternative policy options

1. Assumptions about VET
- Skilled labour is a principal factor in productivity improvement.
- Vocational education and training alone cannot create jobs, but training programmes contribute to job creation.
- A certain level of vocational skill should be made compulsory for each individual.
- Private training markets are important and should be encouraged; the state training system should have a complementary role.
- Vocational participation should be encouraged as much as possible.
- VET should focus on developing total competence in people and preparing them for a lifetime of learning.
- VET avenues should not be a dead-end; they should provide access to higher education and continuing education and training.

2. Sample mission statements of state-run vocational education and training
- To provide job-related knowledge and skills enabling people to find employment;
- To provide vocational knowledge and skills to any citizen who desires them and to increase the proportion of people with formal vocational qualifications;

Box 1.4 (cont'd)

- To ensure a more equitable distribution of national income by providing access to skills for the most disadvantaged groups;
- To support national economic priorities by catering to the economic sectors which are expected to undergo rapid growth of output and employment;
- To contribute to the creation of employment and self-employment.

3. Citizens' rights to public training

- People of 27 years of age and below who are out of work and disadvantaged people of any age have the right to free public vocational training.
- Employees have the right to paid educational leave, the cost of which is co-financed by enterprise contributions and the government.
- The unemployed are entitled to retraining programmes financed from unemployment insurance funds.

4. Responsibility for VET

- Government is responsible for the national skill development process.
- The social partners have prime responsibility for identifying sectoral training needs; they should also participate in setting national priorities and targets for vocational training.
- Training workers is the employers' legal responsibility; the government should ensure that enterprise expenditure on training is maintained at a socially desirable level.

5. Distribution of public training services

- The VET system should provide equal and free access to all who are eligible. For others, public training courses can be provided for a fee.
- Public pre-employment training and upgrading should be provided as a priority for industry growth sectors.
- To ensure equitable access to VET, government training centres should be equally located in urban and rural areas.
- State-financed programmes can be provided by both public sector and private sector training providers (including firms in production), which should be accredited by the government.

The difference between these options is substantial. The choice will determine the system's strategic objectives and target groups, as well as resource allocation. VET policy statements may combine several of these and other options.

Box 1.5 Continuing training policy in France

Responsibilities for training

In accordance with the 1991 industry agreement, the social partners in France have accepted responsibility for continuing training as well as for participation in the creation of VET qualifications. The role of the State in continuing training is primarily to create a legal framework for the effective operation of the industry training system. Industry has a legal obligation to negotiate training at sectoral level and/or at company level. The social partners have accepted responsibility for administering the industry training system through joint management-union bodies, such as the joint national committee for vocational training, or the joint regional inter-industry employment board.

Employees' right to continuing training

Employees have the right to paid training leave. The State supervises implementation of this right through fiscal control of employers' contributions, while the social partners supervise respect for the right through management committees of training insurance funds.

Financing continuing training

Employees' paid training leave is to be financed by their employer. The State will support the employers' wish to have training expenditure treated as an intangible investment. The principle of co-financing continuing training through employee participation should be implemented. Greater account of employees' upgrading should be taken in contracts of employment; corresponding incentives should be established and negotiated between the employer and the employee who undertakes training.

Principles of training provision

The enterprise is recognized as a place for training.

Source: Willems, 1994.

THE MANAGEMENT CONCEPT OF VET

Module 2

Unit 1. Manageability in training systems

Learning objectives

This unit is designed to provide a better knowledge of:

1. Management concepts and activities
2. Strategic management
3. Principal types of VET systems and training modes
4. VET management
5. Constraints on the manageability of training systems

1.1 Principal types of VET systems and training modes

1.1.1 Types of VET systems

The identification of different types of VET systems is necessary for effective management. Vocational education and training systems are networks of organizations providing different training and educational services to different types of clientele and reporting to different national authorities. National training activities are usually split between state, regional and local government levels, as well as between several ministries; they target different groups of trainees; they are financed from separate accounts and administered separately. For the purposes of management and organization, three systems can be distinguished:

- vocational education;
- labour market training; and
- enterprise training.

The *vocational education* system offers long-term technical and technological instruction with a large proportion of academic subjects. It is normally offered in vocational and technical schools, colleges and universities. Institutions of higher education also conduct technician- and engineer-level upgrading programmes. Vocational education systems are usually administered by education ministries. In many countries, general education schools are increasingly involved in the provision of low-level (e.g. hair dressing and cooking) or entry-level (e.g. car maintenance and word processing) vocational programmes for young people.

The *labour market training* system provides a broad range of job-related programmes, including short entry-level courses for young people; short and long individualized courses for the unemployed; and upgrading courses for employees. In labour market training, the principal actors are usually national training agencies administered by labour ministries or specially established national labour market authorities. The agencies usually have a broad network of decentralized offices and training centres which coordinate their activities with local employment offices.

Enterprise training covers instruction provided or financed by employers for their employees, either voluntarily or in compliance with regulations. Countries differ in the role that governments play in guiding enterprise training. Three types of interaction between government and enterprise can be identified: unregulated; self-regulated; and government-regulated.

In some countries, governments refrain from intervening and employers are free to decide whether to train employees and for how long. Enterprises can provide training themselves or contract out to specialist training providers. Employees can also buy training courses themselves and request subsidies from their employers. Industrial sectors may institute industry training organizations that will ensure coordination and cooperation, provide advice and participate in the development of national vocational qualifications and other national consultations. However, where the initiative lies entirely with individual enterprises, there are no formal industry training systems.

In other countries, especially the industrialized countries of Europe, self-regulated training alternatives have emerged. In these countries, enterprise training is strongly influenced by national and/or sectoral labour agreements which provide a certain legal and organizational framework for training. Industrial sectors establish joint management-labour bodies, technical committees, apprenticeship committees and the like, which supervise the agreement, coordinate sectoral training activities, administer sectoral training funds, represent industry training interests before the government and become involved in training needs analysis and even in planning government training courses for the industry.

Module 2. The management concept of VET

In still other countries, government regulations fix a minimum compulsory level of enterprise training expenditure or a minimum percentage of employees to be trained each year. As a result, enterprise training activities are strongly regulated and supervised by government. In some countries (mostly in Latin America), large industry training agencies have emerged that are funded from training levies paid by enterprises and self-administered by industry bodies. However, their activities are also legally regulated and audited by governments.

Different forms of the systems described above have emerged in industrialized countries, but in many developing countries entry-level vocational programmes prevail. They are provided by general education schools (administered by education ministries) and by training centres (administered by labour ministries). These countries often lack institutions offering training for the unemployed or skill upgrading for employees, and their enterprise training systems are often undeveloped.

1.1.2 Training modes

Training modes used in VET systems reflect the *organization* of skills acquisition. The prevailing types of training mode affect the management and organization structure of training (see figure 2.1).

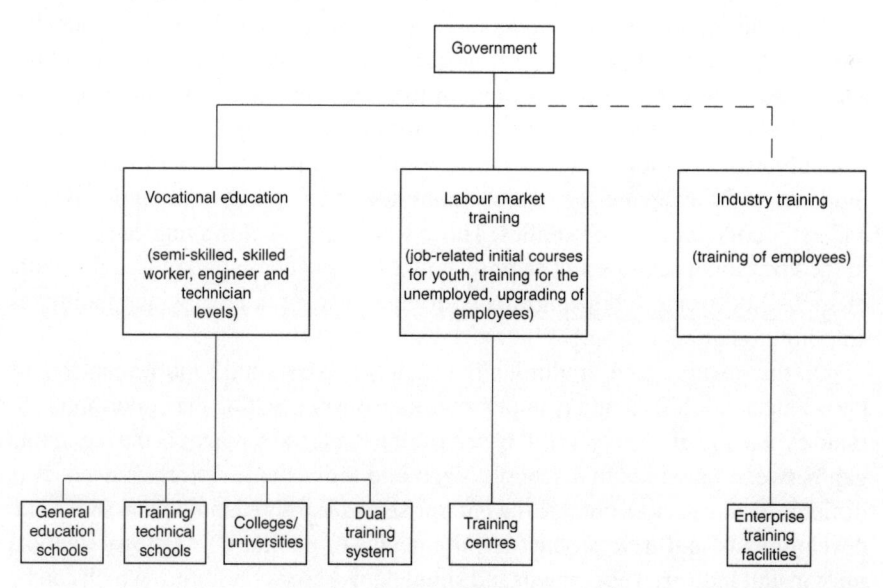

Figure 2.1 Principal VET systems

```
                            Government
        ┌───────────────────────┼───────────────────────┐
        │                       │                       │
  Vocational education     Labour market            Industry training
                            training
  (semi-skilled, skilled   (job-related initial      (training of employees)
   worker, engineer and    courses for youth,
   technician              training for the
   levels)                 unemployed, upgrading of
                           employees)

┌──────┬──────┬──────┬──────┐    │                       │
General Training/ Colleges/ Dual   Training              Enterprise
education technical universities training centres        training
schools  schools            system                        facilities
```

Five major training modes can be identified (de Moura Castro and Alfthan, 1992; King, 1994):

- general secondary schools and comprehensive high schools (sometimes known as the American system);
- vocational school-based learning (often referred to as the French system);
- dual training (often referred to as the German system);
- training centre-based instruction; and
- enterprise-based training (often referred to as the Japanese system).

Comprehensive high schools keep all students, regardless of their aptitude, in the same school until the end of secondary level and add vocational programmes to the academic curriculum. Their learning paths, however, are differentiated. In the United States, for instance, more than 60 per cent of high school students enrol in at least one vocational programme. In other comprehensive high school traditions, vocational training is more structured. For instance, in Sweden the upper secondary classes provide 13 broad vocational options in addition to general education and technician options. In some countries, such as the United Kingdom, the number of schools offering vocational programmes leading to a qualification is increasing. However, there is a tendency to postpone vocational training to the post-secondary stage, with the task being increasingly taken over by specialist organizations – community colleges. Nevertheless, the idea of using regular schools for vocational training has its rationale and many countries continue to apply this training mode.

The tradition of separate *vocational and technical schools* running alongside the general secondary schools is widespread in Europe, Latin America and the Middle East. Separate types of training usually commence after nine years of general education. Pupils are normally sorted out during the lower classes of compulsory education in accordance with their aptitude and school marks. Students with academic inclinations continue in the purely academic streams and enter colleges and universities. Those who prefer skill training can continue in the vocational schools and acquire a qualification corresponding to the years of study. Vocational schools normally offer an academic level which facilitates entering higher education.

On the positive side, traditionally organized vocational schools can impart knowledge and skills to many pupils simultaneously, creating the opportunity for rapid expansion of society's skill base. Among the disadvantages is the inevitable gap between the skills that schools teach and those that enterprises need. It is difficult for instructors outside the enterprise to keep abreast of recent industrial developments and new product requirements. In addition, vocational schools must install industrial equipment and simulate working conditions, which can be much more expensive than the cost of similar learning on the job. The cost of modern equipment alone excludes certain trades from vocational schools.

The *dual system* combines structured training in firms with part-time instruction in state vocational schools. Dual systems are usually administered by education ministries and counted (as in Germany) as part of vocational education. This mode can successfully offer a good combination of theory and practice. Training is organized around employer-trainee contracts, which specify the occupation, duration of training and probation period, amount and method of remuneration, etc. Trainee remuneration is determined in accordance with collective labour agreements. Training contracts are registered by the competent body. The training process and examinations are formal, strictly regulated and supervised; this provides for relatively high uniformity of the training process and high training quality.

The major feature of the dual system is that it is essentially *employer-led*. The number of training places offered is defined by employers themselves and reflects their need for new workers. It is not decided by the government, nor does it simply reflect student demand for training. In the countries which apply the dual system on a national scale, the content and timing of training are centrally determined. Training normally lasts two to four years and ends with a craft certificate. Training under the dual system is co-financed by employers, governments and the trainees themselves.

The dual training system is not entirely publicly administered, although its relative strength derives in part from government policies. It is also far from being a private-sector training system, as the school-based component is directed and funded by the government. The fact that the dual system is "owned" simultaneously by the government, employers and unions creates the case for joint governance, which results in the need for national and sectoral joint management and technical committees, as well as in a significant amount of time for consultation and decision making.

Centre-based instruction is often carried out by national labour market training agencies. Such agencies have a mandate to provide job-related training to young people and to retrain the unemployed for available jobs. Courses typically take place in training centres which, unlike schools, do not offer academic subjects. Training agencies vary depending on their legal status, sources of funding and the way they communicate with enterprises and individuals.

A critical issue in labour market training is that it caters directly to current and expected skill shortages. Training should, therefore, be extremely flexible in terms of programming and resources. On the other hand, the clientele (young people and the unemployed) should be handled on an individual basis. This means that a high level of management flexibility and decentralization is required for the system, as well as individual centres, to operate effectively.

Enterprise-based training entails the initial and continuing in-service training offered by enterprises to their employees throughout their working life. In most cases it consists of practical, on-the-job instruction. Irrespective of the educational level of employees, enterprise training normally adds little to their formal educational profile. In a few countries, enterprise-based training has become the predominant training avenue. Since this kind of training is often entirely financed by employers, it can only take hold in conditions of low labour mobility and smoothly developing markets. It is strongly influenced by the social and cultural tradition of employment and training. Moreover, the role of enterprises as providers of practical instruction to individual trainees, at the request of public authorities, is increasing. Some countries, such as the United Kingdom, where practical training contracted to enterprises is applied on a relatively broad scale, do not have labour market training agencies.

The training modes employed by different VET systems are reviewed in table 2.1. Clearly, the vocational education systems have their specific targets and differ strongly from labour market and enterprise training, which both aim to provide job-related skills.

Table 2.1 Training modes utilized by different VET systems

	VET systems		
	Vocational education	Labour market training	Enterprise training
Training modes	• Vocational programmes offered by comprehensive high schools and general education schools; • Separate training and technical schools, colleges and universities; • Dual training as a combination of structured school-based and enterprise-based instruction.	• Job-related training courses offered by public training centres and private training providers including firms in production.	• Initial and continuing in-service training for employees; • Courses provided by colleges and training centres at the request of enterprises.

1.2 Manageability of VET systems and constraints

1.2.1 The management concept

Management activities aim at changing or maintaining a system's status in order to achieve certain goals. Management is, therefore, *goal-oriented*. Goals must specify the outputs to be achieved by the system within a certain period of time. In order to set objectives the following questions need to be answered: What kind of outputs are going to be produced? What are the priorities regarding these outputs? To be effective, managers must be able to set and meet goals. Otherwise, administrators are unable to determine priorities for resource allocation and justify expenditures, to distinguish more important activities from less important, and to evaluate progress. Detailed programmes can be devised and budgets made to achieve individual targets.

Management decisions are channelled through management and organizational structures. *Management structures* reflect the division of power between levels and individuals who are assigned management and supervisory duties; *organizational structures* reflect the division of technical tasks between parts of the system (e.g. departments and units of the same institution) on the one hand, and between individuals, on the other hand. Management and organizational structures also establish patterns for coordination between the actors involved. These patterns are fixed in organizational rules and procedures that employees and clients are expected to respect.

Routine management activities consist of *decisions* regarding programming and planning, budgeting and financing, staffing, and monitoring the performance of units and individuals. Consequently, effective management requires policies on planning, human resources, resource allocation, wages and other matters. These may be fixed in written rules and procedures.

Management is an ongoing process and its activities are not necessarily sequential. They overlap in time and are linked to each other. Because of uncertainties arising mostly from markets, analysis of the demand for services, adjustment of plans and operations as well as targets and outputs, all need to be continuous. The system has to adjust its goals, strategies, structures and internal management policies to respond to important changes. If one of these is skipped, the management process becomes disordered. If, for instance, the market demand for services has not been examined, the targets and plans become virtually meaningless. If targets have not been set, financial and human resources may be allocated and spent on activities which are not a priority, resulting in low cost-efficiency of operations. In addition, without set goals, it becomes very difficult to evaluate progress and correct systems and operations.

1.2.2 Factors in manageability

The *manageability* of a system is determined by its capacity to use and change its structures, technologies and resources in order to achieve targets. For a variety of reasons, the manageability of every system is limited; the level of manageability is inversely proportional to the existing constraints. Managers should understand these constraints and attempt to reduce them. They should not be held responsible for the management of events which are beyond their control.

The most obvious limits (that are known) are those imposed by the system's legal status and freedom, the competence and commitment of staff, and the availability of resources. More complex constraints are imposed by management and technological *uncertainties* that are less known. Management and organizational systems are, to a certain extent, determined by the nature of the technologies upon which they are based (Woodward, 1958). Management of production, educational services and research differ because their basic technologies essentially differ. Technological uncertainty and the types of technological interaction are fundamental organizational characteristics (Thompson, 1967; Galbraith, 1976).

Technological uncertainty assumes that inputs into the system and internal conditions of operation are difficult to control. High technological uncertainty constrains manageability and, as a result, systems require flexibility and sound management skills in order to operate. Under conditions of high uncertainty, decentralized management structures appear to be more effective. By contrast, very routine technologies usually need simple management and organizational structures which use standard rules and procedures instead of day-to-day management decisions. In practical terms, a reasonable decentralization of power depends on the competence of lower-level managers to make decisions. The possible adverse effects on systems, clients and the environment which may result from a bad decision are important considerations. For instance, nuclear technologies are known for both high technological uncertainty and vast disruptive potential which may be unleashed by poor decisions. Therefore, the organizations dealing with these technologies normally prefer centralized management structures.

Technological interaction concerns the way inputs enter the system and are processed to become outputs. The combination of inputs being processed and the technology applied requires certain patterns of interaction between managers, technicians and workers. These need to be taken into account in organizational and management structures. Some technologies are less "interactive" than others and require less sophisticated organizational structures and fewer written rules and procedures.

Another important factor is *management uncertainty*. In contrast to technological uncertainty, which is internal to the system, management uncertainty may arise from the system's broad environment and internal management practices. For instance, management uncertainty may result if a system's environment is not sufficiently transparent; if sources of funds and other resources are vulnerable; if demand for services is changing rapidly, thereby affecting the managers' ability to set and review targets; or if the government bodies that supervise the system set unclear guidelines, or internal management has established unclear structures and procedures.

1.2.3 Manageability of VET systems

Technological uncertainties. Vocational education and training uses specific technologies for developing and transforming people's knowledge, skills and, sometimes, motivation. These technologies affect the management and organization of training systems and limit their capacity to react promptly to changes in labour- and training markets. They also constrain the extent to which decision makers can manipulate training systems through resource allocation.

First, theoretical learning and practical mastering of skills require a certain amount of time, which may not be reduced. In addition, education and training technologies may apply written curricula and use sophisticated equipment which cannot be adjusted rapidly enough to respond to the labour market demand for skills. Therefore, the education and training process has a certain technological inertia which constrains flexibility of training provision and should be taken into account in management decisions.

Second, different education and training modes affect organizational structures and determine manageability. For instance, school-based vocational education provides knowledge which is less sector- and enterprise-specific and is less subject to change during the programme. As a result, managers of vocational education systems and institutions face fewer uncertainties resulting from change in the labour markets. The providers' organizational structures may have weaker links with enterprises. Since this factor reduces the level of uncertainty, management systems in public vocational education tend to be more centralized. By contrast, labour market training programmes, if they are to be effective, need to be immediately aware of changing job structures and labour market demand for occupations and often have to provide tailor-made courses to industry sectors, enterprises and job-seekers. A management system that delegates tasks such as fund disbursement, recruiting and dismissal of teaching staff to the training centres themselves may be the only viable solution. Dual training assumes strong cooperation and co-funding between government agencies at all levels and industry. As a result, management of this type of VET is based on negotiation and coordination rather than on direct administration. This is reflected in its organizational arrangements (see Module 3, Unit 2, 2.4).

Third, education and training outputs are *intangible* knowledge and skills. Therefore, the performance of a system is difficult to assess until trainees sit for the final examinations and graduates find jobs. However, in contrast to management competence, for example, vocational skills lend themselves more readily to being structured and presented in skill standards, curricula, testing and examination requirements. Consequently, they can be made more observable, demonstrated and tested, which reduces uncertainty in the teaching process.

Fourth, in contrast to production technologies, education and training aim at developing and changing human behaviour, which is always more uncertain than a machine-based process. Trainees' interests, values and attitudes may change rapidly during and after the course, which affects their commitment to training and to the acquired occupation. This in turn can decrease the performance of VET programmes. Individual commitment to training is currently a critical area of study.

Management uncertainties determined by the system's environment. State training systems, as any other public service, operate in a specific environment comprising government authorities, including bodies responsible for policy making and controlling, setting national economic and social targets, budgeting, financing and supervising, as well as local government authorities (co-funding, supervising and service delivery), national advisory bodies (policy analysis and development), job placement structures, the general education system (provider of basic education to trainees), trainees and industry, among others.

All the above entities have competing claims and send conflicting messages to vocational training administrators. The key elements of the VET system environment must be identified; responsibility for establishing and mainlining relations with the important external organizations must be assigned to appropriate units of the system. This involves learning how to satisfy their requirements, expectations and evaluation criteria.

Internal VET management structures and policies, if not clearly developed, may also become a source of serious uncertainty. This handbook aims at helping senior administrators to handle the external environment and reduce internal management uncertainty.

Management uncertainties determined by the demand for services. Education and training services cater to labour and training markets, which introduce significant management uncertainty into VET systems. The major goal of vocational training is to develop skills which will be recognized by labour markets; qualified candidates should be produced to match labour market demand. Labour and training markets, as any other markets, are very difficult to predict. Since the demand for skills tends to fluctuate, it is always difficult to establish operational targets in terms of the number of skilled workers to be produced/upgraded in various occupational qualifications at a certain point in time. Therefore, training managers may need to formulate major operational targets simply to maintain a certain equilibrium in the market with regard to observed skill shortages, rather than to fix the exact proportions of skills to be developed. The need to reflect on movement in the labour market and to follow or even foresee change is one of the most difficult challenges to the manageability of VET institutions. This indicates the need for flexible and decentralized systems.

System flexibility. The ability of a system to respond adequately and rapidly to the demand for services and other changes reflects its flexibility. Achieving high flexibility is an important part of the manager's job. National training systems are large organizations which, in terms of management, are significantly different from smaller ones. Unlike an individual organization, a large system comprises many organizations which exchange services. It therefore operates as a network. It is assumed that all parts of a large system have to move in the same direction on the basis of established policies, objectives and strategies and, through this concerted action, they are expected to produce specified outputs. However, in large systems this is very difficult to achieve. Large systems may be *more wasteful* than smaller ones due to a lack of integration and coordination. In addition, they have a particularly *strong inertia*; making them change direction or start moving towards certain goals may require considerable time and powerful management techniques such as decentralization, incorporation of individual organizations, measurement of organizational performance and outputs, rewards and sanctions. This should be taken into account in the planning and change process.

Individual training institutions are often known for their limited ability to keep up with firms' changing skill requirements because too much time is needed before changes are recognized and incorporated into courses and even more time is needed before students complete the new curriculum. Several ways to improve flexibility have been developed.

First, improved manageability (a system's capacity to use and change its structures, technologies and resources) will create a basis for high flexibility. For instance, considerable budgetary freedom, allowing institutions to manage a proportion of funds at their own discretion in order to recruit part-time staff and develop new courses, can result in a more flexible response to market demand.

Second, strengthening the autonomy of training providers through decentralization or incorporation in conjunction with the involvement of industry managers improves flexibility. The traditional management style, based on authority, control and a chain of command, although useful in many ways, may not be effective in managing large systems, since commands, when they reach operational level, are often belated, misinterpreted or unclear to operators. Administrators have to set guidelines for autonomous training providers that clearly announce their targets, define conditions of financing and allocate the resources needed for meeting targets, set evaluation criteria and link them to the corresponding rewards and sanctions (see also Module 6).

To achieve greater flexibility, the following key responsibilities must be assigned to training providers: (a) *in planning and programming*: developing an institutional strategy, setting targets and offering or closing VET programmes; (b) *in budgeting and financing*: managing resources of various kinds, modifying pay systems, retaining earned income, spending revenues and borrowing funds from banks; (c) *in staffing*: hiring and firing full-time and contract staff and signing employment contracts with the staff; (d) *in technical support*: conducting labour market and job analysis, accessing central and local sources of information on employment opportunities, industry development, enterprise working conditions and pay; developing curricula and teaching materials; introducing flexible curricula, training technologies, timetabling and organization (see box 2.1).

Third, systems with more financial, material and intellectual resources have a better capacity for flexibility. For instance, the availability of well-developed training programmes and staff with superior technical and supervisory skills will speed up adjustment to market changes. Therefore, the capability of VET managers to develop resources, particularly human resources, becomes very important.

Box 2.1 Flexible training programmes in the Netherlands

Flexibility of training provision has expanded in the Netherlands. Most programmes now consist of modules that students can follow at their own pace. A set of completed modules can be exchanged for a vocational diploma.

Opportunities for flexible programme entry/exit, as well as for shifting students between educational and vocational courses, were created. This has increased flexibility and helped reduce drop-out rates.

Practical training has been introduced into the vocational curriculum, leading to new arrangements between training providers and enterprises.

Source: Hövels and Meijer, 1994.

Module 2. The management concept of VET

> **Box 2.2 Approaches for improving the manageability of VET systems**
>
> Numerous steps can be taken to make training systems more manageable, including:
>
> - Reducing uncertainty about training throughput by extended periods of vocational guidance and counselling. This will result in fewer drop-outs and better graduate commitment to the acquired occupation;
> - Coping with uncertainty about labour market requirements for skills through: (a) involving industry-based bodies and the social partners in the development of national skill standards, VET qualifications and examination requirements; (b) delegating responsibility for identifying skill shortages and planning job-related training to industry bodies; (c) strengthening the foundation knowledge component of training programmes and delaying occupational specialization until later in the training programme; (d) increasing the role of enterprises in job-related training; and (e) involving the social partners and local authorities in the administration, control and assessment of VET providers;
> - Improving the measurement of trainees' practical achievements through a competence-based assessment of skills which will be carried out more reliably by independent bodies;
> - Improving the technical and management competence of the staff through developing professional VET administrators capable of applying strategic management and other modern techniques;
> - Improving staff manageability through reducing the proportion of staff operating within civil service rules; and
> - Developing training providers' capacity for self-management, promoting their autonomy through decentralization or incorporation, setting clear national guidelines for their operations, introducing performance measurement, and linking funding to outputs and outcomes.

Approaches to improve manageability through reducing uncertainty and other measures are summarized in box 2.2.

1.2.4 Decision-making criteria

Professional management is based on the organization of knowledge and the competent application of this knowledge to problems featuring considerable complexity and uncertainty. Managers, therefore, always seek clear criteria to which they can refer in making decisions. VET managers, too, need certain

Managing vocational training systems

criteria against which management and organization decisions can be weighed. In the countries where governments apply mature management systems, guidance for operational decisions is mainly provided by a national training policy statement, strategic development plans and national targets, funding mechanisms and institutional performance measurement criteria.

In the countries where management systems have not yet matured, management decisions can be based on broad criteria incorporating universal assumptions and values. Decisions should, at least, ensure that:

- vocational participation is increasing (or is not decreasing);
- graduate employment prospects and earnings improve;
- employer and trainee demand for training is satisfied;
- trainees graduate at higher certificate levels;
- training unit costs diminish or remain stable; and
- the access of low-income and other disadvantaged groups to training is increasing (or, at least, not decreasing).

These criteria are general and they apply to any country. However, the priorities set for the above criteria will differ from country to country and may change over time even for one country. A list of decision-making criteria needs, therefore, to be established and checked whenever important decisions are to be made. On the basis of these criteria, proposals need to be assessed and their advantages and disadvantages compared. As many countries face budget constraints, the decision-making process should refer to the costs involved. Decisions promising greater outputs for high-priority criteria and at lower cost should have a better chance of acceptance.

1.3 Strategic management

1.3.1 The strategic management concept

Most public service systems tend to react to immediate problems. Consequently, public administrators often operate without clearly defined targets, so that outputs become casual and may not correspond to priorities. In some countries, governments direct their public services towards operational targets which are numerical and deal with one- or two-year periods. However, the need to think about the future is apparent. Many public service problems remain the same the year after year and a new management approach is required in order to develop the long-term perspective (Chandler, 1962; Kubr, 1982; United Nations Department for Development Support and Management Services, 1993).

In contrast to short-term operational management, *strategic management* is the process of defining and implementing long-term choices regarding objectives, structures and internal policies. This concept assumes, for instance, that the economic environment, social and demographic conditions for employment and training may change in the future. This change may affect the system's objectives and the way it operates. The strategic management concept is highly relevant to public service systems; where governments think about the future, the concept is successfully applied (see Module 4).

Strategic management involves four basic elements:

- defining the system's mission;
- making an internal audit;
- strategic planning; and
- formulating and implementing a strategy.

All systems and organizations exist for a purpose, which is reflected in their *"mission"* (Adams, 1986). A mission statement gives a certain understanding of what the system is for. In governments, a statement of the public service mission is usually developed by senior executives at minister level. Most policy decisions may be confirmed and strengthened through national legislation; others may change from time to time. When the environment in which the system functions changes, the mission statement may need to be reviewed.

Internal *audits* aim at recognizing a system's environmental circumstances, qualities and resources. An audit of the system can be implemented along the following lines:

- environment and major clientele;
- links with government and other organizations (suppliers, support institutions, etc.);
- opportunities and threats to its operations that occur in the environment;
- resources and capabilities, including people, know-how, capital, equipment and funds;
- management and organization system, including structure, style, planning and budgeting, incentives, performance monitoring and assessment; and
- main achievements and failures, critical strengths and weaknesses in responding to expectations and demand for services from government and clients.

The system's audit should conclude on the need to overcome perceived weaknesses and develop strengths in order to achieve strategic objectives and accomplish the mission.

Strategic planning refers to setting objectives and programming to achieve these objectives. It is based on forecasts and makes risk-taking decisions based on the best possible knowledge of the future. However, as forecasts are only informed guesses, they are inevitably imperfect. Strategic planning should arrive at decisions which take account of various limitations such as a shortage of public funds in comparison with needs for service or possible changes in government priorities. Strategic planning involves the following steps:

- forecasting developments in the relevant economic, educational, demographic, legal, political and socio-cultural areas and noting trends;
- estimating the future need and demand for services, which will be determined by the above;
- understanding the need to change the system's mission statement and future mission – its "vision" – as a result of foreseen developments and identified trends;
- establishing priorities for services and drafting strategic delivery objectives and activities;
- drawing conclusions, on the basis of the audit, regarding capacity to meet strategic *delivery objectives*. It may, for instance, be concluded that the system does not have the capacity to implement the planned change and that the strategic delivery targets need to be lowered. As a result the system's *development objectives* are set, and become part of the strategy.

A management *strategy* determines how the system's current and future mission is to be accomplished. It reconciles what a system *should* do to accomplish its mission and achieve strategic objectives (what its managers want it to do), what it *might* do in terms of opportunities, and what it *can* do in terms of strengths. Since there are many ways of achieving the same result, setting objectives and developing strategies to achieve them are different things. However, the same strategies can simultaneously contribute to different objectives. Each strategy may represent a combination of decisions regarding the system's organization, legal changes, resource allocation, monitoring and related matters. For instance, equity in public VET services may be improved through: (a) building more institutions or (b) providing education programmes for badly educated and poor people, enabling them to compete for training places. These strategies would require different organizational and management arrangements, resource allocations, programming and time to accomplish. Each strategy will therefore have its own cost and feasibility.

When several strategies leading to the same objective are available, they can be *evaluated* on the basis of the following criteria:

- political feasibility – a judgement on the extent to which the strategy will correspond to established national policies;
- projected effectiveness – a determination of the extent to which the strategy will contribute to the corresponding strategic objective(s); and
- budgeted cost of resources needed to implement the strategy.

Strategies can be compared through building a matrix where alternatives are presented in rows and the above criteria in columns; the intersections are rank ordered or given different weights.

1.3.2 Strategic management of national training systems

National training systems, like many other public services, lend themselves to strategic management since they operate with huge public funds and target large populations. In addition, VET activities are appropriate for long-term planning as education and training is a continuous process and as skilled and highly skilled occupational qualifications often require long lead times. Since government training activities provide substantial inputs to national economic and social development, strategic management would have an effect on the economies of scale.

Strategic management will involve the steps outlined above. First, the main purpose of the training system must be formulated in a mission statement. This may entail a review of the whole national training policy framework.

Second, an in-depth audit of the system will have to be conducted. This will make it possible to identify its strengths and weaknesses and to specify the need for reorientation and improvement.

Third, strategic planning should start with building *development scenarios* with the aim of assessing future needs for skills. These needs, and thus the priorities for meeting them, will be determined by many factors, including economic development trends and population trends. Some elements of national economic, social and demographic development are fairly reliable, others are merely speculative. Although the people who may require training can easily be predicted for a period of ten years, little is certain about the future trends of industry growth and demand for training. It is therefore difficult to make precise predictions. However, for shorter periods of, say, three to four years, more certain predictions of trends in industry can be made. The fact that wholly accurate predictions cannot be made should not discourage thinking about future training demand and the national system's future mission.

On the basis of the identified political, economic, social and other trends, a new vision of the national VET system in the future must be formulated. This may result in changes in the national policy framework. For instance, the government may decide that in ten years it would be able to change its mission statement from the "provision of job-related knowledge and skills to people, enabling them to find employment" to the "provision of vocational knowledge and skills to any citizen who wishes it". It is clear that the latter mission is much broader than the former, would require more funds and a more developed delivery system, and is linked to the human resource development concept rather than to the employment concept.

Strategic planning should result in setting objectives and establishing corresponding activities. On the basis of identified future needs and within a formulated mission statement, *strategic delivery objectives* need to be devised which will determine the priority target groups and the outputs and outcomes that the VET system is going to produce in the future.

The national training system needs to be directed and upgraded on a continuous basis, regardless of the predicted need for individual qualifications. The technical support structure should be maintained even if the demand for courses is not known. VET administrators should aim at improving the quality of services, reducing unit costs and increasing flexibility. In order to respond to future market demand properly, the curricula, training standards and assessment techniques need to be updated continuously, and qualified instructors have to be made available. As a result, the system's *development objectives* need to be geared to achieving the above delivery objectives.

Fourth, specific plans for achieving strategic objectives need to be formulated. They should specify the way in which the financial, human and other inputs to the VET system will be combined. They may also envisage changes in management and organizational structures, as well as in internal management policies such as planning policy, staffing policy and remuneration policy. Programmes must be developed for implementation of each objective. The cost of activities covered by programmes should be calculated; this will provide a basis for budgeting and resource allocation decisions. On the basis of strategic objectives, operational targets may be established for each individual provider if necessary. Implementation needs to be monitored through an assessment of the system's performance and outputs.

Management is an unending process. The environment in which previous VET strategies have been developed may change over time. New industrial sectors may emerge, new markets may open, different training objectives and policies may be adopted, attitudes towards training may change, and new training technologies may be developed. Training administrators must respond to these changes by adapting strategic objectives, reviewing management strategies and regularly identifying critical areas or client groups which will need attention.

1.3.3 Management strategies applied by national VET systems

The management of national vocational training systems aims at productivity, responsiveness, flexibility, efficiency, continuous improvement in the quality of training and increased access to training. Some strategies used in national systems for meeting these requirements are listed below.

Greater *responsiveness* and *flexibility of delivery* can be achieved through the:

- diversification of training providers through involving private-sector institutions and enterprises, which can be accredited in order to deliver publicly funded courses;
- development of a variety of delivery methods and training paths in order to serve groups with various needs;
- decentralization of responsibility for programming and resource management to providers, while retaining central control over setting national priorities and targets, financing and quality control; as long as training providers are able to make decisions independently, government authorities should intervene as little as possible;
- regular review of graduates' labour market performance and client satisfaction;
- award of vocational certificates which recognize trainees'/employees' prior learning and experience; and
- involvement of industry and other client groups in identification of training needs and priorities, planning of training delivery, resource allocation, and management and technical decisions.

Increased *efficiency* may be achieved through the:

- introduction of assessment indicators and financing mechanisms focusing on training outputs and outcomes, rather than on activities;
- development of capital investment mechanisms which take account of the providers' use of existing facilities and equipment;
- introduction of competitive tenders for public VET funds; and
- encouragement of public providers to partly commercialize their services.

Enhanced *training quality* may be achieved through the:

- introduction of national competency-based skills standards, examination and assessment requirements, and curricula;
- creation of standing industry bodies that participate in the development and maintenance of skill standards and examination requirements;

- establishment of quality-related targets and other performance indicators as part of performance agreements between providers and government authorities; and
- promotion of best practice and benchmarking for quality delivery (see below).

Improved *training access* may be developed by means of the:

- identification of groups under-represented in training;
- recognition of their specific needs; and
- targeting of these groups through planning, resource allocation, delivery and reporting.

Unit 2. Improving the accountability of VET administrators

Learning objectives

This unit is designed to provide a better knowledge of:

1. The concept of management in government
2. Differences between policy making and operational levels of government administration
3. Approaches to improving public managers' accountability

2.1 Management in government

2.1.1 Policy making

Democratic governance has classically been understood as the mission of public administration. Public administration has to pursue simultaneously the goals of democratic accountability, public policy effectiveness and operating efficiency. This concept accepts administrative inefficiencies in order to attain the goal of accountability (Perry, 1989). The strengths of VET administration tend to be: policy development, regulation, prevention of discrimination in schools, equity management in support of education and training for students from low-income families, and stability in public services. By contrast, the weaknesses of public services are thought to include: an inability to perform complex tasks, take risks, adjust rapidly to change or be innovative; failure to be highly productive or cost-efficient; and a tendency to deliver services that become obsolete quickly (Osborne and Gaebler, 1992).

Management in government should be distinguished from policy making, which involves policy analysis and development. Policy analysis aims at identifying and comparing policy options (United Nations Department for Development Support and Management Services, 1993). It starts with identification of the need for a government service or problems with existing services. The identification of public need can be surprisingly difficult. The formulation process will be affected by the values and goals of policy analysts and decision makers. In addition, political leaders always insist on controlling the way in which the public need for a government service is defined and interpreted.

Policy development aims at influencing alternative future trends. Alternative policy options need to be studied and scenarios predicting future developments must be produced. Policy options are evaluated on the basis of certain criteria set by the government, including public reaction to each policy option. The option perceived as most suitable by the government will be approved as a policy decision.

Policy decisions should, as a rule, aim at establishing and reviewing the *mission statement* of a government service (see Unit 1 of this Module). In other words, policy decisions should answer the questions "What is this government service for?" and "To what public needs should this government service respond?" A policy decision should also set priority areas and target groups for the government service that will provide an input to budgeting and resource allocation. In countries where governments apply strategic management of services, policy decisions involve setting national strategic objectives to be achieved by the corresponding public service system. Strategic objectives will specify measurable outcomes and outputs to be achieved through provision of government services to the targeted population in a particular period. Corresponding policies may also be outlined with the aim of further developing the public service system, as well as achieving the outputs and outcomes. The policies which offer the greatest outputs within the resource allocation will be approved. Matching services to changing public needs remains an important role of policy makers.

A developed national policy becomes the basis for managing service operations. From this point, a responsible administrator (who has been involved as an advisor in policy formulation) begins to implement practical policy decisions. Depending on the type of structure adopted, management functions are assigned to various levels of the public administration. Two main levels of public administration may be involved in managing services: chief of the ministerial department or office and chief of the government service agency. In some countries, ministers are involved in the direct administration of services.

2.1.2 New concept of public management

There are several reasons why a government cannot be run like a business and why public administrators should not be expected to operate at the same level of efficiency as private sector managers (Commonwealth Roundtable, 1992). From the above priorities of public administration (e.g. democratic governance and public accountability) stem barriers to effective performance and constraints on management practice. Among the barriers are the following:

- Centralized decision making reduces the responsibility of lower-level administrators.
- Public administrators are very dependent on politicians; this militates against clearly defined objectives and hence against effectiveness.
- Public administrators are rarely paid or promoted on a performance basis (Kakabadse et al., 1988).

A new management concept aiming at improved effectiveness and accountability of government services and at strengthening the managerial culture of public administrators has recently been tested in OECD countries (OECD, 1994b). This concept emphasizes the *accountability* of government departments and agencies for their performance and outputs. The purpose of public accountability is responsiveness.

The new concept divides responsibility and accountability for public service administration between three groups: (1) ministers are exclusively involved in policy formulation and monitoring of implementation; (2) chiefs of government departments are responsible for providing policy advice to ministers; and (3) chief executives of national service agencies administer public service operations. Service contracts determine the operational role of these actors. This arrangement also introduces mechanisms based on market forces, such as the commercialization of services and use of contractual services, into the provision of public services in order to incorporate elements of efficiency into government. As a result, the measurement of public service activities focuses on outcomes. Explicit, quantifiable objectives and performance indicators are established to serve as the basis of management decisions.

The countries which have adopted this concept, including Australia, New Zealand and the United Kingdom (Elliott, 1996), have made considerable changes in organizational and management arrangements for the provision of public services. The implications of such a concept of public administration to the government training system are presented in table 2.2.

Table 2.2 Traditional and new management concepts in public VET administration

Traditional concept of VET administration	New concept of public VET administration
• Governance by short-term targets	• Governance by strategic objectives
• Government-owned and government department-administered training institutions	• Government-funded but autonomously operated training agencies/providers
• Little use of market forces in the provision of services	• Use of market-type mechanisms and competition between public and private training providers
• Hierarchical organization of tasks and responsibilities	• Service contracts between the government and public training agencies
• Resource allocation per institution	• Resource allocation per delivery target to be achieved in line with strategic objectives
• Little assessment of providers' performance	• Measurement of training providers' outputs against the targets with management decisions made on this basis
• Delivery of courses responding to student demand	• Delivery of courses on the basis of identified national priorities and target groups
• Government training providers as spending units	• Government training providers as spending and earning units

2.2 Improving the accountability of government departments and agencies

2.2.1 Accountability of government departments

Recent organizational reforms in some industrialized countries have made a clear distinction between the outcomes and outputs of government services, separate policy advice (provided by government departments), and operational service delivery (implemented by government agencies). Government departments are accountable for policy advice expressed in terms of the services' expected impact on society (*outcomes*). The government decides which outcomes it wants to achieve and selects the appropriate outputs (targets). In contrast to outcomes, *outputs* are defined as the government agency's direct results and may be expressed in terms of quantity, quality, cost and time of delivery. Operational agencies become responsible for the outputs, rather than outcomes, while government departments become responsible for advice and are no longer in charge of operations (OECD, 1994a, 1994b).

Analysis of performance outputs provides a basis for measuring the degree to which quantitative operational targets have been achieved. However, it can only partly determine whether the outcomes are essential and positive. Outcomes can be identified when the following questions have been answered: "What has been the effect of VET operations on customers?" "What unexpected effects have appeared?"

The reforms described above resulted in the introduction of *contractual arrangements* between ministers who have become responsible for outcomes, on the one hand, and heads of government departments, on the other hand, who have become responsible for policy advice. Policy advice is provided to the responsible minister, the cabinet and its committees. Another type of contractual arrangement has emerged between ministers and the chief executives of government agencies responsible for operations. The reason for separating policy advice from service delivery was primarily to improve the management of both government departments and service agencies. One objective was to ensure that policy advice would not be dominated by operational concerns. Another concern was the high cost of policy advice *purchased* by the government (see box 2.3).

2.2.2 Accountability of government agencies

Contractual arrangements can also be established between ministers and national service agencies. In such contracts, the responsibilities of each party are clarified and their formal commitments are established. The ultimate aim of introducing management contracts is to generate productivity gains through better resource utilization and improved accountability. Delegating management autonomy means that training agencies and providers may be required to deliver more services for lower budget allocations. Resources are allocated to VET agencies in accordance with the outputs to be produced. Outputs could be promised in return for specified funding and a certain level of agency autonomy.

Box 2.3 Contractual arrangements in New Zealand

The New Zealand VET sector has undergone major changes over the last decade as part of a comprehensive reform of the entire state sector. Reform is based on the principle of minimizing the differences between state sector entities and those in the private sector. In 1989, state agencies became subject to a special reporting and accountability regime which established lines of responsibility for the efficient use of financial resources in government departments and state agencies. Management reform includes provision for the appointment of chief executive officers (CEOs) of departments of state and state agencies. Each CEO has a performance agreement with the responsible minister. The agreement specifies key results that should be given priority, and includes, as an appendix, a purchase agreement that specifies the outputs to be supplied by the department or state agency as well as their quality, quantity, price and timeliness. Performance agreements take the form of contracts and they bear on the employment contracts of CEOs. The chief executive reports to Parliament on the performance of the service, which is subject to government auditing. CEOs are employed on fixed-term contracts and their performance is assessed by the State Service Commissioner rather than by a minister.

In the VET sector, the Department of Education was replaced in 1989 by a smaller, policy-focused Ministry of Education. The Ministry's most important function is the provision of policy advice to the Minister of Education on all aspects of education, including VET. The Ministry also oversees the implementation of approved policies, and advises on the best use of the resources allocated to education at all levels. The Education and Training Support Agency (ETSA) has been established as a state operational agency with its own Board that, apart from the CEO, is appointed by the Minister of Education. The primary function of ETSA is to administer education and training programmes as the Minister determines. The Secretary for Education is the CEO of the Ministry of Education. The CEO of the Ministry of Education and the CEO of ETSA have performance agreements with the Minister of Education, and negotiate purchase agreements that specify the outputs that these agencies are required to deliver in each financial year.

One of the important arguments for separating policy advice from implementation was the high cost of advice, which, like any other service, must be purchased by the Government. For instance, policy advice

> *Box 2.3 (cont'd)*
> products were estimated to cost the Government of New Zealand over $400 million in 1993/1994. As the present policy agenda is more complex than ever before, in terms of fast response, sophistication of situations and their implications for the public, the Government seeks to assure the quality and timeliness of advice, and the efficiency of resource use in preparing it. To ensure efficiency, standard costs for the provision of policy advice have been drafted. A system of measurable indicators has been established, enabling CEOs to produce policy advice matching expected indicators. In addition, management principles have been applied to the policy advice process. As a result, certain divisions of responsibility have taken place in the policy advice services, with the following key qualifications distinguished: policy analyst, policy manager (requiring a higher level of supervisory skills) and policy technician (a person possessing scientific/technical expertise).
>
> Sources: Hunn, 1994; Irwin, 1996; Preddey, 1996.

Government service agencies acting on management contracts with the corresponding ministers should not be held directly accountable for outcomes since they work under short-term (often one-year) contracts. Assessment of outcomes should be perceived as a matter for the responsible minister. The analysis of outcomes is more broad-based and takes dynamic economic, political and labour market factors into account. In some countries, management contracts emphasize the importance of an agency's knowledge of outcomes, although the agency is directly responsible only for its outputs. Agency involvement in measuring both outputs and outcomes may be required, and the indicators are specified in the contract. The allocation of resources to agencies can also take account of both outputs and outcomes. The problem of differentiating between outputs and outcomes often appears when a VET agency has achieved its targets (outputs) but, due to a deteriorating economic situation, the projected impact of training on employment has not been achieved. In this case the responsible ministry has to review its training targets and reallocate resources accordingly.

Under such contracts, the ministry is no longer involved in the direct administration of the agency's operations; rather, it sets objectives, provides technical assistance, measures results and makes decisions. Management contracts spell out the negotiation process between the parties rather than their direct subordination. Contracts also determine the agency's performance indicators and reporting arrangements to ensure improved accountability.

Agencies acquire the freedom to choose their method of operations, while the ministry guarantees resources. Negotiations on the agency budget will be closely linked to targets and performance results. In due course, contracts between the administration of the national agency and its autonomous operational centres may be introduced, specifying national priority groups, VET enrolment and other targets, the list of authorized programmes to be provided, the providers' measure of staff and payroll flexibility, and the financing mechanism.

The scope of responsibilities delegated to an agency's chief executive may vary. Full managerial autonomy will cover setting VET operational targets, managing funds, recruiting staff and reorganizing the agency and training providers. The following responsibilities could be delegated to service agencies under the management contract:

- saving or overspending 3 to 5 per cent of the budget and carrying this amount over to or deducting it from the next year's budget;
- converting funds (with or without predetermined limits) from recurrent cost to capital cost and vice versa;
- staffing and staff management, including the ability to recruit and dismiss full-time and part-time staff in accordance with employment legislation;
- determining scales for the pay of staff;
- using authorized revenues for financing operations and agency development activities (Fortin, 1996).

Government agencies in Canada receive a single operating budget for their programmes that includes wages, running costs and minor capital expenditure. Ministries may carry over 2 per cent of their budget from one year to the next. In Finland too, agencies under management contracts are free to allocate a budget between wages, running costs and minor investments as they wish. Finnish law divides services into two categories: mandatory services and market-type services. Ministers have the power to decide which public services will be provided free of charge or for a fee, and they also set prices. In principle, charges should cover the internal costs of running the service. The unit cost control system has been utilized since 1989. In Australia, revenue retention incentives are provided for revenues raised from user fees and sale of surplus assets. The VET unit costs for different states are compared and the states known for high unit costs may see their federal government training allocation reduced. One of the most sensitive areas is agency autonomy regarding staff management; the agencies' administration, under the pressure of management contracts, tends to abandon the principles of civil service employment for their staff. For instance, in the United Kingdom, since 1994, the agencies dealing with VET have been registered as corporations limited by guarantee, and their staff no longer operate according to civil service rules. (Examples of government-VET agency management contracts are given in boxes 2.4 and 2.5.)

2.2.3 Monitoring management contracts

A monitoring mechanism should be specified in the management contract to ensure the operational autonomy of the agency and to avoid day-to-day interventions by the responsible government department. The contracting parties should define who is accountable for what and what information will be collected, processed and shared between them. Effective control cannot be exercised without rewards and penalties. Contracts may specify that ineffective managers will be replaced or that the next year's budget will be cut for agencies which have overspent their resources for the year. In addition, the terms and conditions of the agency's management autonomy may be reviewed. As far as incentives are concerned, a management contract may provide that savings can be retained, spent on local area development projects or used for internal agency improvements. It may also introduce a performance-related element in the pay of professionals and supervisors.

Management contracts require solid management skills on both sides – the government department and the training agency. Agency staff should be concerned with performance targets, unit costs and efficiency, and quality of services. Senior administrators should be prepared to spend time with their subordinates on joint diagnosis of performance indicators. In addition, an agency's central unit should be properly organized and allow for further delegation of management powers to lower-level "centres of responsibility".

Governments in many industrialized nations use management contracts. For instance, the public accountability of government agencies has improved in the United States, because of performance contracts between agency chief executives and the administrators of government departments. For most federal agencies, productivity indexes are calculated and published. The productivity measure used is a ratio of the number of units of output to the amount of employee time utilized (McCaffery, 1989). The results of agency performance measurements are used for holding public administrators accountable for service quality, quantity and efficiency. Performance measurement results are often used to document accomplishments as part of performance-based pay plans, which are increasingly being applied at all government levels; actual performance is compared with objectives and specific indicators as part of performance appraisal. Performance measurement data are also used to justify agency requests for funds (see also box 2.6).

Module 2. The management concept of VET

> **Box 2.4 Government-training agency management contract in Belgium**
>
> The Flemish Employment and Vocational Training Service (VDAB) has the legal status of an independent public body and provides training for job-seekers and employees. It is administered by the Management Committee, in which employers' and unions' organizations are equally represented. A management contract for 1995-96 was signed between the Flemish Government and the VDAB which obliged the VDAB to achieve certain targets in exchange for greater autonomy in the use of funds earned through the sale of services in the market.
>
> The state based its allocation for the VDAB on the following performance indicators, which were set out in the contract:
>
> - *The overall number of training hours and hours per instructor.* It was assumed that the VDAB's productivity would improve and that, over the course of the contract, the number of training hours would decrease by 5 per cent. The time freed from instruction was to be used for activities such as the development of new programmes and quality steering missions.
> - *Participation of certain groups in training.* The VDAB was responsible for ensuring that the long-term unemployed, the unemployed with primary and lower secondary education levels, and migrants accounted for 70 per cent of trainees.
> - *Placement after retraining.* The post-training placement ratio (after 6 months) was to reach 60 per cent for the above mentioned disadvantaged groups and 70 per cent for other trainees.
> - *Earned income.* The income to be earned annually by VDAB in the market was to be a minimum of BEF 40 million.
>
> The contract assumed that the VDAB's obligations would improve its administration. This was to be achieved by shifting from fixed to demand-led training provision. Decision making and funding were decentralized to ensure greater flexibility. Training services were adjusted to the market supply in order to avoid overlap and reduce inefficient investment. Training centres received lump-sum allocations enabling them to contract external training providers and recruit staff on a short-term basis. VDAB staff have become deeply involved in quality control of the training contracted out. New training programmes were developed involving sensitive subjects such as the environment, quality, safety, enterprise-oriented key qualifications and distance learning. A quality steering system was developed to trace trainees' performance in their jobs and thereby facilitate improvements in

Managing vocational training systems

Box 2.4 (cont'd)

courses. The administration was also adapted to involve industry in decision making on needs assessment, planning, curriculum development, and instructor upgrading.

The targets and corresponding allocations were divided between VDAB training centres. The number of training hours to be conducted by each instructor served as the basic indicator for allocating funds. The reporting system applied all the indicators introduced by the management contract. Budget allocations for VDAB were affected by its performance as measured by the indicators fixed in the contract.

Source: Geers, 1996.

Box 2.5 Management contracts in France

In France, employment and training operations are conducted by the National Association for Adult Vocational Training (AFPA), a national training agency, and the National Agency for Employment (ANPE), which is in charge of placement. The AFPA and ANPE are guided and funded by the Ministry of Labour's Employment Delegation, and they are now required by the Government to earn part of their budget in the market. The transfer to the new funding scheme was made in "progress contracts" (actually management contracts) which are to be signed each year between each agency and the Ministry. The contract establishes operational targets and priorities, organization, planned outputs and investments.

AFPA is the leading training agency. It targets young people, the long-term unemployed and those at risk of redundancy. It has 22 regional agencies and 130 training centres staffed by almost 10,000 employees. Beginning in 1947, AFPA was fully financed by the Government, but in 1995 it received only 70 per cent of its budget and was required to make up the balance through selling training services to private firms and Regional Councils. The State is becoming a client negotiating the training services it buys from AFPA rather than simply being its administering and funding agent. Despite this partial withdrawal of the State, AFPA, along with ANPE, remains part of the public employment and training service. It will continue to provide services at the request of regional government authorities, Regional Councils, individuals and companies. Linking AFPA to the training market prevailed over the alternative of having its 22 regional agencies supervised by the Regional Councils. AFPA's regional agencies now operate directly in the training markets and their regional training centres are becoming profit centres.

Module 2. The management concept of VET

ANPE committed itself, under the progress contract, to ensure that by 1998, 40 per cent of all unemployed people registered by the agency on an annual basis found jobs. In return for this, the State commited itself to expanding agency staffing by 300, up to 16,000, and to increase its budget by 5 per cent.

Source: Willems, 1995.

Box 2.6 Monitoring agency contracts in the United Kingdom

In the United Kingdom, 56 executive agencies have been established with 200,000 staff. Nearly half the civil service staff are now working in executive agencies. An agency's chief executive is accountable to the Secretary of State (minister), who agrees the agency's objectives and strategies and its annual business plan. The business plan, which is prepared by the agency's chief executive, should set out:

- general priorities;
- key performance targets;
- strategies to be employed to achieve objectives;
- the work programme, patterns of expenditure for the year and staffing requirements;
- key assumptions underlying the objectives and work programme; and
- a performance measurement framework.

The following monitoring and control methods are applied in agency contracts:

- review of documents at the end of the contractual period by the agency, the responsible government department, the Treasury and the Cabinet Office;
- annual analysis of business plans, financial results and performance indicators;
- regular reports to be submitted to the responsible government department;
- annual audits of the agency's financial statements by the National Audit Office; and
- implementation of internal audit procedures.

Source: Commonwealth Roundtable, 1992.

2.2.4 New legal patterns of VET organizations

Incorporated public agencies and providers. The effectiveness of traditional state-owned public service systems, including VET, was thought to be insufficient in many countries because of, *inter alia*, over-centralization, mismanagement, weak operational and financial flexibility, low staff commitment and high operational cost. In several countries, governments have attempted to shift from the traditional organization of their training agencies and other institutions to new legal patterns which provide high operational autonomy. This process involves deregulation of public services and allows for market competition between public and private VET providers. The VET organizations operating within these new patterns are increasingly required by governments to charge fees for their services, which further strengthens the impact of market forces.

The new legal status applied most frequently is a corporation or a company limited by guarantee. This usually assumes that public institutions are not privatized but become public corporations with operational and fiscal responsibilities limited by government guarantee. These organizations are non-profit, and they receive government service contracts, but their staff are contract employees rather than civil servants. These are important preconditions for raising operational flexibility and improving the employees' commitment to work (see box 2.7).

Private management of public services and publicly funded private schools. Governments in some countries use special types of management contract to provide public services more efficiently while maintaining full ownership and control. In such cases, a private contractor takes over the operation of a public service facility for a specified period of time with the freedom to make only routine management decisions. Management contracts for operating public training institutions spell out the targets, operational conditions, resource allocation procedures and incentives for contractors. In some countries, such as Belgium, the Netherlands and the United Kingdom, it is possible for private individuals and groups to create and administer schools of basic and vocational education. The private schools that conform to public education standards are eligible for public funding as if they were state schools (see box 2.8).

Service delivery contracts. Service delivery contracts are another legal option for increasing the efficiency of national vocational training through private-sector involvement. Under this arrangement a government contracts with private firms to provide a service for a specified period of time. This legal pattern has been

Box 2.7 VET organizations as companies limited by guarantee in the United Kingdom

The most common legal form of VET organization in the United Kingdom is that of a "company limited by guarantee", a wholly independent entity operating under normal company law, outside civil service rules, subject to market forces. The vast majority of VET providers (mostly colleges) as well as management agencies (Training and Enterprise Councils (TECs)) and support organizations have this legal form. While a company limited by guarantee has no shareholders, it does have financial obligations, which are limited to the character of the government guarantee of the company. Usually, the guarantor (government) nominates the directors of the company, who are then subject to normal company law. College boards of directors typically include representatives of employers, educational institutions, the local community or local government, the managing director (college principal), an elected staff representative and a representative of the local TEC.

The Colleges of Further Education (FE) and the Colleges of Higher Education (HE) are the most important vocational training providers in the United Kingdom. Reforms removed the colleges from local government and "incorporated" them as publicly funded but independent, self-governing, non-profit-making institutions with the legal status of companies. The colleges project how much revenue they can acquire for the coming year. They then decide what to spend on staff; heat and light; books, computers and other materials; taxes; building maintenance, gardening and estates; advertising; and promotion. They are responsible for all staffing matters, including hiring, firing and determination of pay levels. The colleges have no recourse to public authorities should they experience financial difficulties. The colleges do still differ from standard private companies in three ways. Firstly, they have recourse to banks for overdraft facilities, although this is limited by statute. Secondly, while they own their assets and buildings, their power to dispose of them is inhibited by their statutes. Thirdly, at the present time, colleges may appeal to the Further Education Funding Council (FEFC) for capital grants for new buildings.

The market discipline to which VET organizations are exposed is harsh. For instance, in 1994, one of the TECs was declared bankrupt. The Employment Department did not intervene with emergency funds. The unfulfilled portions of contracts were re-allocated to neighbouring TECs. Colleges had to proceed through the courts in the usual way and re-negotiate with the surviving TECs. In other words, the commercial failure

Managing vocational training systems

Box 2.7 (cont'd)

of the TEC Company was accorded no status that marked it out from any other commercial failure in a free market.

TECs and the FEFC must contract with the Department of Education. The colleges must, in due course, make service contracts with the TECs or the FEFC. The FEFC makes contracts with colleges that include targets for enrolment with penalty clauses for missing the targets. There is some evidence that the contracts made have become unrealistic in some cases and that they are causing great financial difficulties in some colleges. However, there can be no doubt that the use of service contracts in the relationship between Government and training providers has been a key factor in improving the performance of the VET system.

Source: Russell, 1995.

Box 2.8 Freedom of educational choice in the Netherlands

In the Netherlands, as a result of the policy to ensure freedom of choice in education, almost 85 per cent of senior vocational training schools are now privately run. Private schools which meet state standards are publicly financed according to the same criteria as public schools. The statutory provisions with regard to organization and examinations are basically the same for both public and private schools. Within this broad framework, private schools are free to set their own curricula and to determine the content of teaching, appoint teaching staff and choose their own training materials. Central government monitors the quality of education provided. The Government has delegated control over public allocations to schools to regional and municipal authorities.

Sources: Burgess, 1993; Netherlands Ministry of Education and Science, 1993.

---

increasingly used in labour market training programmes, which are often short-term and individualized.

State guarantees and incentives can reduce the cost and risk for private companies providing government-funded services, while the cost of these incentives for the government may eventually be less than the cost of providing training services directly. Guarantees and fiscal incentives can mobilize private sector resources and expertise that would not otherwise be available or affordable for government VET agencies.

Module 2. The management concept of VET

Unit 3. Developing internal management policies

Learning objectives

This unit is designed to provide a better knowledge of:

1. Internal management policies in vocational training systems
2. The performance measurement concept
3. Performance indicators and criteria for measuring agency performance
4. Benchmarking as a management tool

3.1 Effective management policies in VET systems

Internal management policies are rules and procedures established to make a system operate effectively and reduce the number of routine decisions. Governments commonly establish uniform administrative policies for all public agencies, while individual agencies may develop specific policies. Internal management policies and their underlying assumptions are reviewed below. Such policies commonly relate to:

- organizing systems;
- staffing and managing human resources;
- setting targets, planning and budgeting;
- financing; and
- controlling performance.

Although some internal management policies were developed primarily for business organizations (Goodman and Pennings, 1977; Pfeffer and Salancik, 1978; Peters and Waterman, 1982; Robbins, 1987; Banner and Gagné, 1995), they are widely applied by educational administrators.

Organizing VET systems effectively requires policies aimed at:

- reducing the number of hierarchical levels of power, thereby improving coordination and communication and allowing senior administrators to handle more people;
- converting, where feasible, part of the public service into government-controlled but operationally independent agencies and training providers with staff operating as contract employees. This will improve the manageability of training systems (see Unit 2 of this Module);
- delegating responsibilities to the lowest possible level and ensuring that supervisors are able to operate independently. This will improve the ability of the system to respond to changes in the demand for services;

- organizing work in a product-oriented way whereby objectives are set and activities are structured as programmes or products aimed at achieving those objectives;
- maintaining simple organizational configurations and the minimum staff (see Unit 1 of this Module);
- establishing structures that will identify and serve the needs of "strategic constituencies" (e.g. government agencies, priority target groups, employers, suppliers of services, professional associations, etc.); and
- introducing management analysts to the VET agency, who will study management practice; advise on the effective execution of public programmes; and assist in the introduction of strategic planning and budgeting, market analysis, performance measurement, and office management (see Elliott, 1996).

Human resource management policies should focus on:

- emphasizing that managing primarily means *managing people* and that individuals are the most important organizational element, since only motivated and creative employees can make the system more flexible, effective, and productive;
- ensuring employee job satisfaction and commitment to work, since motivating people to achieve the organization's objectives is a manager's most important task (demotivated employees can be an even greater hindrance to organizational performance than shortage of funds);
- ensuring all managers' participation in target setting and other important decisions;
- sharing with employees key organizational values and goals, which can improve their commitment to work;
- developing professional VET administrators through management training and continuous skill-upgrading;
- holding managers accountable for the success and failure of the organizations and units assigned to them and establishing a system of rewards and penalties; and
- developing a motivating pay system for public administrators. Some countries (e.g. Australia, Sweden and the United Kingdom) have decentralized pay determination in large areas of the public sector to the agencies (Elliott, 1996). Uniform centralized pay systems have been dismantled, and flatter, streamlined structures have been introduced. Performance-related elements have been incorporated into civil service pay systems and are linked to the achievement of long-term objectives.

Module 2. The management concept of VET

Planning and budgeting policies in national VET systems must realistically reflect the sometimes conflicting demands of operational efficiency and political imperatives relating to public funding. Although the purpose of sound budgeting is to determine the most desirable activities and allocate resources to them as efficiently as possible, efficiency is not the only criterion for government decision making. It is not realistic to assume that major decisions will be made mainly on the basis of cost-benefit analysis or other analytical models. Time pressures, shortage of funds and political interests affect the integrity of policy analysis and decision making. A compromise in the budgeting process should be achieved between efficiency and political priorities (Naschold, 1995). Therefore, policies should involve:

- setting measurable, time-oriented and realistic targets, with an eye to long-term results, through strategic planing for the VET system as a whole and for individual providers;
- ensuring that target-setting and planning drive budget formulation and not the other way around;
- avoiding obsolete budgeting practices which allocate resources to government agencies and institutions with no indication of objectives, strategic plans or development processes; and
- introducing modern types of budgeting which could be described as performance-related, multi-year, implying productivity gains, assuming greater accountability and budget flexibility and incentives.

Budgeting for results is an implied contract that links resources provided to outputs promised. Planned outputs, if properly costed, could be used for determining the budget allocation needed to produce them. Budget proposals should be accompanied by a statement of objectives, as well as service performance, effectiveness and efficiency measures. Budgeting for results allows for emphasis on efficiency rather than simple expenditure control (see boxes 2.9 and 2.10). *Multi-year budgeting* helps address the long-term outcomes of current policy and investment decisions which often materialize years after the budget makes provisions for them. Strategic planning is difficult to implement without multi-year budgets. In some industrialized countries budget allocations are also adjusted for *productivity and efficiency gains*, thus requiring improved management. Improving productivity in the public VET sector means emphasizing the importance of productivity in terms of the efficient use of funds, capital and human resources; and considering strategies for expenditure reduction through improved management or reorganization. For instance, in the United States, United Kingdom, and Sweden, agencies are required to establish productivity targets and report on progress. In Australia, all agencies are

Managing vocational training systems

> **Box 2.9 Planning and budgeting in the VET sector of New Zealand**
>
> Guidance in the vocational training sector is provided by the Ministry of Education and two state agencies- the Education and Training Support Agency (ETSA) and the New Zealand Qualifications Authority (NZQA). VET programmes are delivered by tertiary educational institutions (TEIs) which include seven universities, 25 polytechnics, four colleges of education, etc. The common budgeting pattern is *budgeting for results*, in which funds are appropriated to outputs rather than to departments, agencies and institutions. A major development in the management reform of the state sector was an "outcome statement" issued by the Government, outlining its strategic vision for the medium term. This document was followed by the publication of Strategic Result Areas for the Public Sector (SRAs). These determine the priorities of government departments and agencies. For instance, the SRAs for 1994-97 were identified as: maintaining and accelerating economic growth; enterprise and innovation; education and training, etc. The SRAs are complemented by departmental/agency Key Result Areas (KRAs) which are linked to SRAs. The education and training SRA has major implications for the KRAs of the Ministry of Education and of NZQA and ETSA. Following this, detailed expenditure plans for the year ahead are drafted. Portfolio by portfolio, ministers specify the groups of outputs they intend to produce or contract out to government departments and agencies; and the investments they intend to make in agencies in order to achieve specified targets. The KRAs are incorporated in the performance agreement between the CEO of the department/agency and the minister responsible.
>
> It is a requirement under the Public Finance Act of 1989 that state agencies provide for their responsible minister a statement of intent (in effect a business plan). It must specify: the objectives of the agency; the nature and scope of activities proposed; performance targets and other measures by which the performance of the agency may be judged in relation to its objects; and accounting policies. Although departments and agencies estimate the cost of the resources needed for producing the outputs requested, the budget process focuses on outputs alone and does not prescribe the inputs to be used by agencies. State agencies routinely develop and publish corporate plans which replicate all aspects of private sector business planning.
>
> TEIs are not required to negotiate business plans with the Minister of Education, nor does the Minister have any power to intervene in business planning. Nonetheless, TEIs are required to submit a statement of objectives

Module 2. The management concept of VET

to the Ministry of Education for the purpose of determining state funding. The exemption of TEIs from any legislative requirement to negotiate statements of intent with a responsible Minister is currently under review. The TEIs are required to report against defined outputs (statement of objectives) and performance indicators. The outputs do not necessarily have to be measurable in financial terms.

The Public Finance Act, 1989, requires departments and state agencies as well as TEIs to submit audited annual reports, including annual financial statements, to responsible ministers and to Parliament. State departments and agencies are legally required to disclose the full cost of producing outputs and conducting their business. The annual financial statements must allow for comparison between projected and actual performance.

Source: Irwin, 1996; Preddey and Doyle, 1998.

Box 2.10 Budgeting for results in the Government of the United States

Performance budgeting in government has been enacted in the United States by the Government Performance and Results Act (GPRA) of 1993. The GPRA requires federal departments and agencies to produce strategic and annual performance plans with specific performance goals. Budget levels correspond to the level of programme performance to be achieved. Department and agency strategic plans cover a minimum of six years and are to be updated at least every three years. An agency's strategic plan should include:

- a comprehensive mission statement;
- a description of general goals and how these will be achieved;
- a description of the relationship between performance goals in the annual performance plan and general goals in the strategic plan;
- an identification of key external factors that could affect achievement of the general goals; and
- a description of programme evaluation and a schedule for evaluation.

An agency's annual performance plan should contain:

- performance goals for each of the programmes and operations listed;
- performance indicators for measuring outputs and outcomes (about 2,000 performance standards have been created for measuring public service outputs);

> *Box 2.10 (cont'd)*
>
> - a description of the means to be used to verify measured values; and
> - a brief description of the operational process and resources needed to meet performance targets.
>
> The annual performance plans derive their goals from the general goals in strategic plans. Often, the goals in a performance plan are outputs while the general goals are expressed as outcomes. A number of agencies using the above planning format have encountered difficulties in the formulation and control of programme goals and outcomes, reorganization of programme staff and weak performance measures.
>
> Source: Groszyk, 1996.

expected to produce an annual efficiency dividend of 1.25 per cent on their running costs; this is intended to demonstrate improved management. In Ireland, the budgeting process involved reducing the departments' running costs by 2 per cent in 1992 and 1993.

Modern budgeting should promote greater *accountability* through enhanced incentives and opportunities to retain savings achieved by increasing productivity above the budgeted target and to keep the revenues from charging fees; to have a greater budget flexibility in terms of freedom to decide on the mix of inputs (more staff and less equipment or vice versa) and reallocate funds freely between budget lines. For instance, in Denmark, agencies have a single flexible appropriation for their operational expenditure which imposes limits only on pay and on person-years at management levels; agency accounts are interest-bearing. Ministries are allowed to transfer funds from line to line and from less to more productive activities. The agencies also keep half the revenue earned by better cash management. In Australia, for instance, the carry-over provision allows agencies to reallocate up to 6 per cent of their total running costs between years; in Canada this provision is 2 per cent. In Denmark, agency savings on pay can be carried forward and used for staffing, though within narrow limits (Cope, 1989; McCaffery, 1989; OECD, 1989,1995).

Introducing market mechanisms into VET administration may involve:

- using some or all of the following instruments: output-based school financing, vouchers for purchasing training from a variety of providers, company grants offered to VET schools, user charges for public services (in the United States some agencies receive over a quarter of their revenues from fees), contracting out of public services, and publication of school results (Perry, 1989; OECD, 1993; Standaert, 1993);

Module 2. The management concept of VET

- creating internal training markets and requiring public and private providers to compete for government contracts through competitive bidding;
- applying incentives and penalties; and
- closely monitoring external contractors' performance.

Contracting out services can introduce new problems into the administration of vocational training programmes. Monitoring the performance of external contractors can become costly. Poorly prepared service agreements may result in the limited liability of private contractors and, further, in low responsiveness to changing demand. Further, the quality of VET provision may suffer as private contractors tend to economize on staff, textbooks, materials and equipment.

Control of VET systems involves a balance between centralized and decentralized methods and this requires policies for:

- distinguishing the principal options of control: administrative control by ministerial department or inspectorate; decentralized control by local management committees involving authorities, industry and parents; or control by market competition;
- implementing central control through: (a) data collection and measurement of agencies' and providers' performance, outputs and expenditure in relation to established targets; and (b) accreditation of training institutions, certification of teaching staff and school managers, establishment of standards regarding quality of premises and teaching; and administration of examinations;
- devolving, where possible, the power of control to local employers' groups, parents and local authorities;
- decentralizing management power to school management committees which should include representatives of the above local groups; and
- focusing control on activities which have failed to meet targets. All deviations from targets and reasons for failure should be reported on. Through routine performance evaluation as well as a study of failures, any necessary changes in internal policies should be identified.

Developing new management skills is critical for effective public administration (Perry, 1989). Administrators need to develop professional management skills in:

- identifying and prioritizing the demand for services;
- strategic planning which emphasizes long-term perspectives rather than short-term thinking;
- budgeting for results, which stresses outputs rather than performance;

- developing and managing public service programmes and contracts;
- managing public services without actually producing them (i.e. outsourcing services and products to operating agencies and private firms);
- developing and guiding consultation with client and other groups;
- guiding joint management and advisory bodies;
- defining and measuring service performance, outputs and outcomes;
- defining the optimum quantity of government service (which facilitates efficient use of resources);
- managing equity through targeting and consulting groups under-represented in VET;
- introducing market mechanisms into public services;
- using new legal forms for delivering public services (e.g. companies with limited guarantee by government, etc.); and
- promoting training markets and competing with other government agencies and private service organizations.

3.2 Performance measurement as a management tool

3.2.1 Performance indicators and criteria

Measuring the performance of government service organizations has become an important management tool. It aims at improving the productivity and effectiveness of education and training, health care and other sectors by establishing the accountability of public administrators and, to a certain extent, improving the budgetary process. There is no single measure of an organization's performance. A performance profile can be generated with direct performance indicators as well as complex criteria. The indicators and criteria to be applied depend on government values and priorities. Certain measurement indicators and criteria can be fixed as standards against which agency performance is assessed (OECD, 1994a, 1994b).

Direct performance indicators that are commonly applied include:

- number of clients served;
- client satisfaction;
- service quality indicators;
- equity in the distribution of services; and
- earnings from fees charged to users.

Complex performance criteria include:

- efficiency, calculated as the ratio of the cost of utilized resources to the budgeted value of these resources;

- effectiveness, determined through measurement of the deviation of outputs from objectives (an organization cannot be considered effective if expenditures did not exceed the budget but output targets were not achieved);
- cost-efficiency, as the cost of each unit of output; and
- cost-effectiveness, as the unit cost of producing the planned/targeted output. When all organizational outputs meet the set targets, the cost-efficiency of agency performance equals cost-effectiveness.

3.2.2 Performance indicators and criteria in the VET sector

The following indicators and criteria can be used for measuring performance in the vocational training sector:

- retention rate, as the percentage of completers to the total number of trainees enrolled at the beginning of the course;
- student learning outcomes, as the percentage of trainees who graduated with a certificate/at a certain level to the total number of completers;
- the percentage of graduates who found employment;
- utilization of training capacity, as the proportion of training places filled by trainees compared to the total number of training places (this criterion reflects the productivity of staff, capital and equipment);
- staff productivity measures, including staff/student ratios, the number of annual hours of training curriculum delivered per instructor or employee of the institution, and the "module load completion rate", which effectively measures labour productivity by calculating the percentage of annual hours of curriculum for which students are awarded a completion grade or are assessed as meeting the required skill levels (Australian National Training Authority, 1995a);
- measures of equitable access to publicly funded training, including the percentage of public training places created per thousand 16-25 year olds (for initial training) or per thousand people of working age (for labour market training) in each region, and the percentage of public training places filled by people from each disadvantaged group (young people from low-income families, the long-term unemployed, etc.) to the total number in this group as compared to the same ratio calculated for other, non-disadvantaged populations;
- the degree of satisfaction of client groups (employers and graduates);
- measures of revenue earned through selling training services (revenues as a proportion of the total budget);
- the average training cost per student contact hour (OECD, 1996);

- the market value of each VET credential (the percentage of school graduates and adult trainees who completed a certain vocational qualification); and
- private and social returns to training investments (see Grubb and Ryan, 1999).

Another way of measuring an organization's performance is by making comparisons. There are four possible areas of comparison:

- comparing current outputs with past production, since an organization can reasonably be expected to improve productivity and reduce the unit cost per output over time (though improvements might be due to technological advance rather than management efforts);
- comparing the performance of the public agency with private organizations offering similar programmes;
- comparing actual results with what was planned, targeted and budgeted; and
- comparing actual outputs with what could reasonably have been achieved in the circumstances.

Benchmarking is a special type of comparison, which uses measurement results to promote best, rather than standard, performance. Benchmarking means selecting, standardizing and developing best practice. A standard may be defined as a desired state that is used to calibrate real performance. Quantitative standards have an advantage over qualitative standards in that they can be adjusted marginally, in a precise way, whereas qualitative standards tend to be more long term. Common classifications of performance standards include minimum standards, average standards and best practice standards. Minimum standards are commonly regarded as user entitlements and may provide, for instance, that no young person should have to wait more than three months for a training place. Average standards are sometimes used for the internal evaluation of service performance (OECD, 1994a, 1994b).

Benchmarks should take account of realities and be established on the basis of best performance results demonstrated by VET agencies/providers in a particular country. Another basis for setting benchmarks could be users' highest expectations of public VET services, which can shift when the old benchmarks have been achieved. Important features of the service may be ranked differently by groups of customers, by the government and service agencies. All the features that matter to users need to be included in a benchmark. As public servants are struggling with increasing demand and contracting resources, best practice standards can indicate the direction for them to improve performance. A special management development team may be established by the government in order to assist an agency to move towards benchmarks.

Problems of performance measurement

One major problem in measuring effectiveness and cost-effectiveness is the ongoing failure, in many countries, to set objectives for VET systems. Many government agencies simply do not do it or they apply unsatisfactory target-setting techniques. In addition, it is sometimes difficult to express agency or programme targets in quantifiable terms.

Another difficulty in measuring cost-effectiveness and cost-efficiency has been that systems for recording and attributing costs to certain VET programmes and outputs have been difficult to implement. Some agencies receive free services from other government organizations, the cost of which needs to be assessed and attributed to certain outputs. Assessing the actual cost of an agency's capital has also been problematic as its true economic value is the amount the capital can be sold for to other businesses. In order to collect and maintain all these data, a complicated system of financial information needs to be established.

A third type of problem relates to the fact that outputs/outcomes might decline because of unfavourable external conditions, such as an economic downturn.

The cost of measuring performance is another important issue. The cost of setting an agency's performance measurement system has been estimated to account for 1 to 2 per cent of the programme's running costs. Therefore, performance measurement should be undertaken only if the government is strongly determined to use the data for important policy and management decisions leading to improved agency performance.

One way of using results measurement is to improve control. However, the cost of collecting, processing and interpreting the data may be too high to justify the perfection of control alone. Another type of application would be using performance measurement as a basis for VET programming and resource allocation. The best performing agencies and providers may be entitled to greater allocations and incentives, or the more cost-effective programmes will be expanded and less cost-effective ones contracted. So far, however, the use of performance measurement results for management decisions has been limited.

The following are general recommendations for measuring performance:

- Only the most important agency outputs/outcomes should be evaluated.
- Managers' performance should only be measured for the areas under their control.
- A special external unit may be established to measure agency performance professionally. This function is often assigned to national education inspectorates. Agencies may also be required to establish their own specialist units for conducting internal performance measurement (see Module 6, Unit 2).

- Performance indicators and criteria should be consistent over time, simple and easily understood.
- Indicators should allow for interpretation and utilization in management decisions.
- Inputs external to the performance under measurement should be eliminated.
- Employees should be involved in devising performance indicators.

VET MANAGEMENT AND ORGANIZATIONAL STRUCTURES

Module 3

Unit 1. Configuration of organizational and management structures

Learning objectives

This unit is designed to provide a better knowledge of:

1. Configurations of VET organizational and management structures
2. The implications of decentralization

1.1 Management structures

Management structures define the levels of authority and reporting systems, as well as the degree of decision-making power concentrated at the top and at lower levels. They indicate the level at which decisions are to be taken and the degree of control over the lower levels. An organization's power centre determines its organizational objectives and structure, controls resources and information, and has the formal authority to establish internal management policies, plans, and budgets; to control and review performance and outputs; and to make other decisions which direct employees' behaviour. The management line (line of command) begins with the top level administrator and ends with the lowest level supervisor and operator (teacher level, in vocational training organizations). Good management and organizational structures do not, by themselves, produce good results, but poor structures make good performance impossible, no matter how competent individual managers may be.

The centralization of power is the degree to which decision making is concentrated at a "single point" in the organization (e.g. director of the department).

High concentration of decision-making power means high centralization. In centralized management systems, most of the important and many unimportant decisions are made at the top level, and lower-level actors are expected to operate in accordance with these decisions. The vertical division of management responsibility is based on the principle that each management level is responsible only for those issues which cannot be resolved or handled efficiently at lower levels.

Decentralization means that decisions are made by officers who are close to the action and that power is delegated to them. Another way of decentralizing power is to include representatives from various organizational levels on management boards to ensure participation in decision making. Management capabilities at lower levels should improve under a decentralized system.

In well-structured systems, central management authorities are established for each functional area (general management, financing authority, technical authority, etc.). In a national VET system, technical decisions on national qualifications development or assessment and certification can be centralized by assigning responsibility to the appropriate units of government training departments or by establishing a national curriculum development authority and a national testing and certification authority. Those powers could also be decentralized to lower-level operators such as VET providers. In this case, providers must have the necessary technical know-how to implement those functions.

1.2 Organizational structures

1.2.1 Organizational configuration

An organization involves: (a) structures (how the organizational units fit together) and (b) internal rules, regulations and procedures which may prescribe unit performance and employees' behaviour in order to ensure their coordination and integration (Mintzberg, 1979).

The organizational structure has three major functions:

- to divide operational tasks and resources among the system's structural units;
- to assign responsible staff among the structural units; and
- to ensure flexible communication and integration of units and individuals working towards common targets.

Horizontal differentiation is reflected in the qualifications of specialist employees providing support functions such as planning, financing, accounting, bookkeeping, building maintenance, maintenance of teaching equipment, curriculum design, procurement, data processing, personnel practices, etc. Various combinations of operative and specialist functions can also be envisaged. For instance, specialist staff can be attached to the top administrator, or certain specialist positions can also be established in operational divisions. The organization of a VET provider would be influenced mostly by the types of training programme delivered as well as by the technical support functions which are assigned to it. In some institutions, teachers traditionally combine direct instruction with specialist functions. For instance, they may be in charge of producing curricula on the basis of national training standards or maintaining training equipment. The distinction between the operational staff and specialist staff is an area of frequent conflict.

Individual performances need to be coordinated and, finally, *integrated*. One way of doing this is to develop internal rules, regulations and procedures which specify patterns of interaction and communication. These will reduce information distortions, avoid delays in implementing decisions and introduce uniformity and standardization of behaviour. Another powerful way of achieving organizational integration is central control. A special service of inspectors can be established to ensure compliance with internal policies, rules and procedures. Organizational objectives may also serve as strong integrators, as their purpose is to make everyone move in the same direction. Effective coordination may also be ensured through incentive mechanisms which encourage employees to work together in pursuit of common objectives. Excellent systems and organizations have been found to be well-integrated through target setting, control and coordination. Each organization has its own *organizational culture* of shared assumptions and beliefs, which strongly affects the way people work and communicate.

1.2.2 Principles of organization design

Organizational structures are formal arrangements between people, and organizational sophistication depends on the ability of people to use or comply with those arrangements. There are many approaches to organizational design. When formal structures are thought to be unsatisfactory, people can develop informal structures and communicate and make decisions through those. Thus, there are a number of principles which should guide the design of an organization. First, it should be realized that there is no single ideal organizational structure for the same system. In principle, structures should be as simple and transparent as possible. Each additional body/unit created will bring an additional need for communication, control and integration, as well as additional costs and delays in decision making (Banner and Gangé, 1995).

Flexible organizations adapt their structures when the system's mission, major objectives or external environment change significantly.

Second, there are many internal and external variables which determine management and organizational structures. As far as internal variables are concerned, a system's organizational configuration and measure of centralization should correspond to its mission and objectives, as well as to employees' management and technical skills and their commitment to work. The higher the commitment and competence, the more functions may be delegated. Systems providing services commonly require full decentralization. Structures must also be able to respond to complex environmental factors. These external factors, including uncertainty, must be considered in planning organizational configuration. One way of handling complexity is to create a so-called organic structure that assumes low formalization of behaviour and high independence of supervisors and operators. To be viable, this type of structure requires highly competent, self-controlled, responsible and motivated individuals.

Third, the principal criteria for establishing units and dividing tasks between them are objectives, processes, products, clientele and territory. The same system will be structured differently, depending on the relevant criterion. For instance, if the national training system specifically targets certain groups of beneficiaries, such as women, rural people or employees without formal qualifications, corresponding structures can be established which will handle these targets (see section 1.2.3 of this Unit). There are always support activities such as personnel, financing, bookkeeping and maintenance, which do not aim at any specific objective. It often makes sense to group these in separate units. Wasteful organizational overlap arises when two or more units have the same authority to act in pursuit of the same purpose.

Fourth, operational rules and procedures strengthen coordination and integration. In principle, high organizational formalization (i.e. the degree of application of rules and procedures) is more appropriate with routine technologies and with less-educated and unambitious employees. The need for formalization may increase when the organization's resources are very scarce and strict procedures need to be applied to allocate them.

Fifth, with respect to human behaviour, organizational formalization and centralization have limits. Overly formalized and centralized organizations are often unable to satisfy employees' needs for personal development, attractive job content, recognition, team work or competition. Over-regulation may lead to a focus on observation of rules rather than pursuit of common goals. Lack of creativity and initiative is also a common result. The negative implications of bureaucracies and formalization may be addressed through deregulation, team building and participative management.

Sixth, wide spans of control, short chains of command and minimum fragmentation have significant organizational advantages. The span of control (i.e. the number of employees per supervisor) should be as wide as possible. More employees per supervisor at the bottom of the organization means fewer supervisors and fewer layers of supervision. Over-fragmentation means dividing the organization into smaller units and simultaneously creating more layers of power and increasing costs. The weakness of rigid vertical structures with long chains of command is that decisions are delayed and may be reinterpreted as they go down. The maximum number of employees per supervisor depends on the differentiation of their functions and their level of commitment, competence and self-control (Oman et al., 1992).

Seventh, centralized structures appear more appropriate in situations where important, frequent and rapid challenges confront the whole system. There may be little opportunity for decentralized and participative decision-making in such circumstances. However, if a service agency is large, with many functional or geographical departments, then external challenges can be handled by departments with only limited involvement of the central administration. As a system grows, so does the pressure to devolve power to the lower levels. The argument for decentralization is that subordinates know more about their own work than top administrators do.

1.2.3 Types of organizational structure

On the basis of objectives, processes, products, clientele and territory, three principal types of organizational structure may be distinguished (Khandwalla, 1977):

- functional;
- divisional; and
- matrix.

In *functional* (process-based) structures, all people performing the same function (e.g. course development, financing, skills testing or staff development) are located together (see figure 3.1). Technical specialists involved in the development of curricula will therefore constitute the curriculum development unit, for example. The advantages are that the whole organization has access to specialized personnel and that a technical function is easily developed and supervised. However, in this case, responsibility for outputs lies with top management only. Staff may become overly specialized and solely preoccupied with their functional area, which may result in reduced integration and low effectiveness.

Managing vocational training systems

Figure 3.1 Functional organization of a ministerial training department

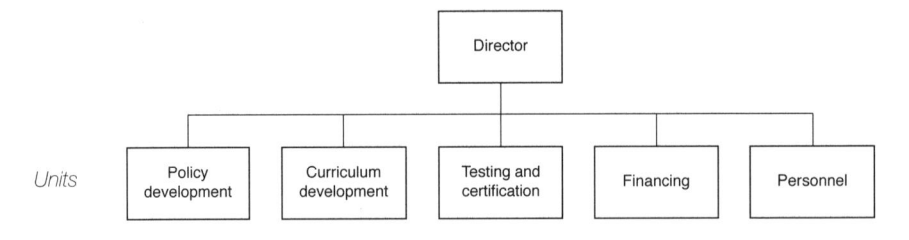

```
                           Director
                              │
     ┌──────────┬─────────────┼─────────────┬──────────┐
Units│ Policy   │ Curriculum  │ Testing and │ Financing│ Personnel
     │development│development │certification│          │
```

By contrast, *divisional* structures bring specialists together on the basis of product or service, type of clientele or geographical area. A product-based VET structure may establish units responsible for the provision of, for instance, agricultural or high-tech courses (see figure 3.2).

Figure 3.2 Product-based structure of a training agency

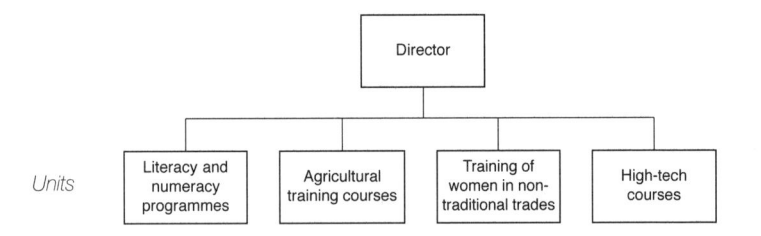

```
                           Director
                              │
     ┌──────────────┬─────────┼──────────────┬──────────┐
Units│ Literacy and │ Agricultural │ Training of    │ High-tech
     │ numeracy     │ training     │ women in non-  │ courses
     │ programmes   │ courses      │ traditional trades│
```

A client-based organization would establish separate units handling programmes for school drop-outs, young people 16 to 25 years of age, supervisors and so on (see figure 3.3).

Figure 3.3 Client-focused structure or a training agency

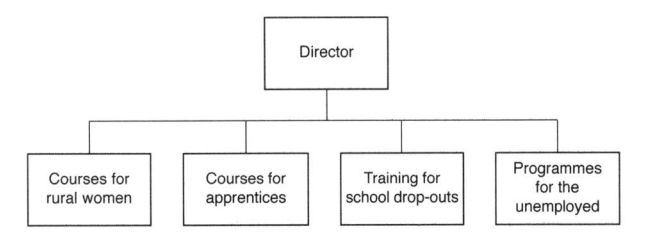

```
                           Director
                              │
     ┌──────────┬─────────────┼─────────────┬──────────┐
     │ Courses for│ Courses for │ Training for   │ Programmes
     │ rural women│ apprentices │ school drop-outs│ for the
     │            │             │                │ unemployed
```

An agency with a geographical structure would establish regional units administering all training programmes as well as technical support functions for individual regions (see figure 3.4).

Module 3. VET management and organizational structures

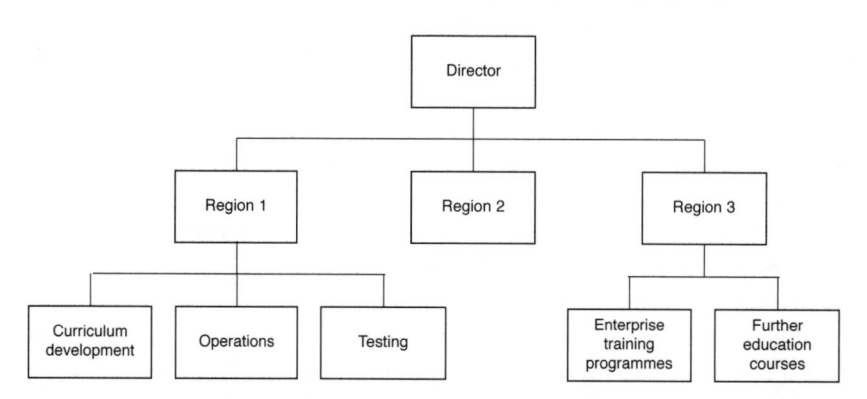

Figure 3.4 Geographical organization of a national training agency

```
                        Director
            ┌──────────────┼──────────────┐
         Region 1       Region 2       Region 3
      ┌─────┼─────┐              ┌──────┴──────┐
Curriculum  Operations  Testing  Enterprise   Further
development                      training     education
                                 programmes   courses
```

The major advantage of a divisional structure is that it focuses on a particular training product or customer group that brings the organizational action much closer to its objectives. It places responsibility for outputs at divisional level through decentralization, and it encourages product, rather than function, development. The disadvantages of divisional organizations are that they require more executives with general management expertise, as well as more technical specialists who are split between divisions, which may result in duplication of effort.

Organizational hybrids combining functional and divisional forms are also possible. For instance, large national *programme-based* structures often combine product- and client-based forms in programmes that usually aim at implementing certain objectives and assume the creation of independent structures. When national VET targets are set, corresponding programme structures can be created aiming at these targets. Each programme may have a separate planning and budgeting process. Although other management and support functions (resource allocation, accounting, etc.) may be centralized, responsibility for achieving individual targets will be delegated to programme managers (see figure 3.5).

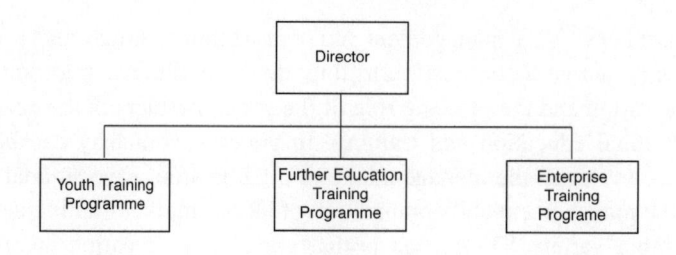

Figure 3.5 Programme organization of a ministerial training department

```
                        Director
            ┌──────────────┼──────────────┐
      Youth Training   Further Education   Enterprise
      Programme        Training            Training
                       Programme           Programe
```

The principal feature of the *matrix* organization is to combine the formal structure (functional or divisional) with an informal team (organic). Temporary project teams are a major feature of the matrix structure. For instance, when a VET agency decides to develop a new type of curriculum, a project team leader may be appointed who negotiates with the managers of functional divisions about using specialists to bring the new product from the idea stage to delivery. Agreements may be concluded on lending functional specialists to the team leader for a certain period of time. These projects should be backed by financial allocations so that the wages of the borrowed specialists are reimbursed to their original divisions. A leader may be in charge of several projects at various stages of completion at any given time. The matrix structure can also be a solution when the organization is performing non-routine, potentially ambiguous work.

1.3 Trends in organizing VET systems

The following structures may be distinguished in governing training systems (see figure 3.6):

- management bodies comprising vocational education/training departments in the education or labour ministry or other bodies governing the system;
- national advisory bodies (e.g. employment and training councils, boards, etc.), usually representing organizations involving government and the social partners;
- technical guidance and support structures providing services to VET management bodies and providers (regarding national skill standards and qualifications, curriculum development, skill assessment and certification, instructor development, etc.) which may exist as part of ministry VET departments or as independent organizations operating under government supervision; and
- VET providers.

It is important to understand this general configuration, as many countries lack or underemphasize certain parts of it, which reduces the system's capability to operate.

A number of VET management and organizational structures have emerged. They vary across countries, reflecting their conditions, tradition of public administration and the growing role of the social partners in the administration of vocational education and training. In general, similarity can be observed across countries in the management and organization of vocational education, while the management and organization of labour market training demonstrates much more variety. The reason is that vocational education involves mostly

Module 3. VET management and organizational structures

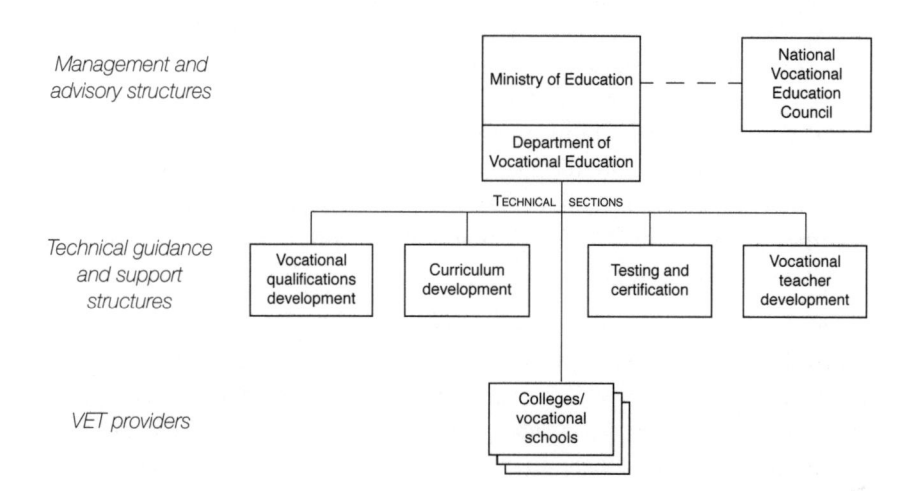

Figure 3.6 Structural components of the vocational education system

Management and advisory structures

- Ministry of Education — — — National Vocational Education Council
- Department of Vocational Education

TECHNICAL SECTIONS

Technical guidance and support structures

- Vocational qualifications development
- Curriculum development
- Testing and certification
- Vocational teacher development

VET providers

- Colleges/vocational schools

school-based teaching, which means grouping students together in classrooms and workshops where they receive visual and written information from teachers. School-based vocational education is highly standardized and repetitive, with little uncertainty. As a result, organizational structures are relatively simple and formal, and assume a central bureaucracy. In contrast, labour market training centres operate in a highly uncertain environment: they have to handle the unemployed and school drop-outs on an individual basis and continuously match the current demand for jobs with the skills which can be developed relatively quickly. As a result, labour market training structures require greater organizational, financial and staffing autonomy.

One of the older configurations has been direct ministerial provision of services. As a result, many national VET departments and training agencies have become horizontally over-differentiated as they combine policy development functions with direct administration of training suppliers and provision of technical functions. This structure is very inflexible and incapable of responding properly to market changes.

To remedy this problem, the following alternative management and organizational options have been introduced in some countries:

- Support functions have been removed from the ministry and national technical support organizations have been established, resulting in improved specialization and greater flexibility.

- Administration of labour market training operations has been removed from ministries and national agencies responsible for labour market training have been instituted. The agency board takes charge of training operations while training policy development remains with the ministry.
- Non-governmental, intermediate management agencies have been created and assigned responsibility for administering public VET operations and funds. They operate on management contracts with the government.
- Public training providers have been established as autonomous institutions or corporations and made fully responsible for operations. The ministry deals with policy issues and funding.

The desire for a comprehensive national policy on skills development frequently becomes an argument for creating a comprehensive national vocational training agency. However, the broad range of education and training activities tends to bear upon other agencies, which can fragment the public system. Along with the education ministry and the labour ministry, the economic ministries may also have a mandate and budget to provide vocational training. Vocational education systems are commonly separated from labour market training systems: each has independent management and advisory bodies as well as technical support organizations; they often have very large, independent delivery structures. As a result, they often compete for government budgets. Separately maintaining different types of provider for vocational education and labour market training can be quite expensive.

The following approaches have been used recently to resolve this problem of coordination:

- placing the administration of all vocational education and training activities under the same government ministry;
- assigning national supervisory (mostly technical) functions to a single agency which is required to endorse and control the quality and unit cost of all government-funded programmes regardless of which ministry delivers them; and
- removing, at least partially, the demarcation between separate delivery structures through the creation of national training markets that require training providers belonging to the different ministries to sell services and compete in the market. Alternative types of provider can also be encouraged. For example, institutions of higher education can provide vocational education programmes as well as upgrading programmes at technician and engineer level. Regular schools can also offer vocational programmes leading to employment. Private enterprises can become authorized training providers, reducing the number of state training schools.

1.4 Decentralizing vocational education and training

1.4.1 Advantages and disadvantages

Countries with a centralized administration and tax system tend to be characterized by weak local government with limited decision-making powers. Generally speaking, the central administration and funding model, which is normally based on standard decisions and uses a standard unit cost principle, is simple and often cheap to implement. However, central decisions and funding schemes that, by their nature, dominate over local initiative lose their operational flexibility and ability to respond to regional and local conditions. They are slow to react to variations in the demand for VET and for corresponding funds. Centralized models are often unable to yield the best possible performance from each individual school.

Local administration of vocational training appears to produce more coherent decisions which are more relevant to local economic growth, labour markets, equity issues and utilization of training capacity. Local governments are normally more flexible and accountable to the local public; they are able to achieve greater cost-effectiveness of decentralized allocations.

In countries with centrally established training quality standards which are incorporated into national skill standards and vocational qualifications, examination requirements and curricula, there is less need for central supervision of teaching. However, when VET providers are allowed to develop curricula themselves and to award qualifications, the need for central inspection of quality is apparent. Some countries apply a model of "reluctant decentralization" under which local decisions, primarily those relating to the disbursement of regional funds, continue to be subject to approval by the regional offices of central ministries.

The following negative results of decentralized administration and funding should be avoided.

- Decentralization may reduce the coherence of national VET policy making and weaken coordination between regions with regard to targets for skill delivery, maintaining national skill standards and skill testing requirements.
- If local authorities do not have sufficient resources and a firm interest in vocational training, or if they favour general education over VET, then the delegation of power may result in a massive reduction in allocations to vocational education and training.
- Because of variations in the local tax base, decentralized administration and funding apparently assumes local disparities. If there is no correction mechanism involving funds from other levels, some regions may be incapable of funding and maintaining the quality of training in their institutions.

- Decentralization of power commonly results in multi-level funding and control. This implies a larger number of decision makers at all levels, some of whom may lose interest in VET if it becomes a low-priority service.
- The creation of powerful local governments may noticeably increase overheads since, in practice, decentralization is rarely accompanied by any serious reduction in staffing. In addition, the coordination of several levels also has its cost and could cause delays in decision making.
- In the transition from centrally planned to market economies, particularly when the delegation of management power is not synchronized with the decentralization of funds, old problems may be aggravated by new developments. For instance, in larger countries, the local cost of maintaining schools may increase considerably due to a privatized local supply of electricity, heat and water. In centralized VET funding mechanisms, this has resulted in a higher funding burden being automatically transferred to the state budget. Because of such local variations, education ministries may be unable to establish standard school maintenance costs and simply have to pay the higher bills issued by local authorities.

1.4.2 Patterns of decentralization

Four major decentralization models have been applied in VET (see figure 3.7). First, responsibility for administration and control can be shared between central ministries (e.g. labour and education) and regional and local authorities. The delegation of management powers must be linked to decentralized resource allocation. This means that central funds are redistributed to regions while local governments are responsible for making more effective use of them. Another option is to mobilize the fund-raising powers of local authorities in order to share funding responsibilities with the state. As a result, a so-called multi-level funding and control pattern can be established where central, regional and local authorities contribute to local training budgets, while each level of authority sets its own conditions for funding, achieving targets and reporting on progress.

Another important condition for successful decentralization is the establishment of uniform technical guidelines for VET operations, including national skill standards, vocational qualifications and core curricula. Although some countries run a decentralized system without national technical guidelines, governments are increasingly in favour of this approach, as such a situation may result in the fragmentation of training systems. In the United States, for instance, state-level skill standards and the corresponding credentials are established through government-private partnerships which enable training providers to respond adequately to local labour markets. Italy, for example, has attempted to decentralize

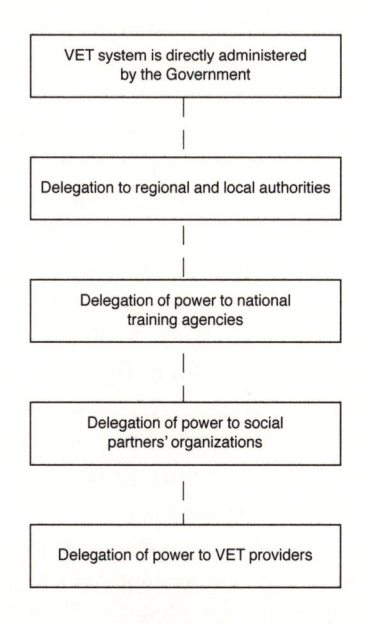

Figure 3.7 Patterns of decentralization in vocational education and training

```
┌─────────────────────────────────┐
│ VET system is directly administered │
│         by the Government           │
└─────────────────────────────────┘
                 │
                 ↓
┌─────────────────────────────────┐
│ Delegation to regional and local authorities │
└─────────────────────────────────┘
                 │
                 ↓
┌─────────────────────────────────┐
│  Delegation of power to national    │
│         training agencies           │
└─────────────────────────────────┘
                 │
                 ↓
┌─────────────────────────────────┐
│   Delegation of power to social     │
│       partners' organizations       │
└─────────────────────────────────┘
                 │
                 ↓
┌─────────────────────────────────┐
│  Delegation of power to VET providers │
└─────────────────────────────────┘
```

training administration to regions receiving authorization. However, the process is impaired, as the national system of testing and certification has not matured and no corresponding technical support has developed locally (Burgess, 1993).

Second, management powers and funds can be devolved to the national training agencies which have been established in many countries, mostly for labour market training. The management boards of training agencies become fully responsible for national training operations, often leaving no role for regional or local authorities, while the government sets operational targets and a framework for the agency's accountability. Other agencies which may be given power to administer public VET operations and funds on behalf of the government are so-called management intermediaries, which operate on the basis of management contracts signed with the government (see Module 2, Unit 2).

Third, the role of the social partners has increased dramatically, with many management and technical functions becoming bipartite or even tripartite. The social partners are represented on both consultative and decision-making bodies in vocational education. They dominate decision-making bodies dealing with employees' skill upgrading and other areas of continuing training. In some areas of continuing training, such as paid training leave, bipartite management-labour boards and funds have become the major authority responsible for the administration of mixed private-public funds and for the implementation of programmes. Social partners' sectoral organizations are increasingly taking the lead in planning industry training, while sectoral plans provide an input to national target setting and planning. In some industrialized countries, the social partners' standing bodies are fully responsible for drafting national skill standards as well as for skill testing.

Fourth, administrative and operational autonomy has been delegated to the lowest possible level – training institutions. Training providers are enabled and encouraged to study the market for services by maintaining close links with local businesses; they are encouraged to programme course delivery, to develop curricula, to sell services and to follow up on placement of their graduates. Only skill standards, vocational qualifications and examination requirements are defined centrally in order to ensure quality training. All this results in schools responding to regional and local needs more effectively. In some countries, the autonomy of providers has been strengthened through legal and funding reforms, resulting in the creation of independent organizations which are required to earn their funds by selling services in the market. Another avenue for decentralization of VET providers is to give the power of founding them to regional and local authorities, employers' and workers' organizations, cooperatives and even private individuals if they comply with national regulations aimed at securing quality training and defending the rights of consumers (see Module 3, Unit 2, and Module 6).

Unit 2. Organizational structures in vocational education

Learning objectives

This unit is designed to provide a better knowledge of:

1. Management patterns and organizational structures in vocational education
2. Limits to decentralization in vocational education

2.1 Government-administered vocational education

Traditionally, vocational education has been part of national education, which, for various reasons, is highly centralized. First, education systems teach fundamental subjects which do not readily lend themselves to change. Therefore, vocational education systems are often less dynamic than vocational training systems and do not maintain close links with labour markets. Second, many developing countries possess only limited financial resources and lack professional educationalists. They need to concentrate financial and human resources and to retain entire control over

Module 3. VET management and organizational structures

the education system at central government level. A certain degree of decentralization has been introduced to vocational education through the establishment of national VET councils and boards with broad representation of ministries, employers and unions and, sometimes, educationalists. These bodies, however, have mostly advisory rather than management functions.

Three major types of government-led administrative structures can be distinguished in vocational education. The first option is *highly centralized* structures, where educational institutions report directly to VET departments of national education ministries which set targets, allocate funds, recruit and dismiss staff. All or most technical support functions regarding national vocational qualifications, assessment of students and national curriculum development are also commonly assigned to ministerial VET departments. Regional authorities have no responsibility for administering vocational education except, perhaps, for general education schools offering vocational programmes. The second configuration assumes a *division of management powers between various government levels* (as in Brazil). This means that independent vocational education structures have evolved in both central and lower-level authorities. The third option is *decentralization to lower authorities,* i.e. partial decentralization (as in France) resulting in only a few management functions being devolved to the lower government levels or total decentralization to the local level (as in the United States).

2.1.1 Direct administration by central government

Centralized structures administering vocational education can have various configurations. In one, the vocational education department of the education ministry has divisions supervising separate types of VET institution (see figure 3.8 and box 3.1). In another, fields of study, rather than institutions, are administered. This can be appropriate when vocational programmes and general education programmes are offered by the same institutions (see figure 3.9).

Figure 3.8 Institution-based structure of vocational education (Republic of Korea, 1995)

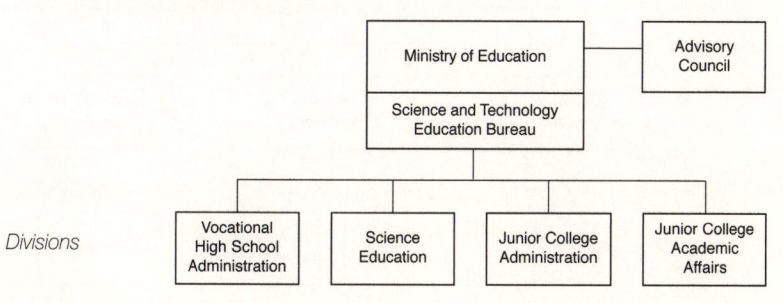

```
                        Ministry of Education ──── Advisory Council
                                │
                    Science and Technology
                       Education Bureau
          ┌─────────────┬─────────┴────────┬──────────────┐
Divisions  Vocational    Science      Junior College   Junior College
          High School   Education    Administration    Academic
          Administration                                Affairs
```

Managing vocational training systems

> **Box 3.1 Management of vocational education in the Republic of Korea**
>
> Vocational education in the Republic of Korea is administered by the Science and Technology Education Bureau of the Ministry of Education (MOE). The Bureau has four divisions responsible for *various groups of institutions*. The Advisory Council focuses on general educational policy. Its 60 members sit on six committees dealing with educational philosophy, academic education, science and technology education, teacher affairs, life-long education and social policy.
>
> Vocational education is provided by vocational high schools (VHSs) and junior vocational colleges (JVCs). High schools offering more than two vocational courses are called vocational high schools. The total number of VHSs in the country is about 900, with a total enrolment of almost 1.1 million. They involve 160 technical, about 240 commercial and 240 comprehensive high schools, and employ more than 53,300 teachers. VHSs offer three-year programmes for graduates from the middle school (nine years of schooling) and produce craft-workers and technicians. Technicians at this level are trained by the technical high schools, which enrol about 220,000 trainees.
>
> JVCs offer two- or three-year courses for graduates of the high schools. The MOE maintains an annual enrolment of about 2.3 million (future craftworkers) in VHSs and 224,000 (future technicians) in JVCs. These figures are not normally affected by changes in industry demand.
>
> Vocational education institutions report directly to the MOE, and local authorities have no power to intervene. Technical support services are centralized. The vocational education qualifications, training curricula and examination programmes for VHSs and JVCs are drafted by the Korea Educational Development Institute and subject to approval by the Ministry. VHSs and JVCs have to teach the approved curriculum and cannot offer any other training programmes.
>
> Source: Shin, 1995.

Figure 3.9 Field-of-study-based organizational structure of education (Flemish Community of Belgium, 1996)

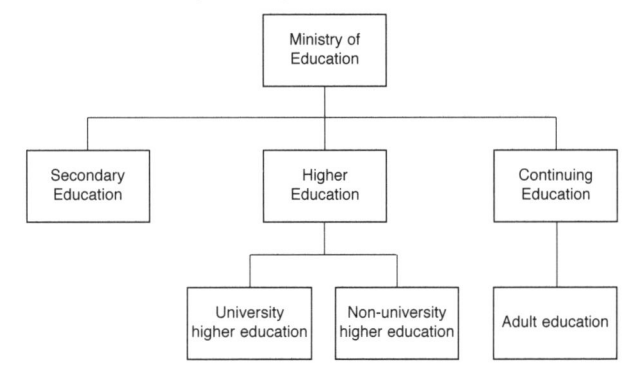

```
                     Ministry of
                      Education
                          |
      ┌───────────────────┼───────────────────┐
  Secondary             Higher            Continuing
  Education           Education            Education
                          |                    |
                 ┌────────┴────────┐           |
             University      Non-university   Adult
          higher education  higher education education
```

2.1.2 Vocational education structures divided between government levels

Relatively independent vocational education structures including supervisory and technical support bodies as well as providers can emerge at several levels of government administration. Some VET institutions may be administered, financed and technically supported by the central ministry, while other providers may be independently funded and administered by other government levels with no link to the central budget or technical guidelines. Each level of government authority (city, state or province) may have its own VET Council, implement supervision and provide technical support to schools. Such structures are commonly exposed to disparities in financial and technical support between schools belonging to different government levels. Maintaining uniformity of national skill standards and vocational qualifications as well as quality of training can be difficult (see figure 3.10 and box 3.2).

Figure 3.10 Vocational education structure divided between government levels (Brazil, 1995)

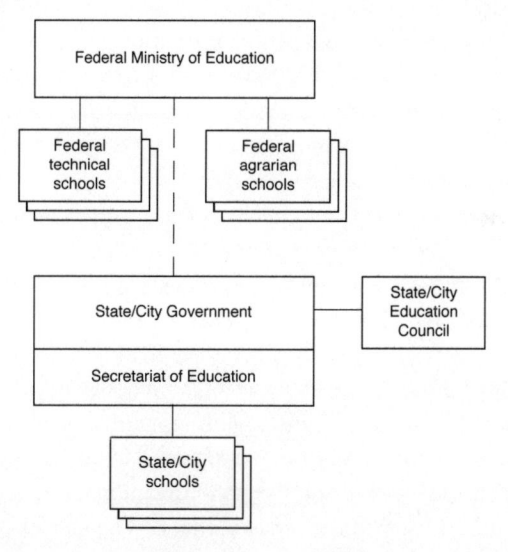

```
              Federal Ministry of Education
                   /           \
         Federal              Federal
         technical            agrarian
         schools              schools
                   |
         State/City Government ——— State/City
                                    Education
         Secretariat of Education   Council
                   |
              State/City
              schools
```

2.1.3 Delegation to lower-level government

In the countries where management power in vocational education systems has been delegated to lower-level government, decentralization is only partial and important functions are retained by the central government. In countries with

Managing vocational training systems

> **Box 3.2 Organization of technical education in Brazil**
>
> Technical education programmes in Brazil leading to the qualification of middle-level technician are taught mostly in the federal and state schools after eight years of primary schooling. The federal system of technical education consists of over 100 institutions with more than 100,000 pupils. The best-organized are the 19 federal technical schools (ETFs) and 37 federal agrarian schools. The federal schools boast high rates of graduation with a large proportion of graduates proceeding to university and entering white-collar jobs.
>
> The *federal* schools are administered by the Technological Education Secretariat of the Ministry of Education, which approves curricula, testing methods and other aspects of operation. Federal schools have a high degree of operational autonomy. Each school has two advisory councils – a superior council and a technical council – which include representatives of the State or City Governments, entrepreneurs and other local leaders. School principals play a significant role in teacher recruitment, but they cannot dismiss teachers. Although in principle the Ministry of Education is responsible for the design of curricula, selection of training materials and school maintenance, most school principals take care of all this directly. The instructors and other staff of federal schools are civil servants.
>
> Another group of technical schools are the *state* schools, which offer a wide range of programmes leading to a full general secondary education suitable for entering college. Most of their vocational courses are for occupations such as teaching, accounting and clerical assistance which involve no heavy machinery or special supplies. State schools are administered by the State/City Secretariat of Education. The Secretariat of Science and Technology or even the Secretariat of Industry and Commerce may also administer technical schools. In addition, there are advisory State/City Education Councils which commonly include representatives from public and private schools as well as industry training institutions. The Secretariats manage education budgets, finance schools and decide on teacher recruitment. Acting through Education Councils, they also authorize vocational courses and approve curricula. The school infrastructural support is entirely centralized.
>
> Source: Leite, 1995.

several government levels involved, one level may be assigned certain decision-making responsibilities and resources, while others may have the legal power of control or of being consulted on capital investment in educational institutions.

Module 3. VET management and organizational structures

Delegation of power to lower authorities may be accompanied by the establishment of ministry offices at the lower government level with the power to authorize and control the expenditure of decentralized resources. In this sense, the structures are quasi-decentralized (see box 3.3).

> **Box 3.3 Delegation of power in vocational education in France**
>
> An attempt to decentralize vocational education in France has resulted in each of the four levels of government administration (national, regional, departmental and communal) sharing control over vocational education:
>
> - The national Ministry of Education is responsible for the most important components of education, including recruitment of teaching staff and provision of wage-related funds, curriculum development and inspection of educational institutions.
> - The 30 educational districts (Académies), which generally correspond to administrative regions, have certain decision-making powers. The chief education officers, who are based in the regional prefect's office, run the districts on behalf of the Minister of Education, while the democratically elected Regional Councils control the operation of lycées.
> - The departments' General Councils control the operations of educational institutions in their jurisdiction.
> - The commune authorities are consulted on the profile of education institutions, their location and equipment.
>
> The regions' responsibilities include programming courses as well as building, operating and maintaining lycées. Regions are required to draw up training and investment plans. The plans for training courses span several years and are designed to coordinate the action of different players and to reflect the region's training needs. Investment plans set out, in order of priority, the number and type of lycées to be built, rebuilt or extended. The state representative uses the region's proposals to draw up an annual list of the major work that will actually take place.
>
> The 22 Regional Councils, with the agreement of the 96 departments, draw up and transmit to the chief education officers the outline education plans (OEPs) for secondary schools and lycées. In turn, the departments' General Councils, with the agreement of the communes, decide on investment programmes for the construction of educational institutions. Implementation of the OEPs is supported by central government allocations to each educational district. However, the expenditure of the regional allocation is subject to the chief education officer's approval.
>
> Source: Kirsch, 1994.

Managing vocational training systems

2.1.4 Full delegation to local level

Management responsibilities and resources for vocational education can be fully devolved to the lowest possible level of government administration. Such structures normally emerge when local governments have the power to collect taxes and generate educational resources. In these cases, central ministries provide guidance instead of administering local VET programmes directly. The intermediate administrative levels provide technical and financial support to local VET programmes. Through their financial support, they exert a certain policy leverage at local level. However, local VET administration does not have to report to higher levels and, in that sense, local systems are essentially self-administered (see figure 3.11 and box 3.4).

Figure 3.11 Vocational education structures at the local level (United States, 1996)

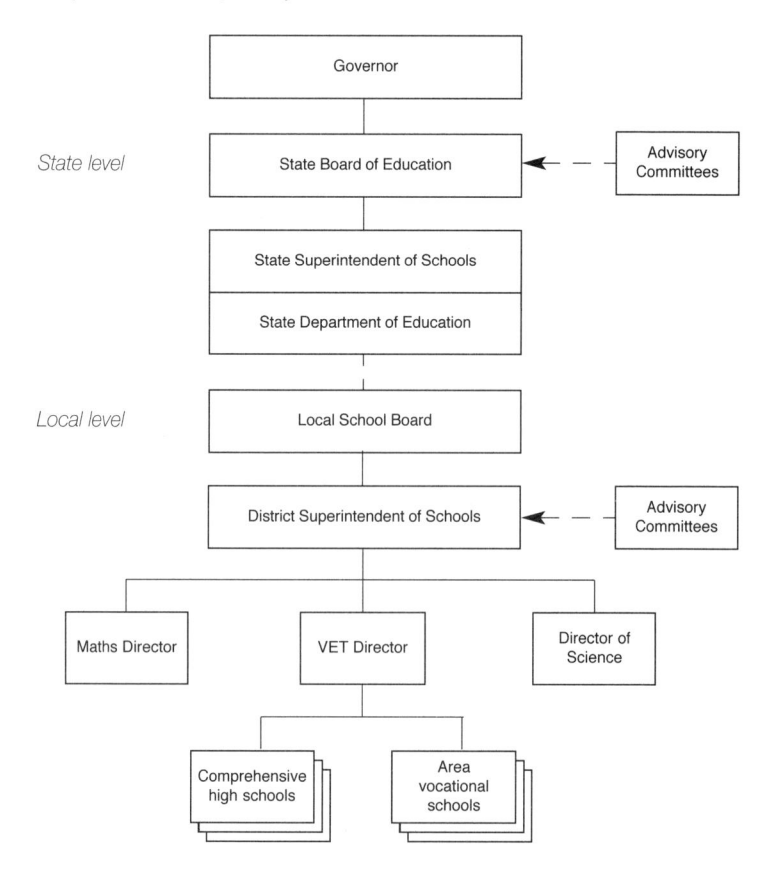

```
                                  ┌─────────────┐
                                  │  Governor   │
                                  └──────┬──────┘
                                         │
State level      ┌────────────────────────┴────────┐        ┌──────────┐
                 │   State Board of Education      │◄─ ─ ─ ─│ Advisory │
                 └────────────────┬────────────────┘        │Committees│
                                  │                         └──────────┘
                 ┌────────────────┴────────────────┐
                 │ State Superintendent of Schools │
                 ├─────────────────────────────────┤
                 │  State Department of Education  │
                 └────────────────┬────────────────┘
                                  │
Local level      ┌────────────────┴────────────────┐
                 │      Local School Board         │
                 └────────────────┬────────────────┘
                                  │
                 ┌────────────────┴────────────────┐        ┌──────────┐
                 │ District Superintendent of Schools │◄─ ─ ─│ Advisory │
                 └────┬───────────┬────────────┬───┘        │Committees│
                      │           │            │            └──────────┘
               ┌──────┴────┐ ┌────┴────┐ ┌─────┴─────┐
               │   Maths   │ │   VET   │ │Director of│
               │ Director  │ │ Director│ │  Science  │
               └───────────┘ └────┬────┘ └───────────┘
                              ┌───┴───────┐
                      ┌───────┴─────┐ ┌───┴────────┐
                      │Comprehensive│ │    Area    │
                      │high schools │ │ vocational │
                      │             │ │  schools   │
                      └─────────────┘ └────────────┘
```

84

Module 3. VET management and organizational structures

> **Box 3.4 Management of vocational education in the United States**
>
> The Federal Department of Education (DOE) administers vocational education funding and legislation through the Office of Vocational and Adult Education (VAE) and the Office of Post-Secondary Education (PSE). Contact with the state-level VET administrative units is maintained through the DOE's ten regional offices, each headed by a regional representative of the Secretary of Education. Their major task is soliciting, reviewing and approving state-level proposals for federal education funds. Policy and practice at both State and local level are influenced by advisory committees and task forces that are appointed by the DOE to explore problems of national importance.
>
> The federal government relies heavily on state governments to administer vocational education and training. In this way it reduces its own administrative costs and programming is more closely aligned to the requirements of states and local communities. A portion of federal funds is used to support state administrative costs, which gives the federal government some administrative leverage.
>
> VET management structures in individual states vary greatly, but three major patterns can be identified. Usually, secondary and post-secondary education are governed by a state board of education (SBE) and administered by a state department of education (SDE) responsible to the board. Secondary and post-secondary education can also be governed by separate boards operated by a state department of education, or the two boards can be completely independent. There are also variations to these patterns. In certain states, community colleges are governed by the same board of directors as four-year colleges. However, in most cases some type of governing board is paired with a state administrative unit. The former focuses mainly on governance and policy, the latter on operations and implementation.
>
> SBEs are either appointed by the state governor or elected by popular vote. They are responsible for policy and planning, setting programme standards, programme review and approval, and general supervision. In addition, they establish graduation requirements and set funding priorities. State-level advisory committees are appointed to develop VET policy. In general, they are composed of representatives from labour, business, government, education and the civic leadership. In some cases, at least half the members must be from the business community. However, the extent to which state boards influence local operations is usually quite limited. The board appoints a state superintendent of schools, who in turn appoints an assistant state superintendent responsible for secondary and post-secondary VET.

> *Box 3.4 (cont'd)*
>
> Local secondary-level VET institutions (high schools and area vocational schools) are part of legally defined public school districts (usually comprising less than 20 schools) governed by elected school boards (usually six to ten members). Local school boards have the major policy-making and budgetary authority. They employ a district superintendent of schools, who is directly responsible to the local school board and has operational authority. In most school districts there are subject-matter specialists, including a director of VET, who must work through the local school principals. The number of districts varies from state to state.
>
> Source: Herschbach, 1995

2.2 Administration through management intermediaries

In several countries, governments administer vocational education and training through professional management bodies which are given an intermediary position between the government and VET providers. These management intermediaries are nongovernmental bodies and may be registered as public companies limited by government guarantee. Their responsibilities and conditions of operation are fixed in a management contract with the government. The government, in these cases, provides governance and funds and supervises the bodies. The mandate of these bodies is to achieve certain targets on behalf of the government by delivering VET programmes and administering public education funds. In order to deliver courses, they contract out to VET providers of all kinds. Management intermediaries usually draw their administrators from business, finance and insurance, and operate outside civil service rules. Management intermediaries also differ essentially from ministerial VET departments in that they do not have their own training providers and they do not offer any significant technical support to providers (see box 3.5; see also Module 2, Unit 2).

2.3 Delegating power to independent schools

Several countries have delegated most management power to providers. The providers' legal status has changed and they have emerged as non-profit companies (as in the United Kingdom) or self-owning institutions (as in Denmark). Delegation of management power can be accompanied by the delegation of technical functions such as curriculum development and, sometimes, testing of graduates. As long as the national skill standards are well established and trainees' knowledge and skills are rigorously assessed, curricula can be developed by schools themselves, provided that instructors are qualified. In some countries, the development of curricula by

> **Box 3.5 Administering colleges through the United Kingdom Further Education Funding Council**
>
> In the United Kingdom, it is the central government tradition to manage public services through intermediary bodies instituted between itself and service providers. The intermediaries have the power to shape, advise, fund and control the system, but they do not govern it. These bodies have the legal form of non-profit-making companies established and wholly funded by the Government with no resources of their own. They do not follow civil service rules; the majority of their boards are drawn from employers. They operate on the basis of contracts signed with the Government. In the field of vocational training, the power to finance and control colleges has been devolved to these bodies from Local Education Authorities (LEAs).
>
> At national level, VET is governed by the Department of Education and Employment. It has established an intermediate management body called the Further Education Funding Council (FEFC) which provides funds and supervision for about 450 Further Education (FE) Colleges offering vocational and technical education programmes. FEFC headquarters has a staff of about 250 and three main operating departments: finance, programmes and inspection. The FEFC employs a large force of full- and part-time inspectors, who report on each college at least once every four years. It also has nine regional offices, where another 150 staff members are based. At 400, the overall number of staff members is less than the staff previously employed in the LEAs and the inspectorate of the Department of Education. Since these intermediate bodies operate on the basis of contracts with the Government, the implications are reduced bureaucracy, higher operational flexibility and greater management competence.
>
> Source: Russell, 1995.

college instructors has become a tradition. Delegation of testing to school staff, on the other hand, has always been criticized as an unreliable mechanism (see box 3.6).

In the management model combining central governance of the national VET system with the full autonomy of training providers, a change in the providers' legal status is not the major precondition for full delegation of responsibilities to them. A decentralized structure can be introduced, and the advantages associated with it can be utilized, with the providers remaining public institutions (as in the Netherlands and the United States). The only authority that the government should retain, if it wishes these institutions to meet national policies and targets, is the administration of funds for purchasing their programmes (see box 3.7; see also Module 6).

Box 3.6 Flat management structure in Denmark

Vocational education in Denmark is administered by the Ministry of Education's VET Department. There are no other intermediary levels between the Ministry and the training schools. The Ministry's management responsibilities have changed dramatically from direct administration of schools to the development of VET policies and targets, promulgation of Education Orders delineating a broad framework for VET courses and regulation of financing.

The reform reduced the VET Department's staff by 20 per cent and changed its functions. Staff involved in the development of rules, inspection of vocational schools and creation of the national curriculum decreased, while staff in the legal office and the planning office grew. The Ministry focuses on the development of training legislation, while the planning office focuses on communication and coordination between the Ministry and the social partners (rather than VET planning *per se*).

Vocational schools are now organized as private, non-profit and independent institutions. They have considerable freedom in the programming of delivery and enrolments, curriculum development and teaching. Individual schools decide which courses to offer and how to organize the teaching within the national guidelines and financial framework. All central regulations regarding class size have been abolished, while regulations covering the number of lessons to be taught to students have been modified. Rules on teachers' working hours have been made more flexible. Instructors' wages and employment conditions are regulated through collective agreements which are negotiated every second year. The independent schools which wish to obtain public funds have to offer programmes which comply with government regulations. Public grants are not earmarked, and schools are free to allocate resources as they see fit. Schools now compete for students and must assess their intake capacity and utilize it effectively in competition with other providers.

Governing boards of six to 12 members manage the schools and administer government grants. Two board members represent the county council and the municipal council, while others represent labour market organizations, usually including a president of the local union and the training department manager of a large enterprise. Teachers, administrative staff and students are represented on the board in a non-voting capacity. The chairperson of the board is drawn from the labour market organizations and normally spends two days a month dealing with college-related matters. The school principal acts as secretary to the board. The board appoints and dismisses the principal, who is responsible for managing day-to-day

Module 3. VET management and organizational structures

operations. It also appoints and dismisses the auditor of the school. On the recommendation of the principal, the board approves the school budget and decides the VET courses and number of training places the school will offer. The school principal is free to recruit and dismiss individual instructors (subject to the board's approval). If the board does not comply with the Ministry's Education Orders, it can be dismissed and its responsibilities will be assigned to a ministry appointee until a new board is elected.

Source: Nielsen, 1995.

Box 3.7 Independent schools in the Netherlands

Senior secondary vocational education schools producing skilled workers in the Netherlands have been reformed. They are now independent and enjoy freedom of operation, organization of teaching, financial expenditure and staff policies. A 1990 law stipulates that schools should provide programmes in accordance with a school work plan, which has become the major programming innovation. An inspectorate assesses work plans and enters into discussion with the school when it finds plans of insufficient quality. Greater flexibility has been introduced into the conditions of employment of teaching staff, with more use being made of people from industry. Schools decide how many people to employ and what salaries to pay. Central regulations on staffing prescribe certain positions assumed to exist in all schools, which, together with student numbers, determine college budgets. The management powers of the school board of governors can be transferred to a central directorate of schools if boards fail to achieve targets.

The attainment targets set by the Government for courses, mainly on the basis of industry advice, have replaced the previous examination syllabi. Schools now have full autonomy with regard to the curriculum. They translate the attainment targets, which include both occupational and general education targets, into teaching objectives which become part of the work plan. They no longer have to apply the timetable supplied by the Ministry of Education, which formerly prescribed the minimum number of teaching periods for each subject. Schools, however, must indicate the links between the attainment targets and the subjects in the curriculum.

Employer influence on teaching and programming has been introduced. The business community is responsible for establishing job profiles and, with educationalists (within the branch consultative bodies), for translating them into training profiles which, along with the attainment targets, are to be incorporated in units of certification. Attainment targets and units of certification are approved by the Minister. Schools are legally allowed to sell

> *Box 3.7 (cont'd)*
> training services to firms. They have to apply to the Ministry of Education for a licence, with minimum standards to be met for courses, examinations and qualifications for entry. The independent training schools now compete in the market.
>
> Sources: Netherlands Ministry of Education and Science, 1993; Burgess, 1993; Hövels and Meijer, 1994.

2.4 Guiding the dual training system

The German-type dual training system features a combination of enterprise-based training, conducted mostly during actual work, and school-based theoretical instruction. School-based instruction is administered directly by government (see also Module 2). The dual system is simultaneously embedded in the national education system and in the market economy. Private firms decide whether to take on trainees and contribute financially. From the management point of view, the dual training system is essentially employer-led and, therefore, market forces-led. The government has no real power over enterprise involvement in vocational training; rather it provides technical support and training incentives to enterprises. The sophistication of this system requires thorough coordination of interests, resources and action on both sides. None of the actors in the German-type dual system actually has substantial management power over the whole system; instead, each actor has the power of participation and control. As in any other system based on consultation and coordination rather than direct subordination, the decision-making process in the dual training system is slow and essentially requires a consensus (see box 3.8 and figure 3.12).

> **Box 3.8 Administration and coordination in the German-type dual system**
>
> There are several major actors in the German dual system: government (federal and Länder (lower-level government)), employers and trainees. Competent bodies representing various economic sectors (e.g. the Chambers of Commerce and Industry, Craft Chambers, etc.) are involved in decision making and training, including practical testing and certification, and approval of training firms.
>
> The Federal Minister for Education and Science is legally in charge of in-plant training and overall coordination, and responsible for issuing training regulations which lay down standards for in-plant training and final examinations. The Federal Government has expert committees dealing with training. The Federal Institute for Vocational Training (BIBB) is involved in the preparation of training regulations and many other technical functions. The

Module 3. VET management and organizational structures

> BIBB has a tri-partite legal body dealing with training regulations with 11 representatives each from employers, workers and the Länder and with five members nominated by the Federal Government.
>
> The role of the Länder is important in that they technically regulate, finance and administer training schools, while local authorities have, in fact, very little management power over schools. The Länder Committees for Vocational Training, supervised by the Länder Ministries, have equal representation of employers, workers and the Länder government; half the committee members must be educational experts. The Committees represent a coordinating instrument at Länder level, whose function is to advise and recommend.
>
> The scale of operation of the whole dual training system is determined by the number of training places offered by enterprises. The Chambers of Commerce and Industry have important decision-making and coordination powers regarding the overall number of enterprise training openings. The Vocational Training Committees include representatives of employers, labour and vocational school teachers and are closely involved in negotiating the content of legal training regulations. The Chambers of Industry and Commerce and the Craft Chambers are legally (but not technically) supervised by the Länder Ministry of Labour or Ministry for Economics.

Figure 3.12 Coordination structure in the dual training system (Germany, 1995)

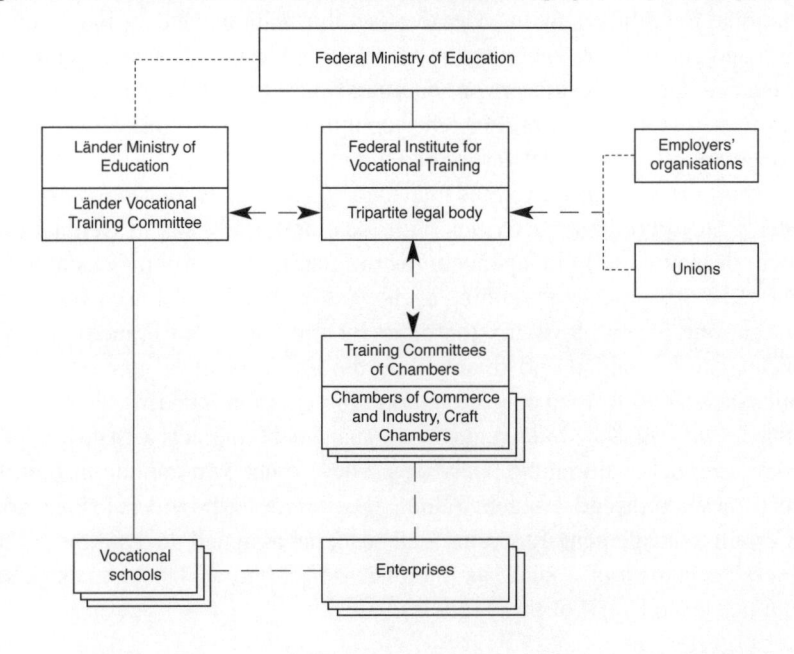

Unit 3. Organizational structures in labour market training

Learning objectives

This unit is designed to provide a better knowledge of:

1. Labour market training systems directly administered by governments
2. The organizational structures that involve labour market training agencies
3. Decentralized structures in training

3.1 Types of labour market training structure

There are four principal options for management and organizational structures in labour market training:

- government administration;
- labour market training agencies;
- intermediary management bodies; and
- workers' and employers' organizations.

Where training is directly *administered by government* at various levels, technical support services can be provided by government departments or specialist public institutions. This type of structure commonly features low operational flexibility, and, in order to offset this, national and regional training boards and councils are becoming increasingly widespread. In some countries, training councils and boards are predominantly advisory and technical clearance bodies (as in Pakistan), while in other countries they have taken over certain management responsibilities (as in the United States).

Decentralized training systems managed by national *labour market training agencies* may coordinate activities with local authorities (as in Denmark and France) or may be fully independent (as in Japan). A country may establish an integrated employment and training agency (as in Denmark) or use two separate agencies, one for employment, the other for training (as in France). Training agencies can be guided and financed by the government or converted into a public corporation fully exposed to market forces (as in Sweden).

Special *intermediary bodies* enter into management contracts with governments to administer national training operations. They do not own training institutions. Instead, they contract government training programmes to providers in the market.

Certain management functions can also be assigned to *employers' and workers' organizations* such as national and sectoral labour-management committees (see Unit 4 of this Module).

3.2 Government-administered training systems

3.2.1 Direct administration of training by government departments

In some countries, labour market training centres report directly to the training department of the labour ministry or regional government. In both cases, government departments are in charge of major administrative, financing and technical decisions. The staff of training institutions are employed by the government and their budget is part of the government budget. A mechanism for sharing responsibility, funds and expertise can be introduced through the establishment of national, regional and local training boards. However, these commonly serve as clearing, evaluating and advisory bodies rather that administrative organizations (see figure 3.13 and box 3.9).

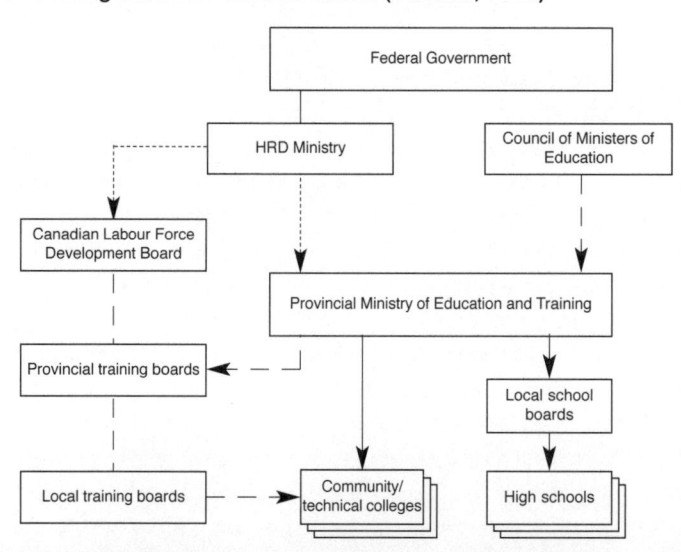

Figure 3.13 Integrated VET administration (Canada, 1996)

```
                        Federal Government
                       /                  \
         HRD Ministry                      Council of Ministers of
        /      |                           Education
       /       |                                |
Canadian Labour Force                           |
Development Board                               |
       |       |                                |
       |       └──> Provincial Ministry of Education and Training
       |                         |
Provincial training boards <── ──┘
       |                         |
       |                         ├──> Local school boards
       |                         |              |
Local training boards ──> Community/            |
                          technical colleges   High schools
```

Box 3.9 Integrated administration of education and training in Canada

The federal Human Resource Development Ministry in Canada (HRD Canada) is responsible for setting the national labour force development strategy, post-secondary VET, overall national coordination and financing of vocational training. It negotiates three-year federal-provincial training agreements with the provincial education and training ministries. Under these agreements, the federal government buys places in provincial training institutions and Canada

Box 3.9 (cont'd)

Employment Centres refer clients to provincial community and technical colleges. Another federal ministry, Industry Canada, gives technical support to the training provided within industry, while Labour Canada supervises and funds apprenticeships. The Council of Ministers of Education provides guidelines and coordination in education and training.

HRD Canada has delegated most tasks related to training policy and technical support to the Canadian Labour Force Development Board (CLFDB), an independent, non-profit organization guided and funded by HRD Canada. The CLFDB mandate is the development of national training policies, skill standards and qualifications and their assessment and certification; the definition of principles of equitable access to VET and eligibility criteria for income support of trainees; and the establishment of guidelines on resource allocation for training. The CLFDB includes the social partners, various social groups and the federal and provincial governments. Its bipartite management structure comprises one co-chair from business and one from labour. Training councils in key industrial sectors have also been established. These are funded jointly by HRD Canada and private industry. (So far, 13 of the 55 proposed councils have been created.)

Although it is divided at federal level, labour market training and education governance is *integrated* at provincial level. Training providers are directly administered by provincial ministries of education and training. Provincial training boards (funded from provincial budgets) and local training boards (funded by federal and provincial budgets) have been set up. Six of the ten provinces now have training boards. Devolution of responsibility and funds for training to the provincial and local levels has been an ongoing process. Coordination between the CLFDB and provincial training boards is facilitated by the fact that representatives of CLFDB and HRD Canada sit on provincial boards.

In the future, decentralization is likely to involve the partial dismantling of HRD Canada and other federal ministries. Some of their operational and coordination functions will probably be transferred to the provinces. The federal government is going to withdraw from direct governance of labour-market training, apprenticeship programmes and workplace-based training. It will no longer purchase training courses, either directly or indirectly, from provincial establishments. Full responsibility for VET will be transferred to provincial ministries of education and training. However, the guiding role of HRD Canada and CLFDB will remain. Provincial training boards will coordinate their operations with provincial ministries of education and training and with the CLFDB.

Source: Wilson, 1996

Module 3. VET management and organizational structures

Most developing countries do not have structures for retraining the unemployed and for upgrading employees' skills. Their focus is on the initial training of young people and the organizational structures of their training systems are therefore limited to this (see figure 3.14 and box 3.10).

Figure 3.14 Government-administered training system (Pakistan, 1995)

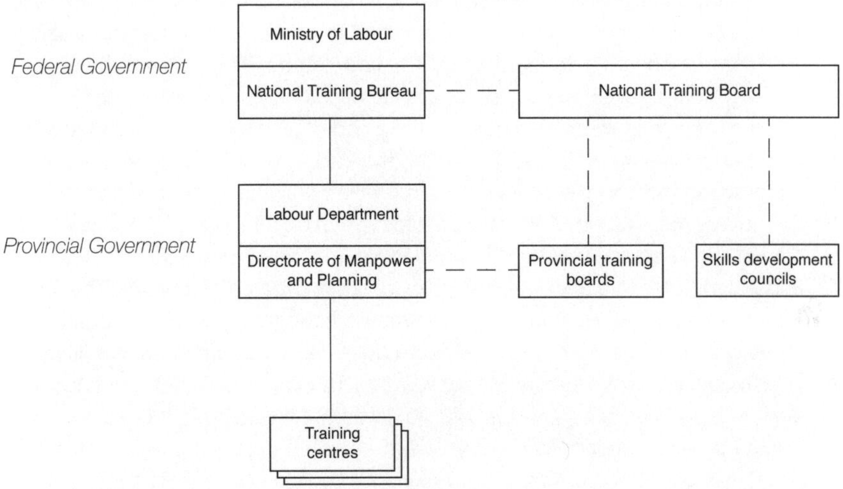

```
                    ┌─────────────────────┐
                    │ Ministry of Labour  │
Federal Government  ├─────────────────────┤         ┌──────────────────────┐
                    │National Training    ├ ─ ─ ─ ─ ┤ National Training Board│
                    │Bureau               │         │                      │
                    └─────────────────────┘         └──────────────────────┘
                                                        │           │
                                                        │           │
                    ┌─────────────────────┐             │           │
                    │ Labour Department   │             │           │
Provincial          ├─────────────────────┤         ┌───┴──────┐ ┌──┴────────────┐
Government          │Directorate of       ├ ─ ─ ─ ─ ┤Provincial│ │Skills         │
                    │Manpower and Planning│         │training  │ │development    │
                    └─────────────────────┘         │boards    │ │councils       │
                              │                     └──────────┘ └───────────────┘
                              │
                    ┌─────────────────┐
                    │ Training        │
                    │ centres         │
                    └─────────────────┘
```

3.2.2 Coordinating the training operations of various government ministries

In most countries, training operations are divided among government agencies (e.g. labour ministries, education ministries, ministries of industry, ministries of youth and sports, etc.). This complicates the coordination of national training operations. All the ministries and their training operations are financed separately by the government. In addition, each ministry tends to establish its own training institutions, set technical requirements and even offer sectoral vocational qualifications. In many countries, fierce competition between ministries for government training budgets has been observed. Another related problem is that various ministries provide similar (though often technically weak) training programmes, whose unit costs vary widely; this reduces the efficiency of the overall national training allocation.

Instead of limiting the number of ministries involved in training, which is commonly proposed, another organizational solution to this problem could be to nominate a certain national training ministry or agency as the lead organization, with

> **Box 3.10 The training system in Pakistan**
>
> In Pakistan, responsibility for the administration of vocational training is shared between the federal and provincial governments. The national training system is governed by the National Training Bureau (NTB), a department of the Ministry of Labour, Manpower and Overseas Pakistanis. The NTB is in charge of planning and developing skill standards, national curricula and trade tests. Training centres report to provincial governments rather than to the central government. Politically and technically, the training system is guided by the National Training Board and, beneath it, four Provincial Training Boards (PTBs). The National Training Board develops policies, assesses needs and plans vocational training, develops vocational qualifications and offers technical support to providers. It is a tripartite body on which federal and provincial government agencies as well as employers' and workers' organizations, such as the Employers' Federation of Pakistan, Chambers of Commerce and Industry and Trade Union Federations of all four provinces, are equally represented. The Federal Minister for Labour and Manpower is Chairman of the board. The NTB Director-General is secretary of the board, while the NTB acts as a secretariat to the National Training Board. The board does not have permanent employees.
>
> Provincial Directorates of Manpower and Training (DMT) of the provincial labour departments administer training centres. In each DMT there are deputy directors responsible for employment exchanges who register youth and the unemployed, and place them in jobs but do not train. The PTBs are guided by the DMTs as well as by the National Training Board. PTB structures and functions are similar to those of the National Training Board. The mandate of PTBs is the provision of technical support to local training programmes. PTBs are required to apply uniform national skill standards and are responsible for curriculum development, skill testing and certification. The provincial labour secretary chairs the PTB, while the DMT director acts as member secretary of the PTB.
>
> A recent organizational innovation has been the creation in provinces, on a pilot basis, of Skill Development Councils (SDCs). SDCs are autonomous organizations reporting directly to and financed by the NTB and they operate in parallel with PTBs. They have been set up in two provinces to focus on the identification of local training needs, development of training packages and selection of providers with whom to enter into service contracts. In contrast to PTBs, the SDCs are staffed with 10 permanent members drawn primarily from employers (50 per cent), with the other members representing local employees, the NTB, DMTs, PTBs and training centres. In terms of operational responsibilities, SDCs resemble the Training and Enterprise Councils (TECs) in the United Kingdom, which are in full charge of administering labour market training operations in their catchment areas (see box 3.16).
>
> Source: Muneer, 1996

> **Box 3.11 The need to coordinate training programmes in the Philippines**
>
> VET programmes in the Philippines are provided by more than 340 government-run institutions. Among the major training agencies are: the Department of Education, Culture and Sports (DECS), which administers high schools and trade schools; the Commission for Higher Education (CHED), which guides state universities and colleges (SUCs), a number of which offer training programmes; and the Technical Education and Skills Development Authority (TESDA), which administers 14 regional and 45 provincial Manpower Training Centres. In addition, local governments own 45 Satellite Training Centres offering basic skills courses.
>
> In order to improve national coordination, the government made TESDA responsible for supervising, upgrading and endorsing, on a regular basis, the technical and financial activities of the entire public VET sector. Annual appropriations for these institutions will be released only if their training programmes are endorsed by TESDA. For this purpose, a one-time allocation was reserved for TESDA, under the National Appropriation Act, 1996, to purchase equipment, retrain instructors and develop training curricula for a large group of education and training institutions. TESDA is obliged to evaluate the technical content of programmes and to recommend ways to improve programmes provided by the above agencies. Financial clearance will require standardization of various courses in terms of outputs, requirements for equipment, materials, administration and teachers. This may eventually allow for standardized programme unit costs which all public providers, no matter the agency, will have to comply with. The SUCs, which are known for the high unit cost of their low- and medium-level programmes, would have to comply with the standard unit cost, which could lead to some SUCs deciding to abandon low-end programmes as cost-inefficient and to expand the up-market, technically sophisticated courses, the standard allocations for which may be much higher.
>
> Sources: TESDA, 1995; World Bank, 1996.

responsibility to examine, supervise and formally approve the technical content and standard cost of all government-funded training programmes (see box 3.11).

3.2.3 Programme-based organization structures

Some governments refrain from direct intervention in labour market training operations. Developing the legal framework and exercising some control over the allocation of funds is sometimes the only role the government retains. (Some managerial power is delegated to lower levels of government, but is still, to some degree, retained.) With this hands-off approach, a central government attempts

Managing vocational training systems

to complement and encourage the training initiatives of lower authorities and to remedy possible regional disparities in their training provision. Such activities may be organized as national training programmes for which special legislation, rules and structures are enacted, which may have time limits (see figure 3.15 and box 3.12).

Figure 3.15 Administration of the federal labour market training programme (United States, 1995)

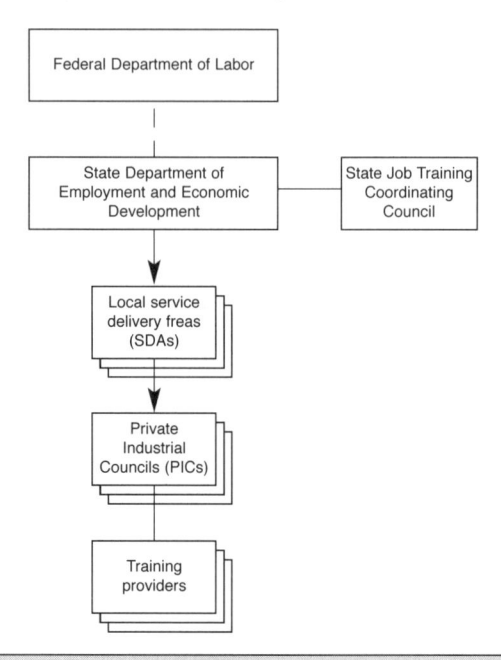

```
             Federal Department of Labor
                        │
                        │
      State Department of          State Job Training
      Employment and Economic ──── Coordinating
      Development                  Council
                │
                ▼
         Local service
         delivery freas
         (SDAs)
                │
                ▼
            Private
            Industrial
            Councils (PICs)
                │
                ▼
            Training
            providers
```

Box 3.12 Programme-based management structures in the United States

The Job Training Partnership Act (JTPA) of 1982 is the largest training and employment programme administered by the United States Government, and it is the only VET programme totally financed through federal funds. While most federal training legislation is permissive rather than mandatory, and states have considerable autonomy regarding participation in federal programmes, most states participate fully because they cannot forgo even modest federal support. The JTPA provides grants to support training for specific categories of disadvantaged people (youth, adults and older workers). The private sector plays a prominent role in administering local employment and training programmes. Federal regulations establish eligibility, the services that can be provided and performance standards.

Module 3. VET management and organizational structures

These standards apply to contractors, programme completers and training placements. The states act primarily as conduits for federal funds and as administrators; local authorities have overall responsibility for programme administration and operation. The federally mandated State Job Training Coordinating Council sets policy and coordinates training activities.

States, in effect, serve as the administrative and monitoring arm of the federal government in implementing particular programmes. A portion of federal funds supports state administrative costs. States also initiate their own labour market programmes to support a wide range of welfare, economic development and training activities. State-funded programmes tend to focus primarily on the disadvantaged (e.g. the working poor, the unemployed, the low skilled, the undereducated and welfare recipients). In general, however, state involvement in direct labour market training is limited. The governors establish state administrative units called designated local service delivery areas (SDAs) which are administered through state departments of economic development and employment. The SDAs determine funding priorities and handle contracting arrangements. Generally, there is one SDA for a population of 200,000 or more. There is no set administrative structure for SDAs, and no fixed number of staff. SDAs can be part of other employment and training organizations or they can be established and staffed outside existing local government agencies.

Each SDA establishes local Private Industrial Councils (PICs) which report to them. Representatives of business and industry comprise half of PIC membership. As with SDAs, there is no predetermined structure for PICs, and both depend on JTPA funds. PICs select service providers for training programmes on the basis of bidding, they monitor quality and evaluate programmes. Service contracts whereby providers are paid only when specific goals are attained are common. A large proportion of training consists of short, inexpensive courses with easy-to-meet performance requirements. Coordination with other public service providers and local employment and welfare agencies is achieved through representation on the PIC, and is covered in the plan submitted to the SDA for funding.

At state and local level there is considerable duplication and overlap in the implementation of federal programmes and the use of funds. There are no common planning and reporting requirements or eligibility definitions. Similar groups and similar objectives are served through various federal programmes. Interest is increasing in achieving greater coordination between agencies in order to reduce duplication and overlap in VET programmes.

Source: Herschbach, 1995.

3.3 Training administered by national training agencies

3.3.1 Managing training as part of labour market administration

Most industrialized countries have national agencies wholly in charge of labour market employment and training operations. Governments set policies and finance and supervise these agencies. Although the devolution of management powers from the ministry to the agency is already a very important step towards decentralization, the agencies themselves decentralize their operations further to their regional and local offices. Integration of the employment and labour market training functions under the same authority results in the possibility of better coordination of operations. An example of an employment and training agency reporting to the national labour market authority and of its regional structures is provided in figures 3.16 and 3.17 and in box 3.13.

Figure 3.16 Regional labour market administration (Denmark, 1995)

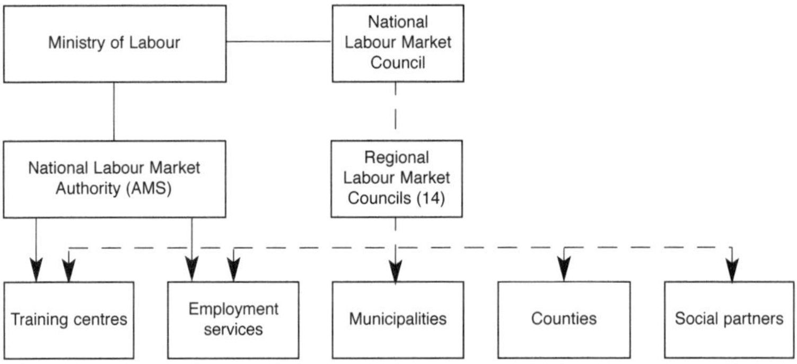

```
┌──────────────────┐           ┌──────────────────┐
│ Ministry of      │───────────│ National         │
│ Labour           │           │ Labour Market    │
│                  │           │ Council          │
└──────────────────┘           └──────────────────┘
         │                              │
         │                              │
┌──────────────────┐           ┌──────────────────┐
│ National Labour  │           │ Regional         │
│ Market           │           │ Labour Market    │
│ Authority (AMS)  │           │ Councils (14)    │
└──────────────────┘           └──────────────────┘
    │   │   │   │                     │
    ▼   ▼   ▼   ▼                     ▼
┌────────┐ ┌──────────┐ ┌──────────┐ ┌────────┐ ┌──────────┐
│Training│ │Employment│ │Munici-   │ │Counties│ │Social    │
│centres │ │services  │ │palities  │ │        │ │partners  │
└────────┘ └──────────┘ └──────────┘ └────────┘ └──────────┘
```

3.3.2 Coordinating separate employment and training structures

In large industrialized countries, employment and training operations are conducted on a very broad scale involving huge financial allocations. Special organizational mechanisms at central and lower government levels are needed to coordinate the employment and training operations. Sophisticated structures are required in countries using separate national employment and training agencies. Employment and training operations have to be integrated under the supervision of either the regional offices of labour ministries and/or regional government.

Module 3. VET management and organizational structures

Figure 3.17 The National Labour Market Authority (Denmark, 1995)

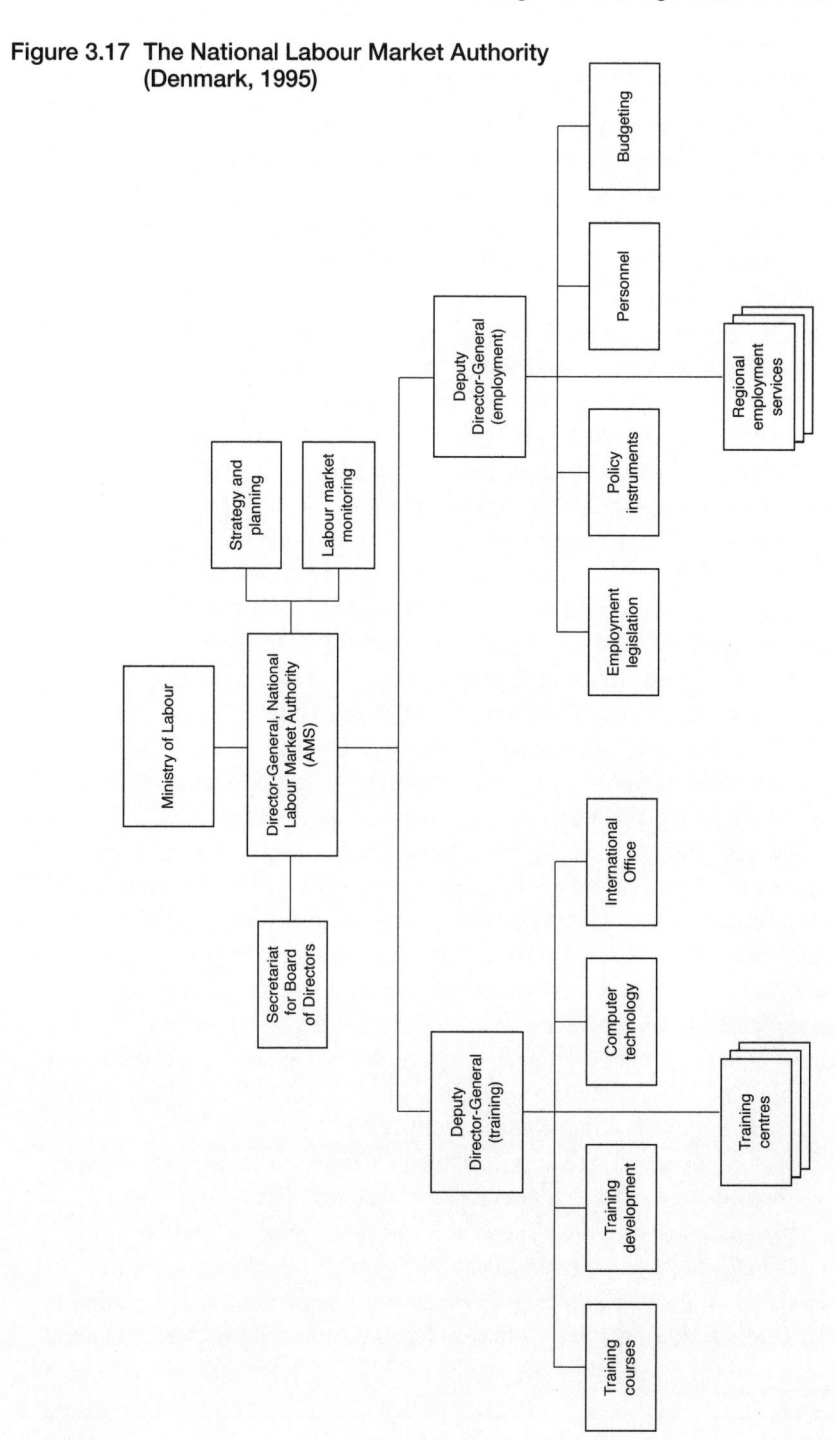

Box 3.13 Labour market training agency in Denmark

Labour market training in Denmark is administered by the National Labour Market Authority (AMS), which is the General Directorate for Employment, Placement and Vocational Training operating under the Ministry of Labour. The AMS is structured around two major groups of function: (1) labour market training and (2) employment and placement. This divide is reflected by the two lines of management and groups of functional and operational units dealing separately with training and employment. The AMS conducts its training activities through 24 centres, most of which have the legal status of non-profit private institutions, while five centres are state schools directly administered by the AMS. Training centres are managed by their boards and, although their staff operate outside civil service rules, they are eligible for certain privileges accorded to civil servants.

On regional labour markets, employment and training activities are guided by 14 Regional Labour Market Councils which set priorities, budget, plan and supervise local labour market operations. Their major preoccupation is combating local unemployment and ensuring a smooth supply of qualified labour. At the regional level, the AMS system is represented by Employment Services and training centres. Employment Services conduct labour market analysis, register the unemployed and provide guidance for retraining. Training centres implement courses at the request of Employment Services and individual enterprises.

Although the Regional Councils coordinate the action of regional training centres and employment offices as well as of other actors, they focus on policy development rather than operational activities. Each Council comprises 21 members, including seven representatives from employers' and seven from workers' organizations and seven from the county and municipality. All members are appointed for a four-year term; the chairperson and a deputy, however, are appointed for two years. The role of county authorities in influencing vocational training is not strong, because of the dominant position of the social partners.

Danish labour market training, although allowing for sound coordination of employment and training operations at national and regional level, is perceived to be excessively expensive. The Government is making continuing efforts to expose training providers to market forces and to intensify competition in training markets. Any operational borders between vocational schools and labour market training centres have been eliminated.

Source: Nielsen, 1995.

Module 3. VET management and organizational structures

The role of the labour ministry, in this case, would consist mostly of political guidance and financing of all or some of the local government training operations (see figure 3.18 and box 3.14).

Figure 3.18 Decentralized coordination of employment and training operations (France, 1996)

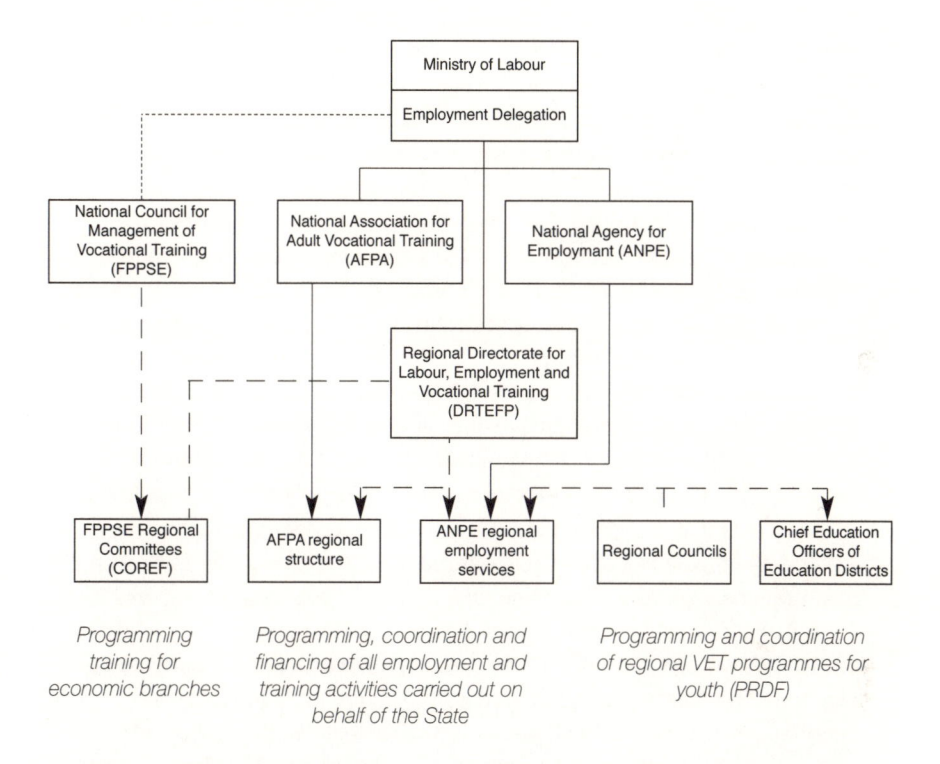

```
                            ┌─────────────────────┐
                            │  Ministry of Labour │
                            └─────────────────────┘
                                      │
                            ┌─────────────────────┐
                   ┌--------│ Employment Delegation│
                   ¦        └─────────────────────┘
                   ¦             │         │
┌──────────────┐ ┌──────────────────┐ ┌──────────────┐
│National Council│ │National Association│ │National Agency│
│for Management  │ │for Adult Vocational│ │for Employmant │
│of Vocational   │ │Training (AFPA)     │ │(ANPE)         │
│Training(FPPSE) │ └──────────────────┘ └──────────────┘
└──────────────┘           │                  │
                  ┌─────────────────────┐
                  │Regional Directorate │
                  │for Labour, Employment│
                  │and Vocational Training│
                  │     (DRTEFP)        │
                  └─────────────────────┘
```

| Programming training for economic branches | Programming, coordination and financing of all employment and training activities carried out on behalf of the State | Programming and coordination of regional VET programmes for youth (PRDF) |

Boxes at bottom: FPPSE Regional Committees (COREF) | AFPA regional structure | ANPE regional employment services | Regional Councils | Chief Education Officers of Education Districts

---

Box 3.14 Coordination of employment and training operations in France

Within the Ministry of Labour, Social Dialogue and Participation of France, vocational training is governed by the Employment Delegation (DE). At the national level, two bodies play a key role: (1) the Permanent Commission of the National Council for Management of Vocational Training (FPPSE), comprising six employer and six union representatives along with 12 representatives of the ministries, with the Ministry of Labour in the leading position (the Ministry is consulted on important policy decisions and has regional and departmental offices); and (2) the Coordination Committee for Regional Apprenticeships and Vocational Training Programmes, made up of representatives from the Government and employers' and workers'

Box 3.14 (cont'd)

organizations, as well as from the 26 Regional Councils. The Committee has a training policy coordination role.

Many institutional actors are involved in employment and training activities. At the regional level, there are four types of policy-making bodies: (1) the Regional Directorate of Labour, Employment and Vocational Training (DRTEFP) representing the Ministry of Labour and responsible for the programming and implementation of regional employment and training activities; (2) the district chief education officer representing the Ministry of Education; (3) Regional Councils, which devise five-year plans for youth training; and (4) employers' and workers' organizations. Regional Councils, which are elected by public vote, have their own training departments and commissions and are legally responsible for training young people and apprentices. At the departmental level, training operations are administered by the 96 departmental labour directorates (DDTEFPs), which purchase training programmes for job seekers over 25 years of age. Funds are allocated to the departments by the DRTEFPs on the basis of regional economic and social conditions, especially unemployment.

The FPPSE's regional VET committees (COREFs) are consulted by Regional Councils and DRTEFPs on the training programmes and policies they implement. A COREF comprises the Prefect of the region, the President of the Regional Council and five representatives from employers' organizations, five from the unions, one from the Federation of National Education Unions (FEN), one from public sector educational establishments, one from the Chambers of Commerce and Industry and two from the voluntary and social sectors. The appropriate Regional Economic and Social Committee consults the Regional Council on VET.

Employment and training operations are conducted by separate agencies: the National Association for Adult Vocational Training (AFPA), which is in charge of training, and the National Agency for Employment (ANPE), which is in charge of placement. The decentralized agencies are both guided and funded by the DE. The AFPA has 22 regional agencies and 130 training centres staffed with 10,000 employees. The ANPE has 25 regional delegations, 103 departmental delegations and 622 employment agencies. It operates on the basis of service agreements with agencies providing registration and guidance of job seekers and with training providers.

In the ongoing process of decentralization, the DRTEFPs will lose some of their coordinating functions to the DDTEFPs. CODEFs, the departmental equivalents of the COREFs, will be strengthened.

Source: Willems, 1995

Module 3. VET management and organizational structures

3.3.3 Incorporated labour market training agencies

Some industrialized countries have been experimenting with the introduction of market forces into labour market training. One approach has been the incorporation of training agencies and providers. The intention is to withdraw from government the direct administration and financing of education and training institutions, and to improve agency effectiveness and reduce the cost of training operations through the professionalization of administration (see box 3.15).

Box 3.15 Incorporated labour market training agency in Sweden

In 1993 Sweden converted the highly centralized, publicly-financed labour-market training agency AMU into a revenue-financed and decentralized corporate concern (which remains state-owned). The need to earn revenues in the market required a profound management reform aimed at increasing operational flexibility and the development of new pricing and marketing policies. The AMU was established under corporate law, with a national parent company (AMU Concern Incorporated, which is responsible for financial management) and wholly-owned regional subsidiaries. This strategy involved preserving the training infrastructure of the AMU Group and at the same time promoting competition in training markets.

The central and local government structures dealing with labour market operations have remained in place while the agency has become a new free-market operator in competition with many other training providers. Most of the AMU's revenues are now derived from selling services to the National Employment Offices and County Labour Market Boards (LANs), which are administered by local governments. The LANs increased their purchase of training services from suppliers other than the AMU, mainly from municipal adult education providers, regular upper secondary schools, universities and colleges, and private training organizations. As it has not competed successfully in the market, the AMU's share of labour market training has declined, while the municipal adult education and private training organizations' share has increased. The AMU, which is still legally required to meet the financial and rental obligations imposed on it prior to conversion into a corporate entity, has reduced its staff and the number of training centres.

Source: Noonan and Söderberg, 1994.

3.4 Administering training through management intermediaries

Some countries apply completely different organizational and management arrangements which involve neither direct administration of public training providers, nor national training agencies. Instead, governments institute intermediate bodies and contract them to administer public services. The government then sets policies and financial conditions for delivering state-funded training programmes and supervises this intermediate body (see box 3.16).

Box 3.16 Administering labour market training through intermediate agencies in the United Kingdom

Nongovernmental agencies similar to the employer-led bodies involved in governing and funding vocational education (see Unit 2 of this Module), have been created in the United Kingdom to administer public labour market training. Training is guided by the government Department for Education and Employment but administered by 82 Training and Enterprise Councils (TECs). The TECs are highly decentralized non-profit-making companies responsible for implementing local training schemes for young people and the unemployed. They are run by boards of directors dominated by local private employers. Like other companies, TECs operate outside civil service rules, but under rigorous financial discipline and the obligations of the market place. They are governed by Company Law. Directors are under the same obligations as all company directors and have to file annual reports at the Companies Registration Office.

The TECs enter service contracts with the Government that specify their responsibilities, targets and funds. Their task is to contract with and supervise training providers who are commissioned to carry out training schemes. Providers could be ordinary firms, sectoral organizations, private training firms or colleges. Each TEC is responsible solely for its own designated territory. Territories can vary in population from about 200,000 to about 2 million. A TEC's staff will number between 50 and 140, but the internal organization varies, as they are all independent companies.

The TECs appear to have considerable power in choosing the private firms with which they place contracts and the industrial sectors for which they develop training. The TECs are also in a pivotal position with regard to strategies for developing local areas. Consequently, college training delivery plans have to be cleared and endorsed by their TEC, which is aware of industry demand for training. The TEC-based organization of labour market training may be a much cheaper option than a national training agency with its own training providers.

Source: Russell, 1995.

Unit 4. Industry-based organization of training

Learning objectives

This unit is designed to provide a better knowledge of:
1. Types of industry training organization
2. Organization of industry training agencies and bodies

4.1 Types of industry training organization

In several countries, certain management decisions in labour market training, as well as responsibility for technical support, have been fully or partly delegated to joint bodies comprising representatives from employers' organizations and unions. The delegated decisions involve: conducting job analysis and drafting skill standards and vocational qualifications; sitting on examination boards and awarding vocational qualifications; analysing industry training needs; setting priorities and planning industry-related training; managing government allocations to industry training as well as employment and training taxes collected from economic sectors; and contracting training providers to carry out government-funded courses for industry. The increased reliance on industry expertise has resulted in the creation of bipartite bodies to handle these functions, often without government participation. In some countries, industrial sectors have established their own sectoral and regional training institutions funded by enterprise contributions and operated autonomously from government VET structures. This has resulted in various types of partnership between the state and industry (Mitchell, 1998).

The most common reasons for increasing the participation of industry in VET have been the following:

- Weak and underfinanced public training institutions have been unable to secure the necessary number of people equipped with entry-level skills. Industry, as the major consumer of skills, intervenes through direct provision and financing of training for its employees.
- Industry has been dissatisfied with the quality of public training and become involved in giving technical support to public training or in the direct provision of courses.
- Increased market competition pressures employers to expand and coordinate their training operations, to develop specific sectoral qualifications and to finance sectoral training.

- Governments and labour unions encourage the employer role in training through the introduction of various types of legal arrangements and incentive schemes, such as collective labour agreements, paid educational leave and training taxes.

Two major patterns of industry training organizations can be distinguished. *Industry training agencies* have their own management and technical bodies and large numbers of training institutions; they become the major, autonomous providers of training to very large populations, mostly employees.

A second pattern is national/sectoral/regional *industry bodies* of various kinds, such as training boards, management-labour boards, sectoral apprenticeship committees, industrial and social funds, and employment and training councils. These bodies may be statutory (legally enacted by the government) or non-statutory (voluntary). They may handle various functions, such as legal representation of industry training interests before the government, administration of funds, technical support and direct training provision. Sectoral training organizations should be distinguished from national VET councils and boards, which act primarily as advisory organizations to the government. Some governments simply want more input from employers and unions, rather than to share management powers. Other governments view employers' and workers' organizations as genuine partners who share responsibility for the development of national human resources.

4.2 Industry training agencies

The most impressive industry training agencies have emerged in Latin American countries. In Brazil, for instance, a wide range of independent private institutions has emerged. Major sectoral training corporations, such as SENAI, SENAC, SENAR and SENAT (the "S" system), were financed through compulsory levies on enterprise payrolls (see table 3.1). Private training institutions have also been established by other sectors, including finance, banking, private and public airline companies, and the maritime industry. These institutions are also financed by sectoral training levies, but are not integrated with the "S" system. In addition, there are private training centres administered and financed by large enterprises (Leite, 1995).

These four major sector-based training agencies are fully employer-led and financed by the compulsory payroll levy. Formally, they are under the supervision of the Ministry of Labour Secretariat of Vocational Education (SEFOR). The agencies also maintain links with the Ministry of Education and the State Secretariat of Education. As private institutions under the Brazilian civil code,

Table 3.1 Sector-based training agencies in Brazil (1995)

Name of agency	Number of schools	Enrolment (thousands)	Staffing	Budget (million US$)	Rate of levy(%)
SENAI (Industry)	930	2 335	15 000 (including 7 500 instructors)	387	1.0 regular, 0.2 additional
SENAC (Commerce and services)	590	1 370	14 800 (including 9 000 instructors)	283	1.0
SENAR (Rural)	n.a.	158	n.a	59	2.5 of production value
SENAT (Transport)	n.a.	n.a.	n.a.	21	1.0

however, sector-based agencies are privately administered and experience little government control. They do not have to comply with the national education laws regarding skill training and certification schemes. Although they are regulated by the same laws and similar rules, they act individually with no coordination between them.

The organized private training sector is the most significant in the country. It offers initial training as well as upgrading courses for workers and the unemployed. Overall, the agencies (excluding SENAT, which is still being organized) have 1,500 training units or schools with 3.7 million training places on medium and short-term courses (from 30 to 185 hours). The state vocational education and training programme at secondary level has only about 800,000 students annually. In contrast to other sectors, the industry sector (SENAI) also has long experience of providing vocational education and apprenticeship training. These agencies supply well-trained and easily employable graduates (Leite, 1995).

The organization and management structures of the SENAI and SENAC are very similar. The SENAI is governed by a National Council comprising the 27 presidents of SENAI's Regional Councils as well as representatives from government ministries (e.g. labour, education, etc.). The president of the National Council is also the president of the National Confederation of Industries. The SENAI has a National Department (headquarters), which is responsible for coordination and provision of technical support to the 27 Regional Departments that operate within each State of Brazil. The National Department is staffed with over 400 people, half of whom are managers and technicians (see figure 3.19).

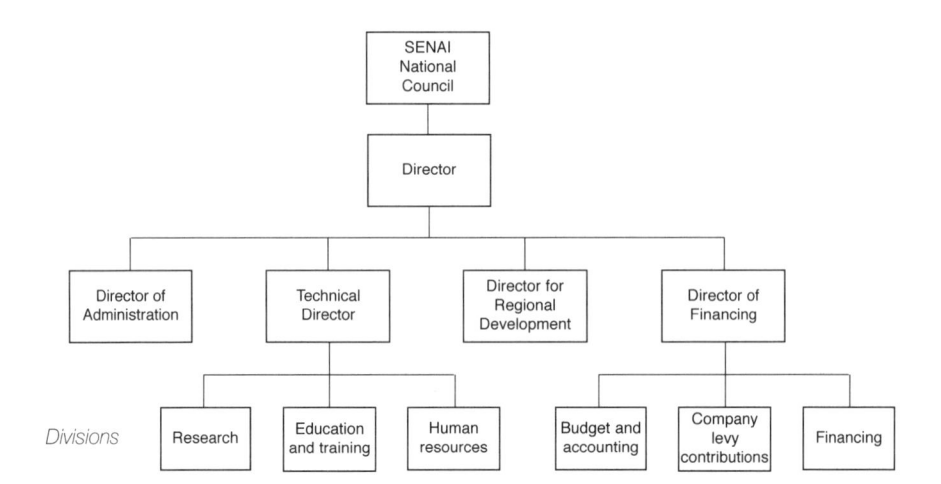

Figure 3.19 Organization of SENAI National Department (Brazil, 1995)

```
                    SENAI
                   National
                   Council
                      |
                   Director
    ┌─────────────┬───┴────────────┬──────────────┐
Director of    Technical      Director for    Director of
Administration  Director       Regional        Financing
                                Development
                   ┌──────┼──────┐       ┌──────┼──────┐
Divisions      Research Education Human  Budget and Company Financing
                       and training resources accounting levy
                                                    contributions
```

The SENAI and SENAC Regional Departments are guided by their Councils. Regional Departments are operational structures: they decide their plans and budgets, develop curricula, hire and fire teachers, administer funds, conduct research and evaluate schools, and maintain linkages with their respective state governments. The SENAI regional structures mirror their national structures. They are supervised by the State Federations of Industry, the presidents of which are appointed presidents of the SENAI Regional Councils. Like the National Council, Regional Councils also include representatives of the Ministry of Education and the Ministry of Labour. For example, the SENAI Regional Department of São Paulo is staffed with almost 750 people, of whom 30 are managers and 440 are technicians and instructors; it administers 100 training schools and employs 4,250 staff. While SENAI offers primarily free courses, the SENAC training schools in São Paulo State operate as "profit centres". They offer mainly short, flexible programmes that can be changed rapidly or cancelled if there is insufficient demand. At SENAC, training schools rely primarily on temporary teachers recruited for individual courses. The recruitment and dismissal of instructors in SENAI is the responsibility of the Regional Department human resources directors (see figure 3.20).

Because of the weak public VET system in Brazil, each agency has developed its own vocational education and training infrastructure. Thus, in SENAI, curricula are developed by the largest Regional Departments (São Paulo, Rio de Janeiro) and taught in all its training and technical schools. In order to

Module 3. VET management and organizational structures

Figure 3.20 Organization of SENAI Regional Department (Brazil, 1995)

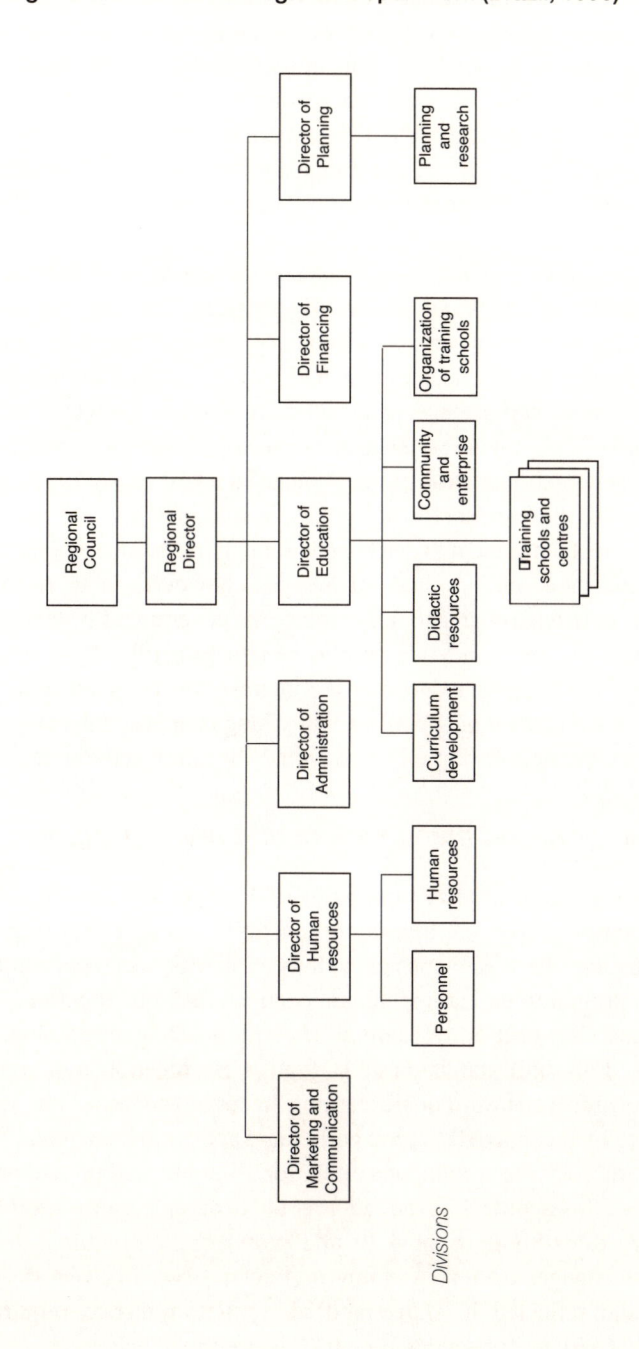

- Regional Council — Regional Director
  - Director of Marketing and Communication
  - Director of Human resources
    - Personnel
    - Human resources
  - Director of Administration
    - Curriculum development
    - Didactic resources
  - Director of Education
    - Community and enterprise
    - Organization of training schools
    - Training schools and centres
  - Director of Financing
  - Director of Planning
    - Planning and research

Divisions

111

draft the curriculum, these departments conduct labour market research and job analysis. For technical education courses lasting up to four years, the curricula must be approved by the State Education Council. The Regional Departments also work out the examination and testing programmes. The skill certificates issued by the SENAI and SENAC technical schools have the same legal status as those issued by the federal and state technical schools. Some SENAI Regional Departments conduct tracer studies of their graduates and provide guidance to schools (Leite, 1995).

Being employer-led institutions, industry training agencies have developed their own particular structures and modes of operation. They have proved capable of training large numbers of workers and young people at different skill levels over short periods of time. Their efficiency was basically due to their technical and administrative flexibility, competence, great autonomy and ever-growing funds. In contrast to the public VET structures, the agencies have been able to recruit qualified technical personnel, pay them realistic, levy-financed salaries and set up adequate training facilities. The close contact kept by these institutions with the production sector makes it possible for them to detect new training needs and respond without delay.

Despite their success and advantages, however, industry-based training structures have been unable to fully replace the government system because of one important deficiency: they are able to benefit primarily those who are already employed, while they have neither the interest nor the mandate to train, on any significant scale, the large population of young people and the unemployed. This remains the prime role of public vocational education and training systems.

4.3 Sector-based management and training support structures

In most of the industrialized countries of Europe, a recent trend has been the reorganization of sectoral training organizations to take over responsibility for certain management decisions as well as to provide technical support to public training programmes leading to an occupational qualification. Sector-based bodies have been set up to examine training needs, plan training, conduct job analysis, draft skill standards and identify examination requirements, assess graduates and even award qualifications. In certain countries, the skill standards developed by recognized sectoral bodies and approved by national VET councils become the basis for training curricula for all public and private providers. The strength of this approach is the fact that the economic sector itself knows better than any external body what skills and knowledge are required to carry out the jobs. The changes occurring in any particular job can be observed by sectoral bodies and reflected in skill standards and examination requirements. The relevant experience of several countries is described below.

4.3.1 Industry Training Organizations in the United Kingdom

In the United Kingdom, the Government has established or identified nearly 200 Industry Training Organizations (ITOs) that have a wide range of functions in identifying training needs and supporting training in their industry or sector. A National Association of Industry Training Organizations has been formed with the active encouragement of the Education and Employment Department and funding for some of its activities. ITOs are registered as companies limited by guarantee, which is the most frequently used legal form of VET organization (see details in box 2.7 in Module 2, Unit 2). Some ITOs have been given additional status as Industry Lead Bodies (LBs). Only the LBs may identify the occupational standards on which the National Council for Vocational Qualifications (NCVQ) approves VET awards. (The Government nominates all the members of the NCVQ's Governing Council and provides funding; NCVQ directors are appointed by the Department for Education.) This has led to the recognition of 160 LBs in small sectors of employment, with some sectors not covered. Many LBs have their development work publicly funded. There are hundreds of voluntary-membership ITOs: about 200 are recognized by the Government and listed for consultation. The NCVQ has approved over 100 Awarding Bodies responsible for developing the schemes and awarding vocational qualifications. Some of these are also LBs (Russell, 1995).

4.3.2 Sectoral Training Committees in Denmark

In Denmark, the Minister for Labour formed the tripartite Adult Vocational Training Council, which considers the policy, organization and financing of adult training. The Employers' Confederation (DA) and the Confederation of Trade Unions (LO) each appoint eight members of the Council and the Ministers for Labour, Education and Industry each appoint delegates for a four-year period. The Council makes annual recommendations to the Minister for Labour regarding issues such as the distribution of resources among industry sectors, groups of courses and procurement of major training equipment (Nielsen, 1995).

The Minister for Labour has also set up bipartite Labour Market Training Committees for four major economic areas: industry, commerce and services, construction and the public sector. For each of these committees the Minister appoints the chairperson, while the DA and LO each appoint eight members. The Adult Vocational Training Council advises on the structure and functions of the Labour Market Training Committees. The annual targets for the labour market training system are set by the Minister for Labour, who usually follows the Council's advice. The Government is not formally represented on these

Committees, which are fully responsible for assessing sectoral training needs, planning and administering training funds allocated by the Government for upgrading courses in their economic sectors. They also have authority to contract out training programmes to any provider in the market. Through the Committees, employers' and workers' organizations have a decisive influence on the planning of upgrading courses.

Continuing Training Committees have been formed within each economic area. Of the current 56 Committees, 25 have been established in industry, 16 in commerce and services (clerical/commercial and financial services as well as transport), 12 in construction and three in the public sector. These Committees develop, plan and monitor training courses for their sector. They conduct job analysis and draft regulations for training courses; they define the targets, duration and timing of courses. The social partners themselves have set up new Continuing Training Committees, which, however, must be approved by the Labour Market Training Committee for the corresponding economic area. Each Continuing Training Committee usually consists of six to ten labour market representatives appointed for a four-year term. The operational costs of these Committees are covered jointly by the social partners, while the Ministry for Labour may also contribute.

4.3.3 Sectoral training bodies in the Netherlands

In the Netherlands, 78 Industrial and Social Funds (ISFs) have been voluntarily established by employers and workers with no intervention from, or obligation to, the Government. The ISFs deal with various issues; financing and promoting training is the main goal of only 23 of them. In the training area, the ISFs aim at raising public and private money to provide financial support for training and related activities, including needs assessment and advisory services; provision of apprenticeship programmes and upgrading courses; and, most recently, training for the unemployed. In addition, the ISFs support employers' organizations, unions and secretariats of collective labour agreements. The Government cooperates with ISFs in promoting training activities which are national priorities (Veeken, 1994).

In addition to the ISFs, most industrial branches in the Netherlands have established Subsidy Funds, the main actors in channelling government subsidies for industrial training. The ISFs and Subsidy Funds are run by boards with representatives from employers' organizations and unions, but no government representatives. It is common for representatives of employers and workers to be board members on both the ISFs and the Subsidy Funds. The Subsidy Funds and, to a lesser extent, the ISFs are granted public money with the aim of conducting particular training programmes. On average, only two-thirds of sectoral training budgets are generated through training levies. The difference is made up by government subsidies from the Ministry of Education, Ministry of Social Affairs or Ministry of Economics and, increasingly, the Employment Services. A recent policy, agreed by all social partners, aims at increasing employment, reducing the costs of the social benefit system and emphasizing the role of industry in training for the unemployed. Training activities can be provided by sectoral Training Boards or by 31 National Apprenticeship Bodies (NABs). The NABs coordinate sectoral training programmes, develop curricula, test for and certify qualifications. They are also administered by bipartite boards and funded by the Ministry of Education.

Unit 5. Management and organization of VET technical support

Learning objectives

This unit is designed to provide a better knowledge of:

1. The configuration of technical support for vocational education and training
2. The management of skill standards and vocational qualifications
3. The national organization of curriculum development processes
4. The management of skills assessment and certification
5. The management of vocational instructor development

5.1 Configuration of support structures

Quality training programmes cannot be delivered without sound technical support. Major technical support functions include:

- development of skill standards and national/sectoral qualifications;
- curriculum and teaching materials development;
- assessment (testing) of skills and certification;
- instructor/teacher development;
- vocational guidance; and
- research and development on vocational education and training.

A national vocational training system missing any of these important functions will lack consistency and quality. Support services provide invaluable technical guidance to VET institutions, both public and private, and to policy makers.

There are several alternative configurations of technical support structure. First, technical support can be highly centralized with major functions implemented by professionals from ministry departments or, along with responsibility for education and training, delegated to lower levels of government. Where training supply structures are highly centralized, technical support structures are usually centralized as well. Thus, most developing countries, and certain industrialized countries, base technical functions in ministry departments. Governments employ technical professionals to develop vocational qualifications and national curricula. This is often done with no input from industry.

The second option assumes that technical support is centralized, but implemented by special government or tripartite institutions. National VET councils/boards can be established to supervise or implement national technical support functions. Such bodies are often bi- or tripartite, including representatives of employers' and workers' organizations as well as professional educationalists. Although the duties of VET councils vary from country to country, they tend to become technical rather than purely advisory bodies and they employ professional staff. Councils often set up national or sector-based technical committees responsible for the development and supervision of national qualifications, curricula, skills assessment and certification. Sometimes separate boards are established by the government for the implementation of individual functions (e.g. national curriculum development boards or testing and certification boards). Creating specialist support bodies outside ministries has a strong advantage since they provide professional services to training institutions on a long-term basis.

Third, following a clear trend in industrialized countries towards the establishment of autonomous labour market training agencies fully responsible for national training operations, the corresponding technical functions are usually assigned to such agencies' technical units.

Fourth, there may be a combination of centralized functions with certain technical work, such as curriculum development and testing, delegated to VET providers.

Fifth, certain functions, such as skill standards development, are increasingly taken over by sector-based employers' and workers' organizations. Responsibility for drafting occupational standards may be left to the sectoral bodies; the development of national VET qualifications may become a responsibility of national VET councils, and providers may be required to develop curricula themselves.

Technical support bodies and procedures for vocational education are usually separate from labour market training systems. However, some attempts have been made to integrate them in comprehensive national VET systems.

5.2 Managing national VET qualifications

Sound occupational qualifications mainly benefit employers, who know what type of people they need to recruit. Well-structured national qualifications also provide a framework for the whole teaching and assessment process. Therefore, some governments retain central management of vocational education qualifications. For example, the French Government reserves the right to award degrees and diplomas (see box 3.17). In Denmark (see box 3.18; see also section 4.3.2 above), the social partners play an important role in the development and steering of national VET qualifications.

In countries where national occupational qualifications are non-existent, each vocational school awards its own certificate. Since vocational awards issued by

---

Box 3.17 Central management of vocational education awards in France

Only the technological and vocational diplomas that are granted by the Ministry of Education enjoy national recognition in France. Consultative Professional Committees (CPCs) are responsible for elaborating national vocational education awards (almost 650 diplomas). There are 17 CPCs corresponding to different economic sectors. CPCs consult with industry in order to define technological and vocational diplomas. They also steer VET qualifications and clear requests for their modification. CPCs evaluate trainees and decide on the basis of follow up whether to discontinue or adjust the criteria for particular diplomas. They also make recommendations on the content of training courses, their duration and certification. Vocational diplomas drafted by CPCs created by ministries other than the Ministry of Education must be reviewed by the Homologation Commission in order to be recognized. If applications are accepted "homologated awards" are given (more than 3,000 exist and between 50,000 and 100,000 people receive them each year). So far, only the Ministry of Labour and the Ministry of Agriculture have established CPCs and entrusted their supervision to the national training agency.

Vocational education awards are elaborated through the following stages. First, an application to develop or amend an award is submitted by a ministry; the CPC secretariat examines the application with regard to the number of persons concerned and consistency with existing diplomas; a report is submitted to the competent CPC, which decides on the course of action. If an award is to be created or if certain diplomas are to be amended, a working group headed by a project leader is established. Second, skill standards reflecting job requirements are formulated with the assistance of professionals. Third, with the assistance of teachers, skill standards are translated into knowledge and skills to be acquired and terms of reference for teaching them. Fourth, modes of assessment of applicants and regulations are defined for the new award.

Box 3.17 (cont'd)

   Each CPC consists of representatives from employers' and craft organizations; the management-labour organization of the branch; the employment department, the vocational education department, and other ministries involved in training; secondary school teachers; the Chambers of Trade and Industry and Craft Chambers; and an advisor on technological education selected by the Minister. The CPC secretariat is staffed by 20 people reporting to a branch chief of the Education Ministry. The secretariat carries out administrative work and supervises external experts. It permanently handles about a hundred working groups of experts, giving rise to more than 700 meetings a year. All nationally recognized VET awards are followed up by the Centre for Studies and Research on Employment and Qualifications (CEREQ), which serves as an observatory for qualifications and reports to the Ministry of Education and the Ministry of Labour.

   The Ministry of Education supports the methodology for developing qualifications, which is based on the duration of training rather than on the skills and knowledge acquired. The economic sectors have limited involvement in the creation of national vocational education awards; they are only consulted on job requirements and diplomas.

Source: Willems, 1994.

Box 3.18 Industry contributions to VET qualifications in Denmark

In Denmark, under the Vocational Education and Training Act, bipartite Trade Committees have been formed by labour market organizations. The Committees are established on the basis of occupational groups with activities and secretariats financed by the employers' and workers' organizations, which have parity of membership. Each Committee has a working group consisting of professional occupational analysts and curriculum developers who assess sectoral training needs, create and revise the occupational profile for the trades concerned, draft attainment targets which are applied as standards for the final examinations, draft frameworks for the curricula which are derived from the above targets, and determine the structure and timing of school-based and practical instruction at the enterprises. They also have the power to approve and abolish courses, conduct examinations and issue awards. Although the Trade Committees submit their proposals for approval to the National VET Council, they do not formally report to it.

Source: Nielsen, 1995.

individual schools are not familiar to employers and not able to reflect real job requirements, industry often does not recognize them. As certificates are issued by many public and private schools, they may not be of great value. Only the bearers of certificates issued by recognized schools are appreciated by employers. The absence of national VET qualifications may become particularly sensitive in countries and regions with significant migration of skilled labour, as in the Asian region and South America. Private employment agencies usually take up this matter and assess skilled applicants against the vocational qualifications applied in the countries that import labour.

In some countries, such as the United States, where the concept of national or state qualifications simply does not apply and graduation requirements in community colleges are devised by individual institutions (Herschbach, 1995), the absence of national qualifications has been, to a certain extent, compensated by industry-based qualifications which are, however, established in conjunction with state departments that issue licenses. By contrast, in the United Kingdom, national vocational qualifications have been developed which are explicitly competence-based (see box 3.19).

Box 3.19 Competence-based national vocational qualifications in the United Kingdom

In the United Kingdom, the national vocational qualifications (NVQs) are competence-based. They involve a detailed statement of competence incorporating the assessment of skills to a specified standard, and the ability to use skills and apply knowledge to relevant tasks. The ability to apply skills and knowledge in practical situations of an unpredictable nature is regarded as vital for a flexible workforce. Emphasis is on core skills: communication, information technology, problem solving and personal development. Assessment aims at ensuring that practical skills are relevant to the workplace. The standards of competence are described in terms of units, which are made up of elements. Each element is individually assessed and certification is available for unit credits (see section 4.3.1 above).

The three-step process of establishing a new NVQ works as follows. First, the National Council for Vocational Qualifications (NCVQ) specifies the criteria for developing competencies (i.e. occupational standards), including:
- a breakdown into units of competence, each of which specifies the elements of competence for that unit;
- the performance criteria and the underlying knowledge for the elements of competence;

Managing vocational training systems

Box 3.19 (cont'd)

- guidance on the range of activities or situations for the competencies;
- guidance on assessment; and,
- for each qualification (award) proposed, a clear definition of the level, from one to five.

Second, a recognized Industry Lead Body consults with its industry and specifies the competencies necessary to perform a certain job in accordance with the established framework. Finally, for each vocational qualification proposed, at least one Awarding Body must be assigned which, on the basis of the competencies, will make detailed specifications for carrying out the skills assessment.

The NVQ specifications are not necessarily very user-friendly from the point of view of the teacher or trainer. There is no guidance on the length, organization or content of training programmes. These decisions must be taken within the teaching or training organization, with whatever help can be acquired. Thus, teachers and trainers are principally responsible for curriculum design. The basic set of assessment specifications must be incorporated into a teaching strategy. The public Further Education Unit (FEU) is available for external support in curriculum development. It uses staff or teams from the colleges to write, advise or undertake action-development projects. The results of project activity are communicated and disseminated to the whole range of colleges. The Awarding Bodies also offer advisory services to schools and colleges for the support of teachers in curriculum development. Some private companies also provide such support.

Source: Russell, 1995.

In summary, the management of national vocational qualifications involves the following elements:
- setting up structures and procedures for establishing and steering national VET qualifications;
- developing the concept of national qualifications (e.g. knowledge-based or competence-based);
- establishing a list of qualifications and qualification levels, linking qualifications to sectoral job and wage structures, etc.; and
- developing occupational standards and skills assessment schemes (i.e. defining the knowledge and performance standards that should be demonstrated in order for a certain qualification to be awarded).

5.3 Developing national curricula

There are several approaches to organizing national curriculum development in vocational education and training. The first option is to establish a fixed national curriculum to be applied by all VET institutions, with teaching materials and textbooks centrally produced and provided. For example, in the Republic of Korea, curriculum and examination programmes for vocational high schools and junior vocational colleges are drafted by the Korea Educational Development Institute (KEDI) and approved by the Ministry of Education. Providers must apply the approved curricula and cannot offer any other programme. The curricula are subject to periodic review by task forces under the supervision of the KEDI. A task force is normally made up of instructors, job analysts, engineers or scientists, and curriculum developers from the KEDI. A task force surveys technical changes which have occurred during the period in question and adjusts curricula to reflect them (Shin, 1995).

A second alternative assumes various combinations of centrally established core subjects with a degree of freedom left to individual institutions to supplement the curriculum. The level of central determination of the national core curricula can vary. For instance, in Brazil, the Federal Education Law prescribes the obligatory minimum curriculum requirements for public technical schools. Its "common nucleus" covers academic subjects while a "diversified part" embraces VET subjects. The latter may vary across schools. The federal law determines 60 per cent of the curriculum content for all education levels, while the State Secretariats of Education and their Education Councils determine the remaining 40 per cent. The Ministry of Education does not issue textbooks but does make recommendations. Each school has the power to adapt textbooks or to choose other training materials. Teachers are required to produce testing materials in accordance with the curriculum. Public technical schools often use privately developed curricula and textbooks (Leite, 1995).

A third approach is to create a technical framework and guidelines for curriculum development which providers can use. For instance, in Denmark, the Ministry of Education issues Educational Orders in which a broad framework for VET courses is laid down; on this basis school instructors devise the curriculum themselves (see box 3.20).

A fourth option assumes that neither national curriculum nor national guidelines exist and that local schools and colleges set the curricula themselves, sometimes, but not necessarily, with guidance from educational authorities. This option is applied in the United States, where most states do not standardize vocational education curricula, except in the most general sense, and where local school districts have full responsibility. State departments of education provide

Managing vocational training systems

> **Box 3.20 Curriculum development in vocational education in Denmark**
>
> On the basis of occupational profiles and draft regulations for each course produced by industrial Trade Committee working groups, the Ministry of Education issues Education Orders which specify the layers of the national curriculum (basic subjects, area subjects and specialist subjects; student attainment targets for various subjects; and provision for skills assessment). Basic subjects comprise instruction in broad general and vocational topics which enhance the personal development of students, qualify them for further studies and convey an understanding of society. Area subjects comprise practical and theoretical subjects relevant to a broad field of the trade and are normally shared by several streams. Specialist subjects comprise theoretical and practical instruction which is specific for an individual trade. All course curricula are required to include basic (one-third), area (one-third), specialized (one-sixth) and optional (one-sixth) subjects. Syllabi are drawn up by schools themselves on the basis of the Education Orders to ensure general uniformity of training qualifications and assessment. However, the specific content of curricula and methods of instruction vary from school to school. Although no database of curricula is available, schools often share programmes.
>
> Schools can set up Local Education and Training Committees (LETCs). The majority of LETC members represent a local branch of labour market organizations appointed and trained by the industrial Trade Committees. The LETCs report to the Trade Committees on important changes occurring in the trades concerned and link schools to industry. They advise schools on:
>
> - occupational profiles and industry training needs;
> - practical training of apprentices and arrangement of training places in the industry;
> - organization of upgrading courses for skilled workers;
> - organization of school workshops;
> - use and purchase of equipment and tools;
> - workshop inspections; and
> - optional subjects to be taught at schools.
>
> Trade Committees and LETCs study changes occurring in industry and their implications for training courses. If any new requirements for training are identified, the agreement of the Education Ministry is sought in order to proceed with redrafting the Education Orders. With assistance from LETCs, schools also take part in this process. In general, schools exercise their limited freedom for modifying curricula mainly through the introduction of optional subjects.
>
> Source: Nielsen, 1995.

only general guidelines for curriculum development. Typically, educational districts form curriculum committees comprised of instructors from individual schools. Local vocational schools and community colleges work out curricula themselves or contract this work to specialist organizations (Herschbach, 1995).

5.4 Managing skills assessment and certification in the United Kingdom

As presented in box 3.19, the United Kingdom uses a system of competence-based national vocational qualifications (NVQs). Trainees' skills need to be assessed in the real-life environment that only specialist assessment bodies can arrange. The function of assessing skills and making awards is therefore separate from training and assigned to autonomous specialist bodies. The assessment (testing) and awarding (certification) system for VET is conducted by, or on behalf of, Awarding Bodies that are independent of the training institutions and the Government. The National Council for Vocational Qualifications (NCVQ) requires that any Award scheme submitted should make no reference to any course of instruction or institution, length of training, entry qualifications, or on-site assessment situation. Only the outcomes, expressed in terms of competencies and their performance criteria can be referred to. Ex-trainees state the name and level of their Award, and perhaps the name of the Awarding Body. Thus a person might say, "I hold an NVQ, Level 2, Award in Food Preparation from the City and Guilds of London". Such a qualification may be taken after training or practical experience with or without formal training. The Department of Education issues no vocational awards and VET awards carry no validating signature from the Department. The Government ensures that the system is appropriate, is meeting the needs of industry and of individuals, is fair, applies good national standards and is reasonably cheap. Otherwise, assessment and certification work wholly through the free market (Russell, 1995).

The traditional system allows any organization or body that wishes to issue vocational qualifications to do so. Over 200 Awarding Bodies exist. But the Government has made key interventions in the system by establishing three large, independent Awarding Bodies – the RSA Examinations Board established in 1854, the City and Guilds of London Institute, 1879, and the Business and Technology Education Council, 1973 – which dominate the system. These organizations make awards and design and control schemes, syllabi and assessment systems. They award vocational qualifications to some 2 million people each year. The Awarding Bodies are registered as non-profit-making companies. Their governing bodies are nominated by the State. Although these bodies are self-financed, they are often advised and guided by the Department for Education.

In addition, the NCVQ has approved over 100 Awarding Bodies which develop the award schemes and offer them in the market. In many cases a government-approved Industry Lead Body may choose to act as the awarding body or it may nominate another body. Colleges, employers and other training organizations can apply to Awarding Bodies for recognition as the assessment centre responsible for certain award schemes. They primarily offer assessment opportunities to their own students, trainees or staff. Some also accept external candidates or candidates from other training organizations. Full-time instructors from the identified organizations will serve as assessors. All the other Awarding Bodies are small in comparison with the major three and address sectoral and specialist markets. Some of them conduct a range of other business for their member organizations. The main recent modification of this system is that these bodies will now be coordinated and to some extent controlled by the Qualification and Curriculum Authority formed in 1997 by the merger of the Schools Curriculum and Assessment Authority (SCAA) and the NCVQ.

The specific occupational standards (competencies) that make up the content of each NVQ are developed by an Industry Lead Body (see box 3.19). Once approved, the competencies enter the public arena and the Lead Body cannot restrict their circulation by the exercise of copyright. Multiple Awarding Bodies may wish to develop and offer schemes for the awards based on the same occupational standards. The NCVQ has approved as many as eight Awarding Bodies for the same scheme. Once an awarding scheme exists it still has to attract candidates in an open market. Any employer, training organization or college has to judge for itself which occupational standards and which awarding scheme best fit its needs. Individual students or trainees will also be selective. There is no pressure from the NCVQ or other agency except the Awarding Bodies, which must approve independent assessment centres for administering their schemes. Awarding Bodies actively promote their products in the open market in the same way as any other provider.

The assessment centres can relate to their Awarding Bodies in two ways. Centres can select a scheme based on an external examination by an Awarding Body. In this case, a written test or examination paper is sent from the Awarding Body to all the assessment centres participating in the scheme. The written products (or scripts) of the candidates are sent back to the Awarding Body for assessment, grading and certification. This is the oldest system and still survives for many schemes. Although regarded by many as archaic and unrelated to the realities of the workplace, the system is seen as maintaining national standards, cheap and reliable. It is still favoured by many employers. This system is often modified by the addition of "course-work" or a "practical test" that is assessed and graded in the centres, subject to approval or moderation by Awarding Body

Module 3. VET management and organizational structures

staff. Alternatively, a centre may devise a teaching and assessment programme within guidelines established by the Awarding Body. Then the programme is submitted for validation, which will include checking the resources available for the learning programme and its assessment. A verifier from the Awarding Body will visit the centre a number of times to check on progress. At the end of the programme candidates for the award will be assessed by the centre using all the evidence of course-work, projects and examinations.

Candidates for competence-based awards must present evidence of competence to the assessors. Evidence of performance at work can only be assessed by immediate observation. Other evidence relies on simulation. In both cases, in order to guarantee future performance, the underlying knowledge must be tested, often by oral questioning. Much evidence will be documentary, consisting of records of performance that are authenticated as having been produced by the candidate. The process of assessing competencies is demanding and requires some guarantee that the assessors themselves have the necessary competence. Furthermore, the system would be hopelessly expensive if all this evidence was new evidence, created outside the normal routines of production and training. The NCVQ has therefore collaborated with the Training and Development Lead Body (TDLB) to produce specific occupational standards and units of competence that relate to the skills needed to run the new assessment processes.

Each assessment of a candidate's performance must be made by an assessor who has demonstrated competence in both the art of assessment and the relevant occupational area. There are three alternative units of competence at this level: one for direct assessment of workplace performance; one using a variety of sources of evidence; and one based on evidence of previous performance. As the assessment format is not standardized, each assessor needs to be trained to develop a variety of practical assessment plans appropriate to particular working situations. Competent internal verifiers must certify assessments. This pattern of assessors and internal verifiers must be coordinated, recorded and managed by a skilled organizer who understands the processes required by the Awarding Body and who keep records in such a way that an external verifier from the Awarding Body can review them. Awarding Bodies determine the number of assessment centres that an external verifier covers. Most external verifiers for NVQs are part-time staff.

Awarding Bodies are self-funded from the fees they earn for assessment and certification. These fees are paid by their assessment centres. The centres try to recover this expenditure from the candidates, the employers who request the assessment and the sponsors of education or training. Since most students in the VET system are government-sponsored, this means that the costs of the Awarding Bodies are included in an overall package fee for the VET programme and are in effect met by the Government.

5.5 Developing vocational instructors in the United Kingdom

Managing vocational instructor development involves the:

- legal definition of instructor status;
- selection and licensing of instructors; and
- establishment of facilities and programmes and allocation of funds for instructor training and upgrading.

For example, in the United Kingdom, the Colleges of Further Education (FE) have been separated by law from general education schools. The supply and certification of school teachers is managed by the Teacher Training Agency (TTA) on behalf of the Secretary of State for Education. In contrast to general education schools, there are no legal restrictions on who can teach or train in VET. The FE Colleges recruit most of their vocational and technical instructors directly from the appropriate industrial, commercial and service occupations, preferably with at least ten years of work experience. Since colleges are now self-governing corporations, the Government does not regulate the qualifications of vocational education and training instructors.

Three structures exist for developing VET teachers. First, there are four specialist centres for the training of technical instructors for further and adult education. The teacher centres have developed into larger multi-purpose institutions of higher education. The core of their work is to provide one-year full-time teacher training for those with a university degree or similar high-level professional and vocational qualification and experience. Industrial and commercial experience is a key factor in their entry standards. They run programmes of part-time and block-release courses for teachers who enter colleges directly and are offered, by their employers, on-the-job training as teachers and educators. About a third of all teachers in further and adult education have been trained in this way. This qualification route does not, however, entitle the person to teach in general education schools.

Second, there is the Training and Development Lead Body (TDLB), which develops and monitors occupational standards for teachers (see the preceding unit). TDLB awards are also suitable for part-time study and are designed for both full- or part-time teachers and trainers. The TDLB occupational standards are used by the entire national VET system. Most further and adult education teachers who were not initially certified as teachers with degree-level qualifications have acquired the TDLB awards. The TDLB and the Awarding Bodies have also developed a series of awards based only on skills assessment.

Third, training providers, and colleges in particular, can themselves provide teacher training which meets the TDLB standards. Further education colleges have for decades made their own provision for part-time courses leading to the awards, which are designed for full- or part-time teachers and trainers.

VET TARGET SETTING AND PLANNING

Module 4

Unit 1. VET planning concepts

Learning objectives

This unit is designed to provide a better knowledge of:

1. VET planning concepts
2. Student demand-driven versus market demand-driven planning
3. Types of VET programmes which need planning

1.1 The need for planning

Planning anticipates future activities. The purpose of planning VET is to establish objectives and translate them into a schedule of operational activities for a set period of time; this will permit budgeting and the distribution of resources. Major planning subjects are the overall number of training places; total enrolment and enrolment per programme; enrolment of targeted populations; outputs (number and type of qualifications to be produced) and schedules for producing them. Regardless of the wealth of a country or the size of its VET operations, planning remains important. As wealthier countries have greater freedom of resources, they can establish and set priorities for long-term needs and demand for VET. On this basis, they can link education and training to national economic and human resources development (HRD) targets. Since educational inputs in less wealthy countries are constrained, the available resources might determine the framework for plans and priorities. Nevertheless, the available, perhaps modest, resources should be used effectively, and for this careful priority setting and planning are indispensable.

Planning approaches depend on the way that national training objectives are set. There are two principal approaches to setting national objectives:

- basing them on current short-term labour market demand and student demand for skills; and
- linking them to national economic and HRD trends so that training objectives become broad-based, long-term and strategic.

There are two corresponding approaches to planning the provision of government vocational education and training: planning based on labour market signals (short-term or operational) and strategic (long-term) planning. All planning, since it is based on future projections, depends on imperfect information. As a result, deviations from planned operations should be expected. If VET availability and labour market demand for skills are particularly volatile, substantial adjustment of plans may be required. Short-term planning of courses assumes the availability of relatively reliable information on current and future job vacancies as well as on student preferences. The major problem, however, relates to long- and medium-term planning, since forecasts of future requirements for professional-worker and skilled-worker qualifications have been found to be very inaccurate. In certain countries, the prediction errors of employment projections are said to exceed 50 per cent (Dougherty, 1990; Richards and Amjad, 1994). Therefore, determining the number of trainees who will be able to enter the occupations which require long-term preparation remains an important issue.

1.2 Planning VET programmes

The following types of programme planning can be distinguished for government training:

- Short-term initiation courses for young people which are conducted by labour market training centres as well as by general education schools. These courses are relatively inexpensive, lead to low-skill qualifications and are commonly offered to young people with only a weak commitment to acquiring skills.
- Long-term training for young people at craft level that is often organized as "sandwich" courses or apprenticeships with the strong involvement of enterprises. These programmes are expensive and should be linked to the market demand for qualifications as far as possible.
- Short- and long-term upgrading programmes for employees which are either requested and financed by enterprises or undertaken by private individuals at their own expense. These programmes do not require any specific planning since they directly reflect market demand.

Module 4. VET target setting and planning

- Short- and long-term retraining programmes for the unemployed. Short courses may last several weeks or months, while the longest programmes may be up to one-year duration. Short courses may train the unemployed for job vacancies known to local labour market authorities. Both long and short retraining programmes have to be planned on the basis of anticipated demand for skills.
- School-based programmes leading to qualifications at craft level, technician, or engineer. These are the most costly and have long lead times. Young people enrol in vocational education programmes in a situation of uncertainty regarding the labour market demand for skills; by the time they complete their studies, circumstances may have changed dramatically.

Detailed forecasts of the market demand and detailed programming of intake are not necessary for low-level skills that require only a few weeks or months to acquire. In addition, less specialized qualifications are more readily interchangeable and, with regard to low skill levels, labour markets can easily adjust to constraints. Therefore, pre-employment short-term courses may simply respond to trainee demand, since their role is vocational guidance rather than the provision of skilled labour. By contrast, the uncertainty of future market developments complicates the planning of long-term VET programmes leading to craft grade and higher skill levels. In addition, these programmes are very costly and mismatches between the qualifications produced and those required may cause a major waste of public resources. Therefore, these programmes in particular require market analysis and planning. Continuing assessment of trends in market demand for higher-level qualifications is needed, as adjustments in VET programming may become necessary.

1.3 Planning driven by individual demand

Training can be sought by private individuals or by enterprises and the labour force. Enterprise demand and individual demand can be identified through different signals, which are handled differently by the public VET system. Planning decisions should satisfy policy priorities. If satisfaction of trainees is the priority, then programming becomes student-demand driven. If the aim is to respond to true skill shortages and improve employment, then programming will attempt to respond to another type of signal. In practice, there are many combinations of signals and responses.

Planning driven by individual demand is the simplest and the cheapest model. It is often favoured by administrators since it means less accountability. This type of planning prevails where national policies grant young people the legal right to freely acquire whatever qualification they wish which, in turn, allows private individuals to acquire skills that may not meet the needs of the market. Such planning assumes that private training decisions take account of labour market information and that individuals will attempt to acquire skills that are really needed. Further reasoning behind this approach could be that since in developed economies labour markets are highly flexible, they can adjust to market moves and constraints provided that the proportion of workers with vocational qualifications is relatively high. Also, in the wealthier countries which apply this concept, pre-employment training is often seen as one of the avenues for the broad socialization of young people rather than a way of catering to labour markets. Governments are not concerned that most college graduates who have acquired vocational qualifications continue their studies in higher education, making little use of the acquired skills.

Student demand-driven programming leaves VET administrators a relatively small role, i.e. to intervene and plan. Under this concept, government training priorities may not be established, except to ensure the right to training or to maximize national training participation. As a result, governments focus on establishing training places nationwide; no enrolment limits are set; and there is no list of government training priorities linked to market demand for skills. Courses which satisfy the minimum standard enrolment will be publicly provided, no matter if jobs are available in the corresponding skill areas. Although administrators may collect data on the demand for courses and training outputs, the decisions they make usually aim to expand the number of training places or institutions and to improve throughput. VET administrators steer the list of authorized public programmes, issue corresponding skill standards and examination requirements, and allocate enrolment-based grants to schools. The best that administrators can do is to attempt to match the programmes to the local need for skills. To do this, institutions may be required to consult local employers before each planning cycle. From time to time, public financing for "leisure" programmes might be suppressed.

In the wealthier countries, VET planning and resource allocation decisions regarding school-based, pre-employment programmes leading to craft and technician levels have been found to respond primarily to individual demand for skills (see box 4.1). This means that government training places and funds actually follow the number of applicants and their individual preferences. Only in a few countries have governments appeared to be selective, making strong efforts to adjust programming to the market demand for skills. In these countries, the courses are limited, while programmes with long lead times are carefully planned on the basis of projected industry growth, market signals and other information.

Module 4. VET target setting and planning

> **Box 4.1 VET programming in the United States**
>
> In the United States, federal, state and local VET programming is conducted on the basis of individual demand and, to a certain extent, market forces. For the most part, little use is made of formal manpower planning data at any government level, either for the allocation of resources or for programming. Manpower data appear to be inaccurate for VET planning purposes in the market-driven economy. As the labour market is very fluid, local or regional data are not very meaningful, and national data are not disaggregated. Consequently, individual demand for training is the major influence in VET programming.
>
> Secondary schools tend to offer general courses in a limited number of occupational clusters (such as electronics, computer applications, automotive technology, business and construction), rather than offering many specific courses for narrowly defined jobs. These programming areas are in high demand and have the potential to employ considerable numbers of people. They provide the foundation for additional future education and training that may be required in real jobs. Many community colleges conduct periodic surveys of local high school *students*, rather than employers, to find out what courses or programmes they would like to be offered after graduation. The purpose is to match college programmes to student demand.
>
> The state government develops priorities for the allocation and use of federal and state VET funds; it determines how funds will be disbursed among local constituencies and it monitors the use of funds. Priority setting is usually a political process involving inputs from advisory committees, VET officials and other professionals. Typical priorities are small business development and export growth, and VET programmes that support these priorities receive more funds. Priorities frequently change. Government-sponsored programmes only train a small proportion of individuals, while the role of private training is very significant.
>
> Source: Herschbach, 1995

In general, the individual demand for courses can be used for programming and resource allocation in countries that have no serious problems with funds and base their VET planning on the policy argument that "the more vocational participation the better". This approach is more easily justified for short-term, inexpensive courses and for the courses producing basic skills, rather than for narrow skill qualifications. In poorer countries, the allocation of scarce public resources should be more targeted and linked to national economic and social priorities. Under the student demand planning concept, training decisions are sub-optimal and low rates of graduates' labour market success may result, as well as low rates of return on public training investments.

1.4 Planning based on market signals

Planning based on market signals aims to respond to the short-term demand for skills. This means that courses must reflect the market demand for skills and change as the market adjusts. In practice, only individual training providers, rather than national systems, can or should try to identify and react to market signals. In planning, VET managers should take account of other training avenues which may be of prime importance to the labour market. The same qualifications may also be acquired at private institutions, in enterprises or by correspondence course and most of these outputs are difficult to account for in assessing the government action needed to satisfy market demand for training. These alternative training systems increase the flexibility of labour and training markets and may react to market signals more rapidly than the public system is able to. Another consideration is that the job vacancies reported by enterprises may not be due to a shortage of skilled people in the market, but to low wages. In this case, the institution which tries to fill such job vacancies will only make the situation worse, as there will be more people with the same qualification and the downward pressure on wages will intensify.

Two principal types of market signal can be distinguished. The first type are generated by enterprises and the labour force, such as job vacancies, unemployment rates, wages, national and local changes occurring in economic sectors. The second type are generated by training institutions themselves through steering student demand for courses, data on training unit costs and the labour market success of graduates. All of these signals should be properly structured, identified and interpreted by the staff of VET institutions trained in market analysis. Due to the high uncertainty of labour markets, the assessment of training demand should be a regular process. Expectations regarding the precision of needs assessment should be lowered. Local labour market administration and VET managers should become market analysts and work together to interpret labour market signals and make flexible decisions on programming and resource allocation. These data are to be supplied to VET providers, private individuals and job seekers enabling them to make informed decisions. By comparing the costs and outputs of their courses, providers can react to the changing market situation. Several types of organization, such as local labour market committees and labour market observatories, have emerged with the specific purpose of collecting and interpreting labour market data and providing inputs to VET programming decisions (see Unit 2 of this Module).

Market signals-based planning is *demand-driven*. Each national VET administrator has to understand clearly which source of demand (young people, employees or enterprises) has priority. Demand-driven training should not be understood literally as training at the request of enterprises. Employers are often concerned with their immediate production needs; if government training system responds to employers' requests alone, the whole national approach to vocational education and training will be too short-sighted.

1.5 Strategic national planning

The approach which attempts to forecast the future and aims at setting long-term priorities, targets and activities is called *strategic planning*. Strategic planning in the area of VET should, therefore, attempt to foresee the long-term trends in national and sectoral economic development and human resources development (HRD) and, on this basis, establish long-term priorities, targets and programme activities to achieve these (see also Module 2). It assumes a long-term and well-structured government intervention in education and training and reflects a deliberate policy to improve gradually the allocation of services to achieve certain economic and HRD outcomes. This approach focuses on future training demand and needs rather than on immediate demand for skills. Long-term government intervention in VET should be linked to economic and demographic forecasts for the country and for economic sectors and areas. It should also take account of the observed trends in market demand and student demand for VET. It should be emphasized that labour market projections, like any other forecasts, are very inaccurate and have to be reviewed regularly.

Strategic planning as an instrument of government management and financial intervention usually aims at:

- supporting economic development objectives such as the improvement of national productivity, moving the national production model towards up-market manufacturing, greater sharing of export markets and the creation of attractive conditions for foreign investors;
- contributing to HRD objectives such as the improvement of educational, technical and vocational preparation of the workforce, reduction of unemployment, achievement of a more equitable distribution of national income and poverty alleviation; and
- developing the VET system's ability to offer quality services, perform with high productivity and respond flexibly to market signals.

These objectives may be seen as closely interrelated or as relatively independent. A frequent stereotype is that public VET expenditure should necessarily result in the greater employability of graduates and improved productivity. Obviously, education and training should contribute to national productivity and income as well as to trainees' earnings. However, knowledge and skills are acquired not only for use in employment but also for social and cultural self-development. One important reason for self-development is that vocational knowledge and skills can reduce a family's cost of living.

Long-term strategic objectives may be only weakly linked to current market demand for skills if the social and private benefits (externalities) from training justify investments which are based on a desired future economic situation rather than a projected one. In this case, planning and investment in skills are themselves instruments to generate change. The short-term demand for public training should be satisfied through operational programming of individual providers. However, a balance between strategic and current needs for VET should be established and time preferences should be recognized. Strategic objectives should not be displaced by pressing current demands for skills.

Unit 2. Planning based on market signals

Learning objectives

This unit is designed to provide a better knowledge of:

1. Market signals in relation to VET planning
2. Planning decisions for VET delivery

2.1 Collecting labour market information

2.1.1 Factors affecting planning

VET managers need to plan ahead both strategically and operationally. *Strategic* VET planning deals with projections of future demand for services and has to identify the activities needed to develop training capacity to meet this demand. It is applicable to both national systems and individual providers; the national strategic plan will set a framework for providers' strategic and operational planning. *Operational* planning deals with individual providers' immediate and relatively short-term training demand. Short-term (i.e. a few weeks or months) courses which focus on entry-level skills do not need the level of scrutiny of market demand that strategic planning necessitates. However, simply planning on the basis of demand for courses in previous years does not adequately anticipate future

Module 4. VET target setting and planning

trends and may result in the ineffective use of public resources. By contrast, the more long-term and costly VET programmes are, the more analytical work and planning are required since labour market demand for skills may change considerably during the programme. Another important consideration is the relative stability of technology and corresponding job requirements. Some occupational fields, even involving long-term training, are relatively stable and the provision of a skilled workforce can be planned more easily. Other occupations are changing so rapidly that without close consultation with industry it is impossible to produce the desired number of qualified people. Tracer studies and reverse tracer studies are useful approaches to understanding the internal workings of labour markets and can help to guide planning (see Unit 4).

Operational VET planning responds to student and employer demand for training. Other considerations include the availability and conditions of government funding, providers' capacity to offer services; managers' willingness to take a certain market position and local competition between providers. Before planning, providers must decide what type of provision they want to offer within the government-approved priorities and which client groups they want to target. Labour market information (LMI) facilitates the analysis and anticipation of training demand in the short term and allows providers to adjust supply to demand. While some education and training needs evolve slowly, for certain skills the balance between supply and demand can change rapidly. In addition, a demand for new skills can emerge. Many sources of LMI are historical in nature and some are subject to wide margins of error (Fluitman, 1997).

2.1.2 Organization of labour market analysis

Labour market information is commonly collected by ministry VET departments, national training agencies and local employment office careers services. Recently regional specialist organizations known as labour market observatories have been established for this purpose. Most of these agencies have labour market specialists and conduct labour market surveys, employer surveys and household surveys of employment status and qualification. In addition, local government authorities may produce demographic and economic forecasts and, on the basis of these, local economic strategies. At national level, numerous studies and forecasts may be produced by central government departments and industry bodies.

Labour market observatories can be useful for collecting broad-based data on employment opportunities, monitoring training outcomes (job placement rates and wages of graduates) and disseminating findings to VET providers (see box 4.2). Perhaps because of inefficiencies born of inexperience, regional observatories have been found to be costly and to have problems with translating labour market signals

> **Box 4.2 Organization of labour market analysis and VET planning in France**
>
> In France, training needs assessment involves observing major labour market trends and drawing pragmatic guidelines from them. National vocational diplomas are defined and updated on the basis of this observation. Three national bodies are involved. The Centre for Studies and Research on Qualifications (CEREQ), which is jointly supervised by the Ministries of Education and Labour, is responsible for studying the relationship between training and employment. The Evaluation and Futures Department (DEP) of the education ministry supplies CEREQ with the results of its statistical research on student flows. The Education-Finance Committee (HCEE) establishes permanent high-level contacts between the education ministry and its partners. It has 24 members appointed by the minister, most of whom come from business and professional organizations. The HCEE aims at finding ways to develop the education system and meet national training needs.
>
> State and regional authorities and the social partners annually update information on trends in employment and qualifications for each economic sector. Data are drawn from employment surveys, which give information on the number of salaried employees in firms, on the occupational structure and on employee turnover. Sector-based analysis of employment trends, public training courses and labour market entry is also conducted. The CEREQ carries out tracer studies of the status of young people five years after graduation from initial training. Studies are conducted by phone, cover a national sample of 26,000 people and include all levels of training and industrial sectors. Seven months after the end of each school year, the DEP conducts an inquiry among school graduates and former apprentices. In 1996 the inquiry covered a national sample of 136,000 young people from 3,000 state and private establishments.
>
> Regional decision makers use the findings of these studies, but each of the 22 regions also has a Regional Observatory for Employment and Training (*Observatoire régional de l'emploi et des formations* – OREF), which supports the development of plans for vocational education of young people (PRDF), provides the Regional Delegation of the National Council for Management of Vocational Training (COREF) with labour market information, and fosters links between VET providers and regional labour markets. OREF boards of directors comprise representatives of state and regional authorities and the social partners. Their reports are circulated to training institutions, which are free to decide whether to use them. The OREFs' 1996 evaluation estimated that about half were producing information that was recognized as useful.

Module 4. VET target setting and planning

> Regions are required to draw up a plan of training courses spanning several years and reflecting quantitative and qualitative training needs. Regional plans focus primarily on the coordination of training programmes provided by various institutions. Therefore, regional VET plans provide guidelines on training courses resulting from a consensus based on evaluation of the local situation, local statistics, needs assessment, forecasts of how the economy and the labour market will develop and discussions between all parties involved. By contrast, the major VET providers are not asked to assess training needs, but to offer the programmes devised jointly by the ministry and the regional authorities. They are encouraged to follow up their graduates in order to determine whether they find work quickly. They are also encouraged to learn whether companies are satisfied with the training that students received.
>
> Source: Kirsch, 1994; Lafond, 1997.

into training decisions. In some countries, industrial sectors have also been active in collecting labour market information and advising VET providers on their training needs (see box 4.3).

Providers themselves should also be encouraged to observe markets and plan VET accordingly. Providers can establish special units to work with enterprises on a continuing basis. The benefit of this approach is that the information collected is more likely to make a direct impact on VET programming. However, training institutions may find that undertaking market research is too costly. Since providers have regular needs for LMI and the process of collecting and interpreting it is costly, they need to develop strategies and assign this duty to marketing specialists. Cooperation with the local employment office, sectoral bodies and research organizations should be sought in order to make data more reliable.

Providers' planning must respond to their *market segment* and be based on:

- the training needs of possible client groups (young people, industrial sectors, adults, special needs groups);
- the capacity of providers to offer the programmes needed; and
- the funds available.

When market segments are mapped according to these factors, the providers' *catchment areas* need to be defined. The catchment area is the market area where the great majority of students are located. Catchment areas may differ markedly depending on the type of provision and client groups. Information on catchment areas can be collected on the basis of the characteristics of existing full-time students as well as through various mapping tools. The identified structure

> **Box 4.3 Organization of labour market analysis in the Netherlands**
>
> Attempts made in the Netherlands by a specially created institution (ROA) to forecast labour market developments on the basis of national statistics were not promising. Traditional statistics failed to provide the data which would ensure inputs to the operational management of national and local VET systems. Therefore, the current focus is on monitoring the match between training and labour markets by means of flexible follow up of students. Regular analysis will be conducted on the rates of unemployment according to education, income range, value of diplomas in the labour market and the vulnerability of occupations in conditions of structural change. Forecasts will be by region at a later stage of development. The data collected are regularly distributed by the National Career Guidance Centre. A CD-ROM prepared by the Centre contains information about 1,500 occupations and 18,000 training opportunities and can be used by individual job seekers.
>
> There are sectoral mechanisms in addition to the national one. The printing sector, for instance, periodically surveys major changes in the industry and examines their significance for the future workforce and training demand. At local and regional levels, both national and local data are used. Another guidance system has been developed that studies the implications of national data for the regions and provides VET schools with this information.
>
> Source: Hövels and Meijer, 1994.

of catchment areas becomes the basis for collecting broader LMI (DFEE, 1995a).

The sources of LMI for each catchment area should be explored. Various sources may be available to providers, including in-house data, local and national research and forecasts, and official statistics. In-house data may be collected on existing profiles of students (age and gender, course preference, areas and institutions they come from, etc.); on typical destinations of students after training and their labour market success (through tracer studies); and on employer demand for skills.

2.2 Identifying labour market signals

2.2.1 Industry signals

Several types of signal have been identified which reflect industry skill shortages. Since these shortages often become known only when they are already apparent, only short-term planning decisions can be based on them.

Module 4. VET target setting and planning

First, employment growth and job vacancies for individual occupations and qualifications should be monitored. Falling job vacancy rates, rising unemployment rates and slowing employment growth for workers with certain qualifications all signal a decline in the need for specific skills. The time needed to fill vacancies and the number of applicants per vacancy also indicate the skills situation. However, even in industrialized countries with well-developed labour market information systems, data on vacancies and number of unemployed have not been found reliable (Richter, 1986). It often happens that wage policies and the structure of remuneration for certain occupations as well as the low prestige associated with them are major causes of high vacancy rates, rather than training shortages. If high vacancy rates are caused by non-training factors (e.g. low wages), no training intervention is required; if high vacancy rates are caused by training factors, then a training intervention should be considered.

In principle, VET managers should react to high vacancy rates by encouraging enrolment in the relevant programmes. However, job vacancy rates should not be equated with training demand requiring a direct response from the government training system, since there may be several ways to remedy the problem. Employers may, for instance, improve productivity, retrain skilled workers or the unemployed, and recruit workers from other firms. In addition, private training firms can react flexibly and produce skilled workers to fill the vacancies. Local education and training leading to certain jobs can be examined through reverse tracer studies (see Unit 4). Government training interventions can produce better results by taking account of these data.

Second, skill shortages among existing employees, as reported by enterprises, can also help identify demand for training and upgrading. However, these data will reflect only the current demand; employers often do not know what skills they will need in future. In addition, some enterprises may be poorly managed and operate with low productivity and profit margins. Employers may take the cheapest labour available rather than that required for the job or they may favour academic over technical qualifications. Therefore, the data reported by enterprises on skill shortages may be affected by employers' imperfect management decisions. VET managers need to consult key informants who know the industry and who can tell what kind of skills may soon be necessary. Employers' and workers' organizations as well as professional associations may serve as key informants on a permanent basis. Additional signals can be obtained from plans for new capital investment and technological change, since the qualification structures required for new technologies may be known from inter-sectoral and international comparisons.

Third, wages and real income across sectors, occupations and qualifications indirectly signal demand for certain skills (Richards and Amjad, 1994). Wage rates are sensitive enough to reflect changes in the demand for skilled labour only in those sections of labour markets that do not have artificial entry barriers and where competitive wages are applied. For example, the growing demand for labour in the United States in 1997 raised national labour costs by 2.9 per cent; at the same time, productivity rose by only 1.7 per cent (Madigan,1998). Increases in wages for certain qualifications may also signal that they are in short supply. By contrast, a decline in wages may reveal that certain qualifications have been over-produced. For instance, skill shortages in the construction sector allowed London bricklayers to command an hourly rate of £8.50 in May 1997, compared with £7 six months earlier (Merriden, 1997). However, in many countries, wages are segmented and the rates for the same qualification may be higher in large factories than in small ones. Wages may also be higher in firms with foreign capital than in local firms. In addition, wage differences may occur across regions as well as across age and gender groups (wage differences by gender, however, diminish rapidly as the level of education increases). Wage rate fluctuations are not necessarily associated with excess demand or shortage of labour. Competitive and flexible labour markets link wages with productivity. As a result, declining earnings may also be a signal of declining productivity and profits. Therefore, wage-related indicators, like other signals, are imperfect; care should be taken in using wage rates as an indicator of the demand for skills.

Fourth, the reaction of labour markets to VET graduates provides very useful information. Tracer studies, reverse tracer studies and rate-of-return analysis can be used to monitor this reaction (see Unit 4). For instance, a tracer study assumes that VET managers follow graduates for a year or two and gather information on placement rates, earnings and hours of work. Estimates of the training unit cost in relation to the impact of training on the graduates' employment ratio help in comparing the cost-effectiveness of training courses. If a significant proportion of the graduate cohort could not find jobs for a year or two or entered other occupations, admission to training for this occupation should be reviewed. Courses which show higher rates of wage employment for graduates should be expanded. Students should be advised on wage and employment rates as well as on average wages for the occupations they have chosen. Another important technique – rate-of-return analysis – helps in examination of the links between the cost of training and improvements in graduate incomes. If a training course results in improved income, this is a sign that training funds have been spent efficiently. Although national training priorities and investments should not be determined solely on the basis of the economic returns on programmes, the courses which produce positive returns on investment should clearly be encouraged.

Strategic and operational planning require information on local employment structures by industry and type of occupation, characteristics of the existing workforce, employment trends by sector and occupation, and any technological

Module 4. VET target setting and planning

Table 4.1 Local sectoral labour market information

Questions to ask	Sources of information	Analysis
How many firms and how many employees will be in this sector in the VET provider's catchment area in 2-3 years time?	• Local employment censuses and forecasts • National/sectoral forecasts from industry boards forecasts can be applied to foresee possible local trends.	• Historical data extrapolated from these sources should be used with caution • National/sectoral employment
Which firms, occupations and qualifications are growing most rapidly, and which are declining?	• National/sectoral forecasts from industry boards • Tracer studies of graduate wages and employment	• Such information can provide a broad national perspective. • Low employment rates and decreasing wages may reflect declining demand for certain skills.
What changes in working practices and technology are expected to result in new training demand?	• National/sectoral forecasts from the industry board • Studies on the sector made in other countries	• Such information can provide a broad national perspective. • It can also suggest ideas for forthcoming changes in the sector.
What types of skill shortage do employers report and which training programmes are they seeking?	• Employer marketing visits	• This provides reliable, short-term information.

Source: Department for Education and Employment – DFEE (United Kingdom), 1995a.

or other developments that could affect employment. Table 4.1. provides a format for collecting and processing these basic data on industrial sectors.

2.2.2 Demand from young people

LMI must be specific in order to be useful in planning student demand-driven VET (see table 4.2). The rates of population growth versus employment growth are the most important basic data. In addition, the number of young people of school-leaving age and their destination patterns need to be examined to project the number of people likely to seek training. When the population growth rate in a catchment area is considerably higher than the rate of employment growth, the problem of youth unemployment and equity becomes acute. Unless the

Table 4.2 Local labour market information on young people

Questions to ask	Sources of information	Analysis
How many young people 16–18 years old will be in the provider's catchment area in the future?	• Local authority demographic forecasts	
What have been and are likely to be young people's destination patterns (e.g. school, VET, employment)?	• Career services data	• Historical data extrapolated from these sources should be used with caution
What types of VET programme are proving more popular with young people?	• Provider records on enrolment and student satisfaction • Career service data	• This information is easily accessible and reliable
Where do student demand and employer need for skills most closely correspond?	• Provider marketing visits to enterprises. • Provider studies of graduate destinations and labour maket success • Local government economic strategy • Local industry employment and occupational forecasts	• The industry view may be the most reliable

Source: DFEE, 1995a.

government creates incentives promoting local business and attracting investors, training can be of little help. In such circumstances, especially when countries are experiencing funds shortages, programmes with low placement rates can be removed from government financing and offered on a commercial basis. Programmes focusing on training for self-employment should be expanded. The number of education and training places designed to produce foundation skills (rather than occupational skills) should be increased.

The applicant-to-admission ratios for particular courses can also reflect the market need for skills, however indirectly, through applicants' expectations for a return on their investment in acquiring particular skills. Individual demand for training very often mirrors the prestige associated with an occupation. Low applicant-to-admission ratios and half-filled training classes may, to a certain extent, signal a low market demand for skills as well as the expectation of uncompetitive wages.

Module 4. VET target setting and planning

Student demand-driven training will continue to strongly affect state vocational training systems. Data on employment and wages across occupations and sectors must be supplied to VET providers, trainees and job seekers in order to inform private training decisions. VET administrators should direct the skills-acquisition process by reducing enrolment in programmes for which there is declining demand. Most industrialized countries base their planning decisions on student demand rather than on labour market data. In other words, government training programmes are provided at the request of young people who may not have a mature knowledge of the labour market. It is assumed, therefore, that public training investments are not necessarily lost even if graduates do not enter jobs but proceed to higher education. The knowledge acquired in vocational courses can make an impact on graduates' ability to choose among further learning avenues and careers. If funds permit, the programmes which feature high applicant-per-place ratios may be encouraged even if the market cannot absorb so many graduates. The best that managers can do is to find the areas where student demand for courses most closely corresponds to employer demand for skills.

2.2.3 Demand for special needs groups

LMI can also be collected on the unemployed, special needs groups and the occupations and qualifications for which a VET provider has solid training expertise and capacity. Making efforts to help special needs groups to organize themselves and consulting their representatives on training needs have proved useful in reducing barriers to their access to training and employment. A format for LMI to be collected on the local unemployed and their training demand is suggested in table 4.3.

2.3 Reacting to labour market signals

The labour market signals which may be generated by industry, young people and adult groups are summarized in figure 4.1, while ways of interpreting those signals and corresponding VET programming and resource allocation decisions are suggested in table 4.4.

2.4 Planning cycle based on market signals

Once collected and interpreted, LMI needs to be incorporated in the planning process. Examples of planning experience in the United Kingdom and the United States are described in boxes 4.4 and 4.5, respectively.

Table 4.3 Labour market information on the unemployed

Questions to ask	Possible sources	Analysis
How many unemployed people are there within the provider's catchment area?	• Population censuses • Employment services	• Employment service information is most up-to-date.
What are the age, sex, previous job and training experience of the unemployed?	• Population censuses • Employment services	• Employment service information is most up-to-date.
What types of training are of most interest to the local unemployed?	• VET providers' own analyses	• Large margins of error may be expected.
What are the key constraints on access to training?	• VET providers' own analyses	• Large margins of error may be expected.
What types of training may lead to jobs?	• Employment services • Data on labour market success of previous groups of trainees	

Source: DFEE, 1995a.

Unit 3. Strategic VET planning

Learning objectives

This unit is designed to provide a better knowledge of:

1. The concept of strategic planning as part of strategic management
2. Different approaches to strategic analysis and planning
3. Strategic objectives

3.1 Systemic strategic planning

3.1.1 Evaluating future demand for VET services

The purpose of strategic planning is to set objectives and a timeframe in which to achieve them. (The concept of strategic management is described in Unit 1 of Module 2.) Strategic planning involves decisions based on forecasts, which are inevitably imperfect. Nevertheless, VET administrators must make informed estimates concerning national economic, social and demographic

Module 4. VET target setting and planning

Figure 4.1 Labour market information needed for local VET planning

Industry short-term needs for skills

Local employment structures by sector and major occupational qualification
Increase/decrease in job vacancy rates by qualification
• Reported skill shortages by occupational qualification • Training programmes sought by employers
Increase/decrease in wages by occupational qualification
Wage employment rates for VET graduates and the occupations they enter

Industry strategic development indicators

Future employment trends by sector and occupation
Rate of firm closings nd new firm formation by economic sector
Large-scale investment projects leading to job creation
Important technological developments leading to demand for new skills or to redundancies
Changes in organization of production systems, new sources of services and supply of products

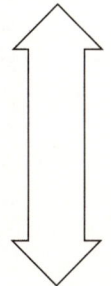

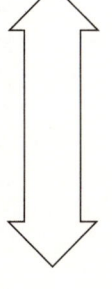

Young people's demand for training

• Number of young people of school leaving age • How many 16-18 year olds will be in the provider's catchment area in the future?
• Young people's traditional destination patterns (education, VET, employment) • How many training places will be demanded?
• Applicant-to-admission ratios for individual VET providers • Which part of the demand for courses could be met?
Where do the student demands and industry needs most closely correspond?

Demand for adult training

Number of groups: • Unemployed • Special needs groups, etc.
Characteristics of adult groups: age, sex, previous training and job experience
Groups' demand for training courses
Key constraints on groups' access to training provision
What type of training may lead to jobs?

145

Table 4.4 Labour market signals and responses

Signals	Responses
1. The local population is growing at a higher rate than employment, increasing the demand for VET.	• Compare the effectiveness of VET courses and shift funds towards courses with higher placement rates. • Increase resource allocation for training programmes for self-employment. • Increase the number of education and training places for courses providing foundation skills.
2. Rising job vacancy rates for specific qualifications reflect an increasing demand for skills.	• Visit enterprises and examine reasons for skill shortages; if they are caused by training shortages, develop the necessary courses. • Conduct reverse tracer studies examining contributions from alternative paths to the jobs in question; focus on VET courses for jobs commonly filled by training graduates rather than from other sources. • Encourage enrolment in courses which produce skills for which there is an increasing demand. • Alert trainees and applicants to labour market changes. • Remember that reported shortages of skilled workers may reflect poor wages and working conditions. • Recall that there may be other avenues for supplying skilled labour that could obviate the need for government training responses.
3. Low employment rates for graduates or graduates entering occupations other than those for which they were trained, reflect a decline in demand for these occupations or low training quality.	• Conduct tracer studies. • Compare local unemployment rates for graduates with national and regional rates for the same occupations. • If funds are limited, maintain only programmes leading to higher employment rates.

Module 4. VET target setting and planning

4. Wage increases for certain qualifications, perhaps indicating a demand for skills.	• Conduct reverse tracer studies regarding the jobs which show wage increases. • Increase allocations and encourage enrolments on programmes leading to these jobs. • Advise students on graduate employment rates and average wages in given occupations. • Remember that wage fluctuations may reflect the movement of enterprise wage policies and profits rather than demand for skills.
5. High applicant-to-admission ratios for particular programmes, indicating the availability of jobs and competitive wages for certain skills.	• Conduct tracer studies. • Attempt to satisfy the demand for courses if the availability of jobs is confirmed by other sources. • Compare the cost-effectiveness of VET courses and reduce admission to costly programmes with low placement rates or else introduce fees. • Advise students on graduate employment rates and average wages in given occupations. • Remember that applicant-to-admission ratios are based on private expectations regarding jobs and wages and can only indirectly reflect the true market situation.
6. Considerable capital investments and/or technological and production changes in certain industrial sectors, pointing to possible future demand for skills.	• Consult local authorities and industry informants (managers, employers' and workers' organizations, professional associations) regarding possible changes. • Examine data from other regions or countries regarding the new occupational structures that may emerge (while remembering to take account of national differences in occupational structures and productivity). • Adjust course offerings and enrolments accordingly.

Managing vocational training systems

> **Box 4.4 Strategic and operational VET planning in the United Kingdom**
>
> The further education (FE) college planning cycle is influenced by the planning framework of the Further Education Funding Council (FEFC), the government funding agency. The FEFC and colleges are involved in a rolling programme of strategic planning and produce plans every three years. If any significant changes to the plan occur, the college need only notify the FEFC. FE colleges start their *strategic* planning for up to three years in the autumn term and it is concentrated between November and February; *operational* planning starts in the spring term and should be in place by the start of the financial year in August. The major planning indicators are student numbers, overall and per programme, and the funds required.
>
> Colleges provide the FEFC with the following information every year (see also table 4.5):
>
> - financial forecasts;
> - statistical information on enrolments/provision;
> - supporting information demonstrating that the projections are consistent with the strategic objectives and information on local market needs; and
> - confirmation that their plans have been agreed by the local Training and Enterprise Councils (bodies which administer training operations on behalf of the Government).
>
> The following areas of education and training provision have been used for college planning and resource allocation: art and design, agriculture, basic education, business, construction, engineering, health and community care, hotels and catering, humanities and sciences. Total full-time enrolments in 1996-97 achieved an approximate 23 per cent increase over 1993-94. Although there are some differences in the level of growth anticipated in each programme area, the distribution of enrolment between programme areas is not expected to change significantly for either full-time or part-time training.
>
> Although FE colleges are relatively free to select provision areas in their locality, their comments on the actual demand for courses are required. The FEFC has reserved the right to earmark funding or otherwise attach conditions to secure particular objectives. The rate of growth of college enrolment is monitored in order to achieve national training targets. Nearly one-third of the colleges use their own sources of market information, student surveys and applications together with local labour market information surveys. For training needs analysis, more than 70 per cent of colleges consult local employers; 61 per cent also consult career services.
>
> The British approach to VET planning, unlike the Australian approach (see Unit 3 of this Module), does not link planning directly to industry growth forecasts or establish national priorities on programme areas. Instead it encourages colleges to follow relatively short-term market signals.
>
> Source: DFEE, 1995a; FEFC, 1994a

Table 4.5 FEFC requirements for strategic planning (3-year rolling programme)

	Statistical information	Strategic plan information	Financial forecast
Feb. 1995	1994–95 estimate and projections for 1995–96 to 1997–98 on: • student numbers • changes in provision	Commentary on statistical information	Mid-year financial forecast
July 1995	Confirmation of statistical information supplied in February 1995	Annual review of strategic plan; outline of provision 1995–96 to 1997–98; risk analysis	Financial forecast 1995–96 to 1997–98
Feb. 1996	1995–96 estimate and projections for 1996–97 to 1998-99 on: • student numbers • changes in provision	Commentary on statistical information	Mid-year financial forecast
July 1996	Confirmation of statistical information supplied in February 1996	Annual review of strategic plan; outline of provision 1996–97 to 1998–99; risk analysis	Financial forecast 1996–97 to 1998–99
Feb. 1997	1996–97 estimate and projections for 1997–98 to 1999–2000 on: • student numbers • changes in provision	Commentary on statistical information	Mid-year financial forecast
July 1997	Confirmation of statistical information supplied in February 1997	Annual review of strategic plan; outline of provision 1997-98 to 1999-2000; risk analysis	Financial forecast 1997–98 to 1999–2000
Feb. 1998 onwards	Repeat cycle		

Source: FEFC, 1995.

> **Box 4.5 Client-driven management in Fox Valley Technical College, Wisconsin (United States)**
>
> Fox Valley Technical College serves 45,000 part- and full-time students in Wisconsin. In 1985 the college administration created the first total quality management programme for their employees. Since then, they have almost completely restructured college operations around market needs. To identify those needs they conduct an annual Student Satisfaction Survey in which 650 students rate teaching effectiveness, instruction methods and student services such as admission and counselling. Each division of the college must take action appropriate to the students' evaluations. A serious problem of course cancellations was solved through this system of evaluation.
>
> The college also surveys its business customers. It has roughly 1,200 separate contracts with business, industry and Government each year. Using a computerized system, it can inform businesses that request training within a few hours whether the curriculum already exists for the programme they want and, if not, how long it would take to develop, how much it would cost and when the course could begin. The college tracks the labour market success of its graduates to see if its programmes are in fact preparing them for jobs in demand. Almost 93 per cent of the 1988–89 graduates surveyed found jobs within six months; of those, 87 per cent did so in their area of training.
>
> To force instructors to act upon the requirement to prepare students for real jobs, the college decided in 1990 to offer students a guarantee. If graduates cannot find a job in an area related to their training course within six months, the college guarantees up to six free credits of additional instruction (two or three courses), plus free support services (e.g. counselling and career development). The college also guarantees the quality of training for business customers. If a customer is not satisfied, the course will be repeated for free, with a new instructor. The college periodically surveys its business customers to see whether they have received quality training. This has resulted in more thorough student counselling, recognition of greater need for instructor competence and greater operational flexibility. Most instruction is individualized; more than 150 different computer-assisted instruction programmes are offered. Flexible entry and exit programmes have been developed; in some programmes students can enrol daily. As a result of these measures, the student dropout rate has decreased by 22 per cent.
>
> Source: Osborne and Gaebler, 1992.

Module 4. VET target setting and planning

trends in order to plan development scenarios. While it is difficult to predict demand for vocational training beyond a period of roughly five years, and it is even more challenging to forecast industry trends, it is vital to be aware of trends relating to training demand, as they may affect the system's mission, objectives and programming.

Trends in population, economic sectors, demand for vocational education and training and the effect of these trends on a VET system's mission should be reviewed in order to plan future activities (see figure 4.2; see also Unit 2 of this Module).

Population trends should be analysed so that forecasts regarding the groups which may request training services can be made. Such forecasts should try to

Figure 4.2 Stages of national strategic VET planning

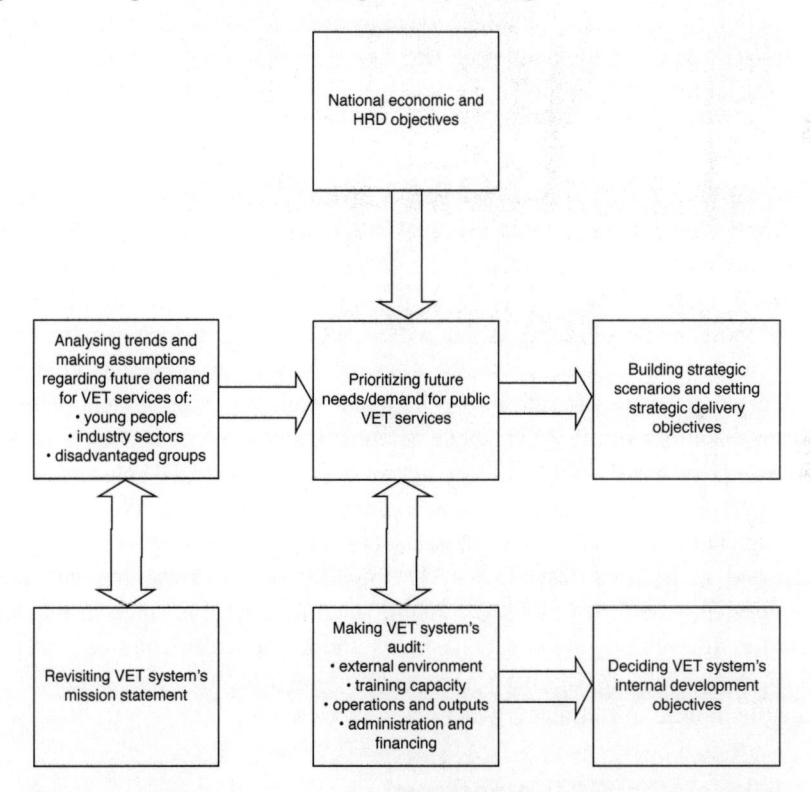

```
                        ┌─────────────────────────┐
                        │ National economic and   │
                        │    HRD objectives       │
                        └─────────────────────────┘
                                    │
                                    ▼
┌──────────────────────┐  ┌─────────────────────┐  ┌──────────────────────┐
│ Analysing trends and │  │                     │  │  Building strategic  │
│ making assumptions   │  │  Prioritizing future│  │  scenarios and setting│
│ regarding future     │─▶│  needs/demand for   │─▶│  strategic delivery  │
│ demand for VET       │  │  public VET services│  │  objectives          │
│ services of:         │  │                     │  │                      │
│ • young people       │  │                     │  │                      │
│ • industry sectors   │  │                     │  │                      │
│ • disadvantaged      │  │                     │  │                      │
│   groups             │  │                     │  │                      │
└──────────────────────┘  └─────────────────────┘  └──────────────────────┘
           ▲                        ▲
           │                        │
           ▼                        ▼
┌──────────────────────┐  ┌─────────────────────┐  ┌──────────────────────┐
│                      │  │ Making VET system's │  │                      │
│                      │  │ audit:              │  │  Deciding VET        │
│ Revisiting VET       │  │ • external          │  │  system's internal   │
│ system's mission     │  │   environment       │─▶│  development         │
│ statement            │  │ • training capacity │  │  objectives          │
│                      │  │ • operations and    │  │                      │
│                      │  │   outputs           │  │                      │
│                      │  │ • administration    │  │                      │
│                      │  │   and financing     │  │                      │
└──────────────────────┘  └─────────────────────┘  └──────────────────────┘
```

predict the percentage change in the population of various groups according to age, sex and educational level. Attention must be paid to the number of young people approaching school-leaving age. Statistics on the educational level as well as the formal qualifications of the entire population and the working population should also be collected. The demand for vocational training will be determined by young people's destination patterns (see box 4.6). Trends in enrolment in higher education versus vocational training, as well as school leavers' direct entrance to employment, must be identified. Statistics on VET participation rates, drop-out rates, repetition rates and overall number of graduates must be collected.

Economic sectors should be monitored so that forecasts can be made regarding output, productivity, employment and unemployment in various industries and the principal qualifications that they employ. Those sectors and regions which are likely to experience growth or decline in output, productivity and employment should be identified so that programmes aimed at producing the relevant qualifications are adjusted accordingly. The private participation in training should be assessed. Large-scale capital development projects and major technological and production changes must be noted so that the need for skilled labour can be met. Established workers' need for skills upgrading must also be identified. Trends in sectoral demand for training for new skilled labour and for the existing workforce must also be charted. Changes in the size of disadvantaged groups and their demand for and access to public training should be monitored.

Rethinking a VET system's mission involves contemplating whether the mission statement needs to be changed in light of demographic and economic trends and their effect on demand for training.

Once trends relating to training demand have been identified and assumptions made regarding which will affect planning, priorities must be set. Demand for VET usually exceeds what the public services can provide. In deciding on priorities for the future, national economic development plans and human resources development plans should be considered. In fact, a training system's priorities should be viewed as part of the national HRD plan and should contribute to national economic development priorities as far as possible. The training demands of industry, students and disadvantaged groups should be evaluated in light of these plans. The identified future training needs and priorities may lead to a revised mission statement. At this stage in planning, priorities for future public VET services and a confirmed mission statement should be in place. On this basis, strategic training objectives can be drafted (see example of systemic strategic planning in section 3.5).

3.1.2 Setting VET objectives

Delivery objectives should reflect the identified demand for VET services and related priorities. They are commonly expressed in terms of national enrolment, level of vocational participation and achievement, hours of curriculum and placement of graduates. The objectives should express the

> **Box 4.6 Questions to ask in assessing future demand for VET services**
>
> 1. Concerning young people's future demand for courses and the number of training places needed to satisfy the projected demand:
>   - Is demand for VET programmes going to increase?
>   - Can the government afford to fully satisfy this demand?
>   - Which courses should become priorities?
> 2. Concerning sectoral and regional demand for new skilled labour:
>   - Which economic sectors or regions will need new skilled labour, if any?
>   - Which qualifications will be most needed?
>   - Will more training be provided by employers?
>   - Should the government provide or support programmes for growing/declining sectors and regions?
>   - Should the government provide or support programmes for workers in employment?
>   - What will be the priorities?
> 3. Concerning disadvantaged groups' training needs:
>   - Who comprises these groups and will their numbers increase?
>   - What are these groups' future needs for VET and which should have priority?
>   - Can the government afford to satisfy these needs?
> 4. Concerning future needs for public VET:
>   - Which training needs are priorities for government training?

hoped-for impact of VET operations on target groups. For example:

- Training attainment targets aim at achieving final training outputs (e.g. "By the year 2000, 75 per cent of all employees in export industries will have formal vocational qualifications.").
- Training participation targets aim at a particular number of people or specific groups in training.
- Job placement targets aim at achieving outputs which are commonly thought to be beyond the control of VET administrators (e.g. "By the year 2000, the post-training placement rate after 6 months for the long-term unemployed and low-educated people will reach 60 per cent, and 70 per cent for all other groups of trainees.").

Operational targets should be drawn from strategic objectives. Being short-term, they should be more quantitative and lend themselves to direct verification. Although, in principle, operational targets are directly linked to strategic objectives, in the short-term perspective, new operational targets may be established reflecting actual situations.

Development objectives are set for two reasons. First, they aim to overcome the training system's weaknesses and maintain its strengths. Audits should help to assess whether the system has the capacity to meet future delivery objectives. If the system is unable to develop needed capacity, the delivery objectives will have to be lowered. Development objectives should be based on the priorities expressed in the service delivery objectives, which they are supposed to support.

Second, whatever the predictions on labour force needs and individual qualifications, public training systems need to be directed and upgraded on a continuous basis. Technical support structures should also be maintained even if the demand for courses is not known. In order to respond to future demand properly, the curricula, skill standards and assessment techniques need to be updated regularly and a new supply of qualified instructors must be trained.

Development objectives are usually expressed in terms of system capacity and performance. For example, objectives could be stated as follows:

- to enhance the quality of training (e.g. "To introduce incentives for training centres which have managed to achieve graduation at higher qualification levels");
- to improve the flexibility of training delivery (e.g. "To decentralize, by 2005, decision-making powers to regional training centres");
- to improve access to training (e.g. "To build, by 2005, ten additional rural training centres in isolated areas");
- to improve the cost-efficiency of training (e.g. "To decrease national training unit costs by 5 per cent over 5 years");
- to enhance the system's capacity (e.g. "To establish, within 2 years, 50,000 additional entry level training places");
- to achieve a certain level of income by selling public training services (e.g. "To earn 40 per cent of the budget by providing commercial training services").

The principles of setting objectives are as follows:
- The objectives should be based on established priorities for service delivery.
- A reasonable timeframe for objectives should be established and the need for time preferences should be recognized. Strategic objectives should not be displaced by pressing current demands for skilled labour.
- The objectives should reflect demand for services rather than what the agency has actually been doing. A frequent mistake is for any measurable performance to become the objective.
- The main objectives may be set along with complementary ones. A common problem is setting many objectives but failing to establish priorities for them.

- Strategic objectives should be translated into annual operational targets which are measurable. National targets may be translated into national programme targets and individual organization targets.
- When determining objectives within limited resources, it should be understood that targets may produce conflicts and that achievement of one target may interfere with meeting another. For example, it is often difficult to target simultaneously the provision of equitable access to training (usually a very costly objective) and a high rate of economic growth (which focuses on skill training for better educated groups).
- The objectives must be explicitly linked to the government budgeting process. If not, targets and priorities are not likely to be implemented.
- Although outputs tend to deviate from objectives, objectives should be regularly reviewed in light of the outputs and outcomes produced (United Nations Department for Development Support and Management Services, 1993) (see box 4.7).

3.2 Strategic planning involving rate-of-return analysis

The contribution to economic growth and productivity of each dollar invested in education and training can be seen in the *rate of return* to this investment. Social and private rates of return help to measure the cost-efficiency of investment in training programmes and suggest a basis for making investment and programming decisions. The rates of return are calculated on the post-training *earnings* of graduates from the programmes. Rates of return can be estimated on the basis of information collected through a tracer study.

In several countries, rates of return to educational and training investments have been used in strategic planning and resource allocation. This approach bases strategic planning decisions on estimates of rates of returns to investment in various engineer/technician specializations that are likely to prevail in the planning period and on estimates of future growth/decline in industry sectors that put upward or downward pressure on these rates of return. While manpower forecasting with all its limitations remains part of this approach, it is used to detect the most likely changes in economic sectors and the implications for employment and demand for education and training rather than to calculate the number of skilled workers needed in the future. The forecast is not used to set enrolment targets for specializations, though VET enrolment and programming decisions are influenced by comparing the programmes' rates of return (for examples of the application of this approach see boxes 4.8 and 4.9). Basing strategic planning on rates of return has considerable conceptual and technical limitations (see section 4.5 in Unit 4 of this Module).

> **Box 4.7 Checklist for formulating objectives**
>
> Objectives should be checked against the following list:
>
> - Are the objectives verifiable, measurable and controllable in terms of quantity, quality, time and cost?
> - If they are qualitative, what are the standards for verification?
> - Are the objectives reasonable and realistic?
> - Are they assigned in order of priority?
> - Are the short-term objectives consistent with the long-term ones?
> - Are the underlying assumptions of the objectives clearly identified?
> - Are the objectives merely a description of activities which will be carried out anyway?
> - Do they provide a challenge?
> - Have the objectives been clearly communicated to those who will be affected and who will be involved in their implementation?
> - Have subordinates been given a chance to contribute to the formulation of objectives?
>
> Source: Ferrari and Lankaster, 1992.

3.3 Strategic planning involving policy considerations and international comparisons

International comparisons of occupational skill structures can be used as an instrument for VET programming. They are also relevant to planning enrolment in courses with long lead times, and they are particularly useful in technology transfer projects. This technique is valuable when patterns of sectoral investment and employment growth become clear. The local or sectoral need for more engineers and technicians, for instance, can be identified through comparison with countries with relatively similar conditions and with mature industries. Well-prepared project documents for technology transfer usually have sections on the workforce and occupational structure and, therefore, allow for an assessment of future employment growth and the need for qualifications. In principle, this can inform VET planning and enrolment targets. Since skills can be acquired through various routes, such forecasts should be translated into predictions of growth by field of study.

The problem with this technique is that suppliers of new, transferred technologies normally anticipate the quantity of labour needed and design its occupational structure on the basis of the country of origin, usually a developed country. However, labour and machine productivity in industrialized countries

Box 4.8 Setting strategic objectives in Indonesia

Indonesia's economic future depends on human resource development (HRD). Improving the skills and quality of life of the Indonesian people through education is a major national goal for the next 25 years. Education is seen as a way to achieve faster economic growth, realize more equitable distribution of income and reduce poverty.

Facing low per capita incomes (of $500 a year) and high inequality in incomes, Indonesia hopes to provide for growth by investing 30.17 per cent of its GNP in physical capital, one of the highest among the ASEAN countries. However, government investment in education is very low, at 2.95 per cent of GNP, the lowest in ASEAN, where the average invested by central governments is 4.2 per cent of GNP.

Rates of return to education have been higher than returns to investment in physical capital, demonstrating the utility of increased investment in education. Real rates of return to basic education in the period 1986–90 were estimated to be 27 per cent in rural areas and between 11 and 16 per cent in urban areas, whereas the real rates of return to investment in physical capital was on average 9.4 per cent. Investment in vocational education is also productive. For graduates entering small business, all types of senior secondary vocational education yield a very good return, averaging 34 per cent. Commercial high schools achieve rates of return of 37 to 51 per cent for males and 24 per cent for females. The unemployment rate of secondary school and college graduates falls sharply to 3 per cent and below after age 26. Underemployment is much higher among those with less education than it is for high school and college graduates.

Other reasons for increasing investment in education have also been identified. For one, Indonesia's main competitors, Malaysia and Thailand, spend more on education. Further, equity has not been attained. Drop-out rates are high, especially in rural areas. Teacher remuneration is irregular and there are high repetition rates in some areas. Access to junior and senior secondary schools is still quite limited.

Indonesia's goals for improving access, equity, quality and efficiency by the year 2018 include enroling 100 per cent of the population (now 91 per cent) in primary education by 1998, 100 per cent (now 41 per cent) in junior secondary education by 2008, 80 per cent (now 22 per cent) in senior secondary education by 2013, and 25 per cent (now 6 per cent) in higher education by 2018; providing aid to under-served schools; improving teacher training and the quality of teaching and teaching materials in core subjects such as maths and science; instituting teacher pay incentives;

> Box 4.8 (cont'd)
>
> revising the curricula and setting higher achievement outcomes at all educational levels; improving internal efficiency within schools; expanding investment in cost-effective programmes; and forging links between education and job markets. Indonesia hopes to reduce degree completion times, and raise higher school attendance. Better quality education in low-income areas will greatly reduce the dropout and repetition rates.
>
> These goals represent a national investment strategy which combines economic and equity development. They will require sizeable public (from 4 to 7 per cent of GNP) and private (family) investments (from 16 to 19 per cent of GNP).
>
> Source: Boediono et al., 1992.

Box 4.9 Planning education and training programmes with long lead times in Malaysia

Planners in Malaysia combined their assumptions about employment growth, technological and productivity changes, and patterns of specialization in industry sectors with assumptions about engineer intensity (based on international comparisons) to forecast the number of engineers per branch by 1995. On this basis forecasts of the stock of engineers in selected sectors were produced. The forecasts regarding engineers and technicians as a whole were then translated into forecasts by field of study. These facilitate estimation of current social and private rates of return by area of specialization and the expected direction of change in that rate over the planning period. As can be seen in table 4.6, the fastest growth in the rate of return was expected for industrial efficiency engineering and the slowest for architecture and town planning. Demand for all other specializations was expected to grow at a fairly steady rate. These analyses can be used to determine which programmes should be expanded and which should be scaled down.

Source: Godfrey, 1994

---

may be two to three times higher than in the country receiving a new technology, which can result in serious mismatches. In other words, the labour/capital ratio (number of workers per unit of machinery) may be much higher in less-developed countries using similar machines. For example, data on the labour/capital ratio for modern spinning machines indicate that an average Latin American plant needs twice as much labour per unit of machinery as a plant in

Module 4. VET target setting and planning

Table 4.6 Planning engineer/technician level programmes in Malaysia (1985-95)

Programme	Rates of return in 1985 (%)		Expected direction of change	Reasons for expectation
	Private	Social		
Architecture/town planning	9.4	6.0	Down	Fall in manufacturing, deceleration
Civil engineering	12.4	7.9	No change or down	Below average growth, deceleration
Electronic engineering	13.1	8.3	Up	Growth of electronic sector and related sectors.
Mechanical engineering	15.5	9.9	No change or down	Growth at average rate, deceleration
Industrial efficiency	17.4	11.1	Up	Above average growth, slight acceleration
Other engineering sectors	13.5	8.6	No change	Average growth, slight deceleration
Total	**13.5**	**8.6**		

an industrialized country. Relative productivity in modern weaving technology has been estimated in the Philippines at 55 per cent and in Kenya at 68 per cent of that in industrialized countries (Pack, 1987).

International comparison of sectoral labour forces for VET planning must also consider important possible differences between countries. These include the division of tasks between engineers, technicians, skilled workers and supervisors; possible differences in occupational structures; differences in productivity; and the common practice in many developing countries of using old machines along with new ones that may have differing workforce and skill requirements. Even if a certain technology largely determines the workforce size and structure needed in a capital project, these differences can significantly affect the true demand for labour and its skill structure. This should be taken into account in VET planning and programming decisions based on international comparisons.

Strategic training targets are often established by comparing national levels of vocational participation with the attainment of formal qualifications. A country concerned with international markets may identify the nations which are thought to be its principal competitors. Assuming that the average skill level of the working population determines, to a certain extent, national competitiveness, strategic objectives can aim at matching or surpassing competitors' levels (see boxes 4.10 and 4.11).

3.4 Common problems in strategic planning

A number of common problems with national educational planning and resource allocation have been identified (UNESCO, 1970). First, the adoption of a national development strategy remains a major problem. Development strategies determine whether public resources are used as efficiently as possible (in terms of generating revenue) or used to reduce social inequalities. It can be difficult to establish the links between indicators of national economic development and indicators of educational achievement, and to plan and budget accordingly. Consequently, resources for education and training programmes are often allocated, not on the basis of a specific concept of national development, but in response to comparisons with other countries.

Box 4.10 National VET targets in Denmark

National vocational education targets in Denmark are set by the Ministry of Education after consultation with the Vocational Education and Training Council; targets for labour market training are set by the Ministry of Labour, which consults the Adult Vocational Training Council.

Vocational education targets

One of the major policies regarding youth training is "education for all". Since about one-third of young people do not have a skilled-worker level vocational qualification, the following national target has been set: by the year 2000, 90-95 per cent of the youth cohort will have accomplished a compulsory education programme and proceed towards further learning avenues (as compared to 77 per cent in 1990).

Continuing training targets

In the area of continuing training, a target for development has been set: between 1993 and the year 2000 an extra 60,000 annual training places (full-time equivalents) should be developed. This will double the public system's training capacity.

Source: Nielsen, 1995.

Module 4. VET target setting and planning

Box 4.11 National VET targets in the United Kingdom

In the United Kingdom new targets have been set for improving international competitiveness by raising vocational training standards and attainment. By the year 2000, it is hoped that:

- all employers will invest in their employees' development to achieve business success;
- all individuals who wish will have access to education and training opportunities leading to recognized qualifications; and
- all education and training will develop self-reliance, flexibility and breadth, in particular through fostering competence in core skills.

To achieve this, the following targets concerning *foundation learning* have been set:

- by age 19, 85 per cent of young people will achieve five GCSEs at grades A-C, an intermediate general national vocational qualification (GNVQ) or a national vocational qualification (NVQ), level 2;
- by age 19, 75 per cent of young people will achieve level 2 competence in communication, numeracy and information technology; and by age 21, 35 per cent will achieve level 3 competence; and
- by age 21, 60 per cent of young people will achieve two GCE A Levels and advanced GNVQs or a level-3 NVQ.

Targets for *continuing training* have also been set:

- 60 per cent of the workforce will reach NVQ level 3, advanced GNVQ or two GCE A level standards;
- 30 per cent of the workforce will have vocational, professional, management or academic qualifications at NVQ, level 4 or above; and
- 70 per cent of all organizations employing 200 or more employees, and 35 per cent of those employing 50 or more, will be recognized as "investors in people".

Source: DFEE, 1995b

Second, as the whole process of strategic planning is based on forecasts of future demand for training, strategic plans risk being very inaccurate. Both forecasts and plans need to be reviewed annually to take account of new trends. The uncertainty of the labour market demand for skills can be managed by: delegating responsibility for assessing skill shortages and planning job-related training to industry bodies; strengthening the foundation knowledge component of training programmes and delaying occupational specialization until the later years of a training programme.

Third, national educational and training objectives are rarely expressed in practical terms. Frequently used formulations of national educational goals, for instance, include: integrating education with national development; correlating education to national economic, social and cultural needs; improving the quality of education; and ensuring equality of educational opportunity. When it comes to the practical aspects of resource allocation and implementation, such goals are too vague. Additional difficulties arise when countries do not have clear national occupational qualifications.

Fourth, strategic VET planning and management cannot be implemented in isolation from the national budgeting process, but education and training ministries often have poor connections with finance ministries. The budgeting process in many governments has its own logic, and it is often on a short-term basis, which may not support strategic planning and management of education and training. National training objectives that are not included in the budgeting process are of little use, even if they appear well-defined.

Fifth, national training budgets often focus on maintaining existing capacities and structures, rather than on achievement and development targets. When a national budget is approved, administrators often discover that 80 to 90 per cent of resources are already committed to recurrent costs and continuing functions and projects. It is very difficult to redirect resources towards new targets.

Sixth, the economic sectors which are the ultimate direct beneficiaries and consumers of public training services are often insufficiently involved in the planning process. Most state vocational training provision used to be primarily concerned with young people; this policy constrained the planning process, as it eliminated one of the most important aims of skills acquisition, i.e. national productivity improvement. Recently, in some countries, the role of industry in training needs analysis and strategic planning has been recognized and institutionalized. Industry has become a key source of advice.

Seventh, following the trend towards decentralization, some governments simply delegate planning and funding responsibilities to regions without developing any national strategic planning framework. This results in the failure of regions and, eventually, the country to focus on national priorities or achieve important training outcomes (see box 4.12).

Module 4. VET target setting and planning

Box 4.12 Decentralized planning in Italy

In Italy, the planning of training is the responsibility of regions, some of which view skills acquisition as a lever to develop local economic sectors, while other regions emphasize the geographical distribution of training. Plans are drafted by the regional authorities and submitted to Advisory Committees comprising representatives of the social partners and training providers. Regional Councils approve the plans. In many regions planning functions are delegated to provinces. Regions produce guidelines for provinces, which in turn make proposals regarding the regional plan. This procedure often results in fragmented regional planning and a lack of national strategies.

Central planning guidelines only prescribe that regional training plans must favour innovative VET programmes (which are difficult to define); gradually redirect resources from the basic training of young people with low educational levels to training for people with an upper secondary school certificate; and focus on training women, immigrants and the disabled.

The following problems have been identified:

- The training needs which should be addressed by the public training system are not adequately expressed. As a result, most regional training activities focus on graduates from compulsory schooling (age 14) and drop-outs from the first years of upper secondary school, ignoring the need for continuing training.
- Regional labour market observatories intended to examine training needs and provide inputs to VET programming and planning show little success. Most training courses in state-financed institutions are linked to the skill profiles which their instructors possess. This does not allow a response to labour market signals and more long-term demand for skills.
- Regions operate in uncertainty regarding financing sources and allocations. The locally raised tax-based funds are very limited, as are the funds received from the state. Most regional training programmes are financed by the European Social Fund, which sets conditions that limit regions' freedom in VET programming and planning.
- Additional complications in the planning process result from the lack of nationally recognized vocational qualifications. Labour unions disagree with the government definition of qualifications, while regions have some autonomy in defining qualifications. Consequently, more than 5,000 types of skill certificate exist, although they are not always recognized by the labour market.

Source: Bulgarelli and Giovine, 1994.

3.5 An example of systemic strategic planning: Australia[1]

3.5.1 Strategic planning at federal level

In Australia, strategic planning is used to develop the vocational training system in a coherent way, to make entry-level programmes industry demand-driven rather than student demand-driven by linking resource allocations and programming to industry outputs and employment projections. Strategic planning is also used to focus on upgrading established employees as well as producing new professionals and skilled workers, to ensure equitable access to training for disadvantaged groups, and to distribute resources equitably between industries.

Strategic planning at national (federal) level is implemented by the Australian National Training Authority (ANTA). National economic and employment projections have been developed to map out industrial and employment trends by industry and by major occupation. The industry forecast for 1991-2001 suggests that mining, construction and manufacturing will have above-average growth in output. There will be above-average growth in employment in recreation and personal services, retail trade, community services and business services, while no growth or declining employment is expected in some other industries (Monash University and Syntec Economic Services, 1995). The trends suggest that particularly strong employment growth is expected for sales assistants, personal service workers and clerks, while little growth is forecast for plant and machine operators.

The principal issue is how changes in the workforce will influence demand for vocational training. Employment growth is likely to continue, implying continued growth in demand for entry-level training; the number of long-term unemployed has fallen significantly and this trend may also continue. However, it is difficult to relate industry employment growth to the need for certain occupations and qualifications. Further, the industries experiencing low growth do not necessarily require a reduction in training efforts. The above projections indicate the occupations where employment growth is likely to be strong, but provide only broad guidance. More complete information is needed for effective planning. State Industry Training and Advisory Bodies (ITABs) were encouraged to examine sectoral trends in economic and employment situations and demand for training services. States were requested to produce plans (State Training Profiles) for each year and projections for coming years.

On the basis of the forecasts a national strategy has been developed which uses target groups, delivery objectives, system development objectives and priority areas.

---

[1] Based on Australian National Training Authority, 1994, 1995a, 1995b and 1995c

The national *strategy target groups* include young people, the established workforce (i.e. low-skilled employees, primarily at the operative level, and middle-skilled employees with low formal qualifications) and groups traditionally under-represented in VET for whom improved access to training and jobs will be secured (women; ethnic minorities; people with inadequate social, literacy and numeracy skills; people with disabilities; rural and isolated people; and the unemployed). Target groups are selected primarily on the basis of skill shortages that create barriers to high productivity. Equity is also a consideration. For instance, a discrepancy was found between government training for operative-level workers (clerks, sales staff, plant and machine operators, labourers and related workers) and this group's share of the total workforce (about 56 per cent). This group has low earnings and faces a high risk of unemployment; it is especially vulnerable to economic downturn and technological change. Another priority is female workers, who make up over three-quarters of the part-time workforce. Female employment is linked to service industries such as education, health and community services and retail trade. In order to increase their participation, flexible delivery of training and commitment to child care facilities have been adopted.

Delivery objectives are geared towards training participation and attainment. The targets have been formulated on the basis of existing trends. By the year 2001, 95 per cent of 19-year-olds are to be participating in or have completed grade 12 or have completed grades 10 or 11 and be participating in formally recognized education and training. By the year 2001, 60 per cent of 22 year-olds are to be participating in programmes which lead to level 3 awards, or have attained level 3 or higher qualifications, or be participating in or have completed higher education studies (degree and diploma levels).

Development objectives for the year 2001 include making the system more responsive to education and training needs, enhancing the quality of training, improving accessibility and increasing efficiency and cost-effectiveness. The system should offer incentives to those who achieve higher standards, ensure that those who want and need training can get it and be accountable. A balance is sought between industry sectors, between the existing workforce and new entrants, and between those who are under-represented in training and those whose training needs are traditionally being met.

Priority areas are determined for each year on the basis of the development objectives and approved by the Ministerial Council. While training development priority areas are *short-term* and reflect the current situation, continuity is maintained in developing them from year to year. For instance, for 1996, the following five development priority areas were set up: (1) promoting best practice and quality assurance; (2) strengthening the influence of industry and other client groups on training resource distribution; (3) focusing on disadvantaged and under-represented groups; (4) developing the training market; and (5) strengthening accreditation, assessment and recognition of training.

For each priority area, specific activities and their qualitative outcomes were planned. For the first priority area state training systems were expected to develop and implement quality standards and management frameworks for providers and agencies receiving public funds and to develop and promote descriptions of best service practice. For the second priority area improved planning techniques were sought to ensure the allocation of resources according to the needs of industry and other client groups. For this purpose, improvements were sought in specific areas of activity, including communication on training needs and capacities between industry, providers and state training agencies; identification and monitoring of skill shortages and gaps; and resource allocation for capital investment decisions and for the distribution of recurrent resources within and between industry sectors. The third priority area dealt with improved accessibility, and women and ethnic minorities were selected as priority target groups for 1996. Acquisition of information on these groups, consultation with representatives and recognition of prior learning experience were the activities planned. Priority area number four aimed at encouraging training to become more responsive to industry demand. Expected outputs included the introduction of resource allocation on the basis of competitive tendering and the expansion of colleges' commercial services. The fifth area called for an improved system for collecting and verifying information concerning education and training achievements.

Implementation of the national training strategy is *decentralized* to the states, the State Training Profiles being the primary planning vehicle. Each state may have its own priorities, and these may differ in some ways from those in the national strategy. States must, however, commit themselves to the national strategic priorities and targets as well as their own priority areas. Therefore, each State Training Profile outlines the activities aimed at achieving national strategic initiatives. It reflects the strategic objectives, strategy target groups and each year's priority areas. For each priority area, VET activities need to be developed with the corresponding resource allocations and expected outputs identified.

A State Training Profile provides a single operational plan for the current year as well as indicative figures for the following two years. As a planning and budgeting document, it covers all commonwealth- and state-funded VET activities. Implementation of profiles is supported by funds allocated by state governments and the federal government. State governments are free to distribute their own funds to support their Training Profiles and federal funds are allocated on the basis of the profiles. Profiles must clearly demonstrate the link between industry requirements and other client groups' training needs, on the one hand, and the planned outcomes, on the other. Corresponding training outputs are to be reported to the ANTA.

The aggregated data from the State Training Profiles constitute the basis for the national VET plan. For 1996, for instance, 33.6 per cent of all training activities were directed towards manufacturing, rural areas and construction, 25.5 per cent towards services and 18.1 per cent to general education and training. In terms of individual industries, in accordance with the priorities identified by states and ITABs, major growth in government-funded vocational training was planned in the business and clerical sector (17.1 per cent), community services, health and education (12.7 per cent) and tourism and hospitality (11.9 per cent); almost no increase was planned for manufacturing industry (Australian National Training Authority, 1995a). In terms of occupational level, national training activities were fairly evenly distributed between general education, training for operative workers, trades persons and professionals (according to the group's proportion in the workforce). The states comply with the priorities identified by the national strategy, which ensured that 56.4 per cent of growth operations (in annual hours of curriculum) were directed towards training operative level workers.

3.5.2 Victoria's State Training Profile[2]

State Training Profiles are produced in a uniform format and have two parts. The first part deals with strategic analysis of the economic, demographic and labour market factors that influence training needs and provision. It concludes with the identified needs and priorities for vocational training. The second part deals with plans for activities and resource allocation on the basis of national strategic objectives and the needs and priorities identified in the first part. Victoria's strategic VET analysis and planning, which is governed by the State Office of Training and Further Education (OTFE), is described below.

Patterns of *population growth* must be examined to determine whether training delivery will be affected and, if so, how it will need to respond. Will the number and characteristics of potential trainees change? Which geographic areas will develop and need more funds? Which areas will need less? Victoria's population is forecast to continue increasing at the rate of about 1 per cent per annum. The number of individuals enrolled in grade 12 is expected to remain stable, at around 48,000, through the end of the 1990s. Trends in student demand for courses and enrolments in individual programmes have been examined. According to college enrolment records, the number of students obtaining places in Technical and Further Education (TAFE) colleges continued to increase from almost 14,000 in 1993 to 18,600 in 1994. If the 1992 to 1993 grade 12-to-TAFE transition rate is retained, the enrolments in TAFE colleges are unlikely to remain above 15,000.

---

[2] Based on State Training Board of Victoria, 1995

The *unmet demand* for full-time TAFE places was estimated at 16,300 in 1995. Demand for programmes in skills which the State Training Board (STB) has judged to have low employment opportunities is left unmet as a matter of policy. The overall number of students could remain at the current level without eliminating unmet demand. The impact of the level of economic activity on student demand for training is not necessarily direct. If jobs are scarce there will be more demand for VET by school leavers. When jobs are easier to obtain, more young people will head directly for the labour force.

While productivity in Victoria is expected to grow at about 1.3 to 2.0 per cent per annum, output is likely to grow at 3.9 per cent. Therefore, *employment* is expected to increase by an annual average of 2 per cent until the end of the 1990s. This is lower than the anticipated national rate of growth and unlikely to reduce the 8 per cent unemployment rate (about 200,000 individuals). To avoid the disastrous social consequences of long-term unemployment, communities will continue to demand retraining to try to ensure that labour pools turn around quickly. The increase in the female labour participation rate is expected to continue and offset a slow decline in the male participation rate, which will affect the structure of training demand. The highest rates of growth in employment into the 21st century are predicted for building and construction (2.5 per cent per annum) and tourism and hospitality (2.5 per cent). Within the growing service sector, the highest annual growth is expected in sales and personal services (2.6 per cent). Technological change and lower employment growth in the manufacturing sector will determine growth in the plant and machine operator category. The increased incidence of part-time work may encourage demand for part-time training.

Trends in *training technologies* are expected to have a substantial impact on training capacity. Interactive multimedia are expected to expand and result in the creation of a new educational network. The development of flexible training infrastructures is forecast. In the near future, individuals should be able to connect to the network from home, work or a local community facility (such as a library) and obtain information about occupations, nearby VET providers, courses and their modules, learning outcomes and related information and enrol in training courses. Eventually learners may be able to undertake all components of training, including communicating with trainers, from home. The vocational training system will have to allocate resources for software development and staff training and provide guidance to consumers for this to happen.

Trends in public *funding* have also been very influential. The Government will change the mechanism of capital funding and resource management to ensure cost-efficient use of capital. First, it will charge rent on buildings through a capital or lease charge. Second, the Competition Code for government activities will also

Module 4. VET target setting and planning

affect training in the planning period. Funds will increasingly be provided on the basis of competitive tendering between government providers and other organizations. A clear separation of commercial and non-commercial activities and transparent cost structures will be needed. The introduction of competition will affect relationships between students, staff, managers and VET authorities.

The strategic analysis of demographic, economic and labour market factors conducted for Victoria's State Training Profile resulted in a number of general conclusions regarding VET provision. The main drivers of change in demand for VET over the next few years will not be economic activity or population or resource growth alone. Rather, the crucial factors will be:

- growing demand from students and employers for tailor-made training;
- continuing government demand for greater cost-efficiency;
- changing training technology;
- growing demand for retraining of operative-level employees;
- increasing demand for VET in secondary schools;
- increasing dependence of some enterprises on the public training system;
- extending national competency standards and national curriculum to all industries; and
- the growing need for a multi-skilled workforce and, hence, for continuing learning.

The formulation of VET needs and priorities relied on the following *assumptions* (Australian National Training Authority, 1995c).

- A resource allocation balance between entry-level training and training for the existing workforce must be found.
- The areas of demand for vocational training are different for those entering the workforce and those currently in the workforce.
- The demand for training from industries that employ young people is significantly different from that of other industries, yet state training for young people has been unfairly distributed between industries. Therefore, priority setting and planning of future expansion in public VET will need to address the current proportion of young people in the sectoral workforce and the distribution of training between industries.
- Industries likely to expand in the future differ from those which expanded in the recent past. This will change demand for VET.
- The number of new entrants to the job market will be small, so new skills must be acquired by the existing workforce.
- Almost half of all public VET programmes are not directly linked to a specific industry.

Identification of the Government's training priorities depended on the following *principles* (Office of Training and Further Education, 1996):

- The main priority of the VET system is to respond to *skill shortages*. Skill shortages can exist in both stagnant and growing economies or industries. A skill shortage can be said to exist whenever workers do not possess the level of skills which would allow them to perform with maximum productivity. Industries need to be ranked by the extent of their skill shortages, which is reflected in the proportion of occupations with the lowest level of formal qualification.
- Another important priority is to support *industry output growth*. This means that public training should be delivered to fast growing industries where skill shortages impeding growth have been observed. If the distribution of funds among sectors reflects output growth priorities, it may not correspond to the proportional distribution of people employed by the sectors.
- *Employment growth* is also a priority. Both the industries for which rapid employment growth is predicted and the industries with little or no growth, but which provide a significant share of employment, are to be priorities.
- The Government also recognizes the importance of *student demand* for VET. However, students are often not in a position to judge which programmes most improve their chance of employment. Training of the existing workforce, particularly in the areas assessed by industry as critical to improving outputs, will be accorded higher priority than training of school leavers and the unemployed in skills and qualifications which are not likely to lead to employment.
- Achieving balance in the provision of state-funded training between industries is also important. Each industry's future training needs are to be assessed and compared with actual training provision to guide the determination of priorities.
- Those industry sectors which could provide jobs for new entrants should have their need for education and training of new staff fully met through government funding.
- The identification of skill shortages, training needs and priorities should be based on inputs from the strategy target groups, ITABs, Regional Councils of Adult, Community and Further Education (ACFE) and TAFE colleges. Special consultation procedures with organizations which represent disadvantaged groups are to be established.

Industry training needs are assessed by ITABs and presented in Industry Training Plans covering two to three years. The results of the economic, employment and demographic forecasts and the ITAB assessment are fed into the Victoria

Module 4. VET target setting and planning

State Training Board (STB) *labour market training needs model* which aims to balance the provision of public training between industries and identify priority industries by comparing future training needs with present government-funded VET operations (State Training Board of Victoria, 1995). The following procedure is applied for the evaluation of industry training needs:

- Projections of total employment by industry are translated into projections by major occupation.
- Three categories of worker with different training needs are distinguished: (1) those new to the occupation, (2) those currently employed who do not have formal qualifications and (3) those who are currently employed and have a formal occupational qualification. The number of those new to the occupation is calculated as the net increase in employment in each occupation in each industry over the projection period, plus an estimated yearly replacement component to take account of those leaving the occupation (changes of employer within occupation are not counted).
- The proportion of workers requiring training is assumed to be 100 per cent for staff new to an occupation. For current employees, both with and without qualifications, the proportion requiring training is established in consultation with the ITABs.
- Assumptions about the training need per worker in terms of contact hours (or annual hours of curriculum – AHCs) have also been made in consultation with ITABs. Whereas new staff are usually assumed to need full training programmes, existing employees without certificates but with practical skills acquired on the job will generally require only a fraction of full training. Further training needs for staff with formal qualifications vary significantly across occupations, but are less than for staff without credentials. These assumptions are occupation-specific and constant across industries. The following pattern of hours of training need by occupation has been agreed upon: trade persons, 960 hours; clerks, sales assistants and personal service workers, up to 600 hours; plant and machine operators, drivers, labourers and related, less than 400 hours.
- The total training need for an occupation in a particular industry is calculated as the sum of: New and replacement employment multiplied by the proportion requiring training (new and replacement) and by the AHCs of training required per person (new and replacement), plus existing staff without formal qualifications multiplied by the proportion requiring training and by the AHCs of training required per person, plus existing staff with formal qualifications multiplied by the proportion requiring training (credentialed) and by the AHCs of training required per person.

These calculations are used to identify the industries with significant *training gaps*. In addition, many pre-employment VET programmes were identified where the number of places considerably exceeded the number of available jobs. These calculations are also used to identify (1) industries where the current training provision exceeds the needs of industry (e.g. arts, entertainment, sports and recreation); (2) industries which receive substantially more than might reasonably be considered as a fair share of government-funded training (e.g. electrical trades, electronics, social and community services); (3) industries which receive considerably less than a fair share of publicly funded training (e.g. printing, transport and storage, wholesale, retail and personal services); and (4) all other industries (the majority) where training need is in excess of current provision, but where a reasonable share of government training funds is received (e.g. automotive). The industries understood to have significant emerging training needs (such as printing, transport and storage) are given priority status for 1995-1996 VET planning and resource allocation (see table 4.7).

Some of the *limitations* of this procedure include the following:

- It assumes that all training will be publicly funded; training provided by enterprises is not taken into account.
- Many pre-employment VET courses (e.g. those that confer basic skills) cannot be attributed and allocated directly to individual occupations/industries.
- All new employees are counted as new to an occupation, while the pool of skilled unemployed who may get jobs according to their previous experience and require little training is not counted.
- From year to year the same data on industry occupational structures, based on the 1991 census, are used, while occupational structures may change.
- Trained workers can be employed in other occupations than those in which have been trained.
- Technological changes may reduce or change the demand for skills (Fluitman, 1997).

State Training Profiles plan vocational training activities which are linked to national strategic objectives as well as to the training needs and priorities identified for the individual state. (Examples of activities for implementing the national development objectives are outlined in table 4.8.) VET delivery activities are presented in activity tables and indicate changes from the previous year as well as projected changes for the coming years. Activity tables may also list resource allocations.

Resource allocation to individual industries is based on assessment of training needs and identified priorities. (Examples of changes made in Victoria from 1995 to 1996 are shown in table 4.7.) Allocations relating to occupational

Module 4. VET target setting and planning

Table 4.7 Government training resource allocation to Victorian industries for 1995 and 1996

Industry sectors	1995 funded activities (AHCs)	Planned 1996 funded activities (AHCs)	Change 1996/1995 AHCs	% change
Arts and entertainment	3 711	3 808	+97	+5
Agriculture and horticulture	2 743	2 939	+196	+7
Automotive	2 833	3 077	+244	+9
Engineering skills	4 981	4 981	0	0
Health services	1 614	1 820	+206	+13
Transport and storage	635	794	+159	+25
Further education	8 688	9 102	+414	+5

AHCs = annual hours of curriculum.

Table 4.8 Achieving VET system development objectives

VET system development objectives	Activities	Outcome
Promoting best practice and quality assurance	Quality initiatives used in the state training system are to be documented.	Information on best practice will be disseminated.
Offering priority services to target groups	New approaches for managing access and equity by building recognition of priority client groups are to be developed.	Target groups will participate in VET at rates proportionate to their share of the population.
Promoting user choice and the open training market	The proportion of funding provided through an open tendering process will be expanded. Competitive processes will be used across all resource allocation activities, including curriculum development.	Increased competitiveness in the state training system and in resource allocation will be introduced.
Strengthening accreditation, assessment and recognition of training	Accreditation by a range of approved organizations and multiple points of access to accreditation will be introduced.	Recommendations regarding the accreditation system will be reviewed.

groups are based on determination of qualifications. For this purpose, courses are coded on the bases of the following three categories:

- Category A – industry-specific occupational training;
- Category B – non-industry-specific occupational training (e.g. clerical and computer training); and
- Category C – general education and training (e.g. literacy, numeracy and social skills).

More detailed planning indicators have been established through disaggregation of activities by occupational level:

- professionals (managers and professionals);
- trades;
- operatives/clerical (clerks, sales, operators and drivers, and labourers); and
- general (unspecified).

VET operations aimed at meeting identified industry training needs and priorities are planned in terms of enrolments and AHCs. The State Training Profile presents activity tables outlining overall training provision and planned entry-level courses (traineeships) per industry in enrolments and AHCs. (Traineeships are provided primarily at the operative/clerical qualification levels.) Table 4.9 presents the format for activity tables.

The identified state and industry training needs and priorities guided the development of *college programming* in 1996 in three main ways:

- It was decided that full-time places in the almost 70 courses identified by OTFE should be significantly reduced because of the limited capacity of labour markets to absorb the graduates. Colleges maintaining the number of training places for these courses will need to provide sound evidence of high employment success of graduates.
- The overall number of full-time places in colleges for school leavers was maintained at the 1995 level, but could be increased for courses where there are expectations of unmet demand from individuals and high employment success.
- College training programmes for the existing labour force were to be made consistent with the needs identified in Industry Training Plans.

However, there are some courses which are not planned on the basis of industry needs. Further education courses, for instance, provide general education and basic education for adults. Strategic plans and priorities in the field of Adult, Community and Further Education (ACFE) are developed jointly by the STB and the ACFE board, with some input from Regional Plans and Industry Training Plans regarding language and literacy training. Priority setting and planning are initiated locally

Module 4. VET target setting and planning

Table 4.9 Training provision to industries for 1996–1997

Occupational groups	Activities for 1996				Projected activities for 1997			
	Course activity per occupational level (AHCs)				Course activity per occupational level (AHCs)			
	General	Operative/ clerical	Trades	Professional	General	Operative/ clerical	Trades	Professional
Category A • industry-specific training								
Category B • non-industry-specific training								
Category C • general VET								

through ACFE Regional Councils. TAFE colleges plan this component in their profiles on the basis of local community needs.

Equity management is a major planning issue in both ACFE and the state training system as a whole. Consultation with organizations representing national strategy target groups have made progress in identifying training needs. Through Equity Management Plans, VET providers attempt to increase participation and improve outcomes for client groups who are traditionally under-represented in VET. Industry Training Plans, ACFE Plans, Regional Council and College Performance Agreements are the key planning and funding mechanisms through which equitable access to training is managed. A 6.7 per cent increase in the delivery of AHCs to ethnic minority students was planned for 1996.

State authorities are accountable to the federal government for implementation of their state training profiles. The following performance indicators are assessed and reported on:

- actual versus target enrolments and AHCs;
- module completion rates as a percentage of load (i.e. AHCs for which trainees are awarded a completion grade or are assessed as meeting the required skill level);
- training completion numbers; and
- total recurrent cost per student contact hour.

3.5.3 Funding VET plans

Specific resource allocation supports implementation of strategic vocational training plans. State and federal funds are used to finance strategic and operational activities. States wishing to receive federal allocations must produce Training Profiles that comply with the national strategy (Australian National Training Authority, 1995a). Training services can be purchased from any provider in the market as long as states ensure that economic, social and equity goals are met.

Recurrent VET funds are allocated in two portions: base funds and growth funds. States are required to allocate the major part (70–80 per cent) of total base funding; the remainder is provided by the Commonwealth. *Growth funds* are used to finance increases of training provision (measured in AHCs) in the attempt to meet national targets; they usually constitute a relatively small proportion of total funding (3-5 per cent). For instance, in 1996, the increased delivery financed by growth allocations was directed primarily at training operative-level workers and areas with identified skill shortages. Federal growth funds are allocated to states on the basis of population shares. They are offered on the condition that states maintain their VET expenditure and total AHCs at certain levels.

In 1993/94 Victoria's public VET budget totalled $588 million ($497 million in recurrent funding and $91 million in capital funding). Victoria itself contributed $408 million (70 per cent) and the Commonwealth contributed the balance. From this sum, $442 million was directed to programme delivery by colleges and private providers and less than 10 per cent was spent on technical support (such as curriculum development); 1.5 per cent of the budget went to central administration. Victoria is expected to increase funding for VET annually by 2 to 3 per cent. In 1996, the planned national growth amounted to 32.7 million AHCs. Of this amount, almost 80 per cent was financed by the federal government. For the State of Victoria, the projected increase for 1996 was 2.38 million AHCs with 97 per cent of the increase financed by the federal growth funds. By 2001 funding from the Commonwealth is expected to increase to 44 per cent of Victoria's VET budget. Thus the central government's influence will increase as well. (Australian National Training Authority, 1995a).

Capital funds for buildings and equipment reflect strategic priorities even more strongly than base and growth funds; they are also allocated by both state and federal governments. Regional Profile Capital Development Plans must describe how proposed capital projects relate to the strategic training priorities. The federal portion totals about 60 per cent, while states contribute 40 per cent in capital VET funds. Capital investment focuses on three key indicators: allocation of resources to new training technologies (primarily flexible media);

greater utilization of existing capital infrastructure (upgrading of buildings to support new training technologies); and targeting growth in emerging and priority areas (capital investments to promote workplace training delivery). Construction of new facilities will only be considered if all other options have been fully exploited. More efficient use of existing buildings, leasing facilities and sharing premises with other providers are encouraged. Capital charges on government buildings and training equipment can be introduced. Benchmarks for efficient use of capital resources should be employed. Minimum utilization targets for capital resources are established, and only providers that meet these targets will qualify for further capital funding.

Federal growth funding is affected by states' reporting on *training unit costs*. For instance, the federal government compares delivery costs (unit cost per student per hour) across states and may reduce allocations for states which deliver costly training. In 1996 Victoria achieved the lowest average training unit cost ($8.13 per hour).

Unit 4. Analytical instruments

Learning objectives

This unit is designed to provide a better knowledge of:

1. Techniques for measuring programme effectiveness
2. Tracer-study and rate-of-return analysis for VET programming

4.1 Measuring programme effectiveness

The effectiveness and cost-effectiveness of training programmes can be analysed in order to make planning and resource allocation decisions. In Australia, for example, institutional training providers are required, under performance agreements, to conduct tracer studies as well as client satisfaction surveys (State Training Board of Victoria, 1995). The most effective and cost-effective training programmes should be given priority. The impact of training may be evaluated by measuring the employment and unemployment rates of graduates and their earnings.

Measurement of unemployment rates can consider the *active unemployment rate*, percentage of graduates who are unemployed and actively seeking work; the *inactive unemployment rate*, percentage of unemployed graduates who are discouraged by the market and not seeking work; and the *total unemployment rate*, which includes both. Analysis of employment rates involves distinguishing between the *wage employment rate* of graduates (i.e. the total employment rate without the rate of unpaid family labour), a more market-oriented measure, as well as the *rate of unpaid family labour*. The *total employment rate* includes both. In industrialized countries, follow-up analyses focus mostly on wage employment. In developing countries, however, the concepts of employment and unemployment differ essentially and a considerable proportion of graduates could be absorbed by the unpaid family sector.

Training performance is effective if it results in an improvement in the wage employment rate (or total employment rate) of graduates in comparison with a control group or with the national average for people of the same age, sex and level of education. In contrast, training performance is ineffective if it results in an increase in the total unemployment rate (or active unemployment rate) of graduates in comparison with a control group or the national/regional average for a comparable group of people (Godfrey, 1996; Hunting and Godfrey, 1996). The control groups comprise people who did not participate in training, but who, at the time of survey, had characteristics such as age, gender and education, which matched those of training programme graduates. A measure of a programme's effectiveness can, therefore, be made by deducting the success rate of the control group from that of the graduates, to show the difference made by training. Although in practice it is difficult and costly to form control groups and have available national/regional averages which fully match graduate groups at the time of each assessment, comparison-free assessments could be very inaccurate.

4.2 Measuring programme cost-effectiveness

A programme's cost-effectiveness can be assessed on the basis of its unit cost (cost of producing one skilled person) and its impact on graduates' wage employment. The calculation of training unit cost is a considerable problem. The public cost of training includes direct costs (wages, materials and services received), overhead costs (administration, maintenance and other service costs) as well as the cost of land and buildings. Although certain direct costs can easily be attributed to individual courses, many indirect costs cannot. The costs which cannot be attributed to individual courses could be distributed between them on the basis of the teaching load. An evaluation of the cost of land and buildings requires special surveys of property assets and market prices and can sometimes be omitted. Countries which introduce market forces into public services tend to institute capital charges and lease charges for using public buildings for VET programmes; this makes it mecessary to measure the actual capital cost of government buildings (State Training Board of Victoria, 1995). Taking account of the above costs, a training unit cost may be expressed as an annual unit cost for a full-time student equivalent. The *programme unit cost* is an important measure on the basis of which VET managers can compare programmes and institutions. This internal measure of effectiveness reflects the cost of training alone and ignores the quality of training.

The impact of training programmes could be estimated on the graduates' total unemployment rates, active unemployment rates, total employment and wage employment. Comparing the impact of training on the labour market success of male and female trainees could also be useful.

Three measures of cost-effectiveness can be produced:

- *social cost-effectiveness*, the cost per graduate calculated on the basis of private and public training expenditure;
- *private cost-effectiveness*, which takes account of the private cost (e.g. trainees income forgone, fees, etc.); and
- *public cost-effectiveness*, the public costs alone.

For monitoring and operational planning purposes, the programme cost per public VET graduate may be calculated as a public cost. This means that the cost will include direct and overhead recurrent costs and the estimated annual cost of equipment and buildings, but not the students' private costs. This will indicate public cost-effectiveness. Strategic, rather than operational, decisions should, however, take account of the full social costs.

The measurement of comparative cost-effectiveness – the impact of training courses on graduates' paid employment rates – can be used for operational programming, resource allocation decisions and for contracting out public training programmes. Public providers can be compared with private ones regarding the effectiveness and cost-effectiveness of programmes leading to the same occupational qualification. Cost-effective programmes should have an advantage in receiving public training contracts. If a shorter course, for instance, can achieve the same impact on the rate of wage employment as a longer course, it would be better to offer the short course, which would result in savings. Costly programmes, unless they target disadvantaged groups, should be discouraged.

VET managers should also analyse the cause of differences between cost-effective and cost-ineffective institutions and programmes. Cost-ineffective programmes need to be reviewed and improved. Public providers can be required to improve their cost-effectiveness through the efficient use of facilities and improved access to labour market information, through entering organizational and training arrangements which assume close links between providers and employers, as well as through providers' exposure to market forces. Other measures aiming to reduce operational costs may involve generating revenue by leasing facilities;

reducing permanent staff and introducing staffing and wage flexibility. The duration of some programmes can sometimes be reduced without affecting the quality of output.

Cost-effectiveness criteria and equity criteria can conflict and a balance needs to be found. Training offers for the disadvantaged should focus on placing individuals in jobs. In some cases, training programmes could never be cost-effective. For groups with low potential for employment, continued income support might be a better solution. General education and vocational preparation levels, age and previous employment experience should be considered when these decisions are made (ILO, 1996).

4.3 Tracer studies

The evaluation of effectiveness and cost-effectiveness of VET programmes demands data on trainee placement rates and training unit costs, which are difficult and costly to collect. The *tracer study* technique has been developed to gather information on the labour market performance of VET graduates. It also provides data for another important assessment instrument, rate-of-return analysis (see section 4.5 below). The tracer study's major instrument is a questionnaire to be filled in by VET graduates (see figure 4.3).

Data collected on the basis of the questionnaire for three training courses (A, B, and C) can be tabulated using the model presented in table 4.10 (Hunting and Godfrey, 1996).

The measurement of effectiveness as the impact of training on graduates' paid employment rates may be assessed by the paid employment rate of graduates *after* the course minus their paid employment rate *before* the course (derived from answers to question 12 in the questionnaire in figure 4.3, excluding those who described themselves as unpaid family workers). For initial training programmes conducted for young people, a comparison should be made of the graduates' paid employment rates with those of the control group, or with national or regional averages.

For the purpose of illustration, the effectiveness and cost-effectiveness of three training programmes are compared in table 4.11. For simplicity, it is assumed that trainees with similar age, sex and education participated in all three programmes, allowing the same comparison group to be used throughout. The *effectiveness* of individual programmes could be compared by subtracting the wage employment rate of the comparison group from the graduates' wage employment rates corresponding to each programme. It may be concluded that Programme B has been the most effective, while Programme C was ineffective, as it did not improve the employment rates of graduates.

Module 4. VET target setting and planning

Figure 4.3 Questionnaire: Survey of graduates of training institutions

Part A. Personal data

1. Respondent code number....
2. Name of graduate...
3. Address...
4. Level of training...
5. Type of programme...
6. Starting date...
7. Finishing date...
8. Number of training hours...
9. Date of birth...
10. General education: highest grade completed...
11. Sex....

Part B. Financing of education and training

12. What was your employment status immediately before participating in this course?
    Self-employed...
    Wage/salary worker...
    Unpaid family worker...
    Unemployed (not working and seeking job)...
    Student...
    Housekeeping...
    Not working and not seeking work....
13. Did you or your family pay a fee for the training course in which you participated?
    If yes, how much was the fee for the whole course?
14. Did you or your family bear any other cost related to this training course (hostel fees, transport, etc.)?
    If yes, how much did these payments amount to?
15. Did you receive any grant or other financial support to finance your participation in this course?
    If yes, how much?

Figure 4.3 Questionnaire: Survey of graduates of training institutions *(cont'd)*

Part C. Current labour force status

16. Have you had a job or business in the past week?

    If no, go to question 21

    If yes, are you:

    Self-employed...

    Employer...

    Wage/salary worker...

    Unpaid family worker...

17. What kind of job is it (occupational category)?

18. When did you get this job?....

19. How much did you earn in total during the past three months (both as wages and business receipts)?

20. How useful is your training in your current job?

    No use at all...

    Some use...

    Very useful...

21. If you are not working now, have you worked at any time since you finished your training course?

    If yes, were you:

    Self-employed...

    Employer...

    Wage/salary worker...

    Unpaid family worker...

22. When did you get that job?

23. When did you lose or leave that job?

24. Were you available for work during all this time?

25. Since completing the course described in Part A, have you participated in any further training course?

    If yes, describe the title of the course and give dates.

Sources: Godfrey, 1996; Hunting and Godfrey, 1996.

Module 4. VET target setting and planning

Table 4.10 Summary of tracer study findings

Type of courses	Paid employment rate (%)[1]	Trainees' average earnings ($/ per quarter)[2]	Unemployment rate (%)[3]	Private costs (fees, etc.)[4]	Total cost per graduate	Private cost as % of total cost
Course A						
Course B						
Course C						

[1] The paid employment rate is calculated as the number of those who answered "yes" to question 16 in the questionnaire (figure 4.3), but did not describe themselves as unpaid family workers, divided by the total number of graduates (expressed in %).

[2] Information on graduates' quarterly earnings can be obtained from answers to question 19. Average earnings can be calculated on the basis of the answers of graduates who had a job. (These data will be used in the rate of return analysis; see section 4.5 of this Unit.)

[3] The unemployment rate should be calculated on the basis of negative answers to question 16 as a percentage of the total number of graduates.

[4] Student fees and other private payments relating to courses should be taken as a total of the amounts recorded in answers to questions 13 and 14, minus the amounts recorded in question 15, divided by the number of graduates answering these questions. (These data will be used in the rate-of-return analysis; see section 4.5 of this Unit.)

Table 4.11 Comparative effectiveness of training programmes

Programmes	(1) Graduates' wage employment rates (%)	(2) Graduates' wage employment rates (%)	(3) Measure of programme effectiveness (%) (1)–(2)
Programme A	38.4	34.5	3.9
Programme B	50.1	34.5	15.6
Programme C	34.85	34.5	0.80

The *public cost-effectiveness* of programmes can be measured by tabulating the impact of training courses on wage employment rates in relation to their cost, for instance, per $1,000 of a programme's public cost (see table 4.12). For this, the data from table 4.11 on programme effectiveness need to be utilized along with data on programmes' public unit cost (given for illustration).

Table 4.12 shows the percentage improvement in the paid employment rate of graduates achieved by each course per $1,000 of cost. It may be concluded that Programmes A and B have been the most cost-effective, while Programme C has been cost-ineffective. The effectiveness and cost-effectiveness of VET programmes can also be measured separately for groups with different gender and education levels, provided that data are available.

The advantages of tracer studies are their relatively low cost, easy execution and ability to provide useful information for improving planning and programming. Their major weakness is the demand for detailed information about sample groups or national/regional averages for groups with the same age, gender and educational compositions. In addition, this technique is typically confined to workers' early market experience and findings may be biased.

4.4 Reverse tracer studies

Reverse tracer studies aim at identifying which paths to skill acquisition lead to certain occupations and qualifications; they can be conducted as workplace surveys of employees (Dougherty, 1988). The comparative contribution of education and training avenues leading to particular occupations and qualifications can be assessed and decisions made regarding the programmes to be offered in response to identified skill shortages. Employees need to be asked about prior schooling, training and work experience. An occupational map can be constructed to illustrate the paths of entry into each occupation and qualification. VET managers can then assess the actual contribution of their training programmes to the development of skilled labour most likely to be employed by industry. This knowledge can help VET managers respond to industry signals reflecting skill shortages by creating or expanding corresponding programmes and by selecting trainees with the relevant previous experience and education levels required to enter into specific occupations. A questionnaire which can be used for a reverse tracer study is given in figure 4.4.

The advantages of reverse tracer studies are low cost and the ability to provide information on alternative means of skill development for target occupations. They can indicate the true role of formal public training in developing skills. The weaknesses of this technique include difficulty in obtaining an appropriate sample and securing interviews at job stations, and the

Table 4.12 Comparative public cost-effectiveness of training programmes

	(1) Measure of programme effectiveness (%)	(2) Programme unit cost ($1,000)	(3) Measure of cost effectiveness (1)/(2)
Programme A	3.9	0.5	7.8
Programme B	15.6	1.35	11.55
Programme C	0.35	0.25	1.4

fact that findings relate only to those in employment. There are also complications due to the variety of training paths leading into the same occupation in different economic sectors and in large and small firms.

4.5 Rate-of-return analysis

Rate-of-return analysis is a technique similar to cost-benefit analysis. The idea is to compare the profitability of an investment in skills acquisition to an individual or to a society with the interest paid on savings or other investments (e.g. machinery). This approach can be used to compare returns on public investments in VET with returns on investments in health and other public services, as well as with the returns on alternative education and training investments. Rate-of-return analysis helps determine the most advantageous investment option (Psacharopoulos and Woodhall, 1985; Carnoy, 1994; Richards and Amjad, 1994).

In this type of analysis, the *private* benefits from education investments equal the increase in individual earnings. Private rates of return are essentially individual and the same training programmes may, therefore, show greater pay-off for some individuals than others. Therefore, average earnings need to be applied in programme assessment.

The *social* benefits of investing in education include the private benefits plus various material and non- material benefits which accrue to society as a whole. Material social benefits appear when both individual and national productivity and income improve. The non-material benefits may include better health and less criminality; an abundance of skilled and relatively low-cost labour that is attractive to foreign investors; the possibility for industry to shift towards skill-intensive and high value-added manufacturing that may result in upgrading the national production model; the possibility of greater access to export markets as

Figure 4.4 Questionnaire for reverse tracer study

---

1. Employee's name...
2. Age....
3. Sex...
4. Job title/occupation:
    Electronic equipment assembler...
    Electrical machinery assembler...
    Machine tool operator...
    Metal finisher, plater or coater...
    Mobile materials-handling equipment operator...
    Other skilled operator...
    Precision worker in metal or related materials...
    Metal moulder, welder, etc....
    Toolmaker...
    Cabinet maker...
    Machinery mechanic or fitter...
    Electrical or electronic instrument mechanic or fitter...
    Other skilled trade...
    Foreman, supervisor, junior production manager...
    Chemical or physical science technician...
    Electrical technician....
    Electronics or communications technician...
    Mechanical technician...
    Other physical science or engineering technician...
    Computer system technician...
    Designer...
    Other technician or associate professional...
5. Employment status:
    Casual daily contract...
    Piece worker...
    Permanent daily...
    Permanent monthly...
6. Highest educational qualification obtained:
    Primary...
    Junior secondary academic...
    Junior secondary technical...
    Senior secondary academic...
    Senior secondary technical...
    Senior secondary vocational...
    Polytechnic...
    University...

Module 4. VET target setting and planning

7. Post-school, pre-career training experience:
    a. Agency which provided training:
         Government institution
         Industry training centre
         Private institution
         Other (specify)
    b. Type of training provider...
    c. Specialization...
    d. Duration of training...

8. When did you join this firm?

9. What was your first job on appointment to this firm?
    Unskilled worker...
    Skilled tradesman/operator (specify)...
    Foreman/supervisor/junior manager/technician/ (specify)...
    Other (specify)...

10. What were you doing immediately before you were recruited to your current job?
    At school...
    Unemployed...
    Working for another employer as unskilled labourer...
    Working for another employer as skilled worker...
    Working for another employer as supervisor/technician...
    Working for this firm as unskilled labourer...
    Working for this firm as skilled worker...
    Other (specify)...

11. Training experience since starting work:
    In-plant, on-the-job, watching only...
    In plant, on-the-job, being taught...
    In plant, off-the-job...
    Off-the-job...

12. Have you ever been unemployed?
    Yes...
    No...
    If yes, for how many months?
    Before starting your first job...
    Since starting your first job...

13. Earnings in your present job:
    Basic wage: $...   per: day/week/fortnight/month
    Other wage in cash: $...   per: day/week/fortnight/month
    Other wage in kind: $...   per: day/week/fortnight/month
    Overtime payments: $...   per: day/week/fortnight/month

Source: Adapted from Godfrey, 1996.

well as the possibility of sharing international labour markets. Material and non-material benefits are, however, highly speculative and difficult to express in monetary terms.

Therefore, two measures of the cost-efficiency of educational investments (i.e. two types of cost-benefit ratio) are distinguished. The *private rate of return* on educational investment is calculated on the basis of a formula in which (a) private benefits are estimated using earnings differences before and after training, net of taxes, and (b) private costs are estimated which comprise the trainee's forgone income and the direct training cost borne by the trainee (Carnoy, 1994):

$$R(\text{private}) = \frac{I - I_{for}}{N(I_{for} + C_{pr})}$$

where:
- R = Rate of return;
- I = Graduates' earnings after training;
- I_{for} = Trainees' income forgone;
- N = Length of studies; and
- C_{pr} = Direct private cost of training per student per year.

The measure of income forgone covers the amount which individuals could have earned while attending the course if they were in the labour force instead of studying. Forgone income can be calculated on the basis of the earnings of a control group with age, gender and level of education comparable to that of the trainees. If such data are not available, national or regional averages for earnings could be used.

The formula for assessing the *social rate of return* is, in principle, the same as for private rates:

$$R(\text{social}) = \frac{I - I_{for}}{N(I_{for} + C_{pr} + C_{pub})}$$

where:
- R = Rate of return;
- I = Graduates' earnings after training;
- I_{for} = Trainees' income forgone;
- N = Length of studies;
- C_{pr} = Direct private cost of training per student per year; and
- C_{pub} = Direct public cost of training per student year

Social benefits should be estimated using the same earnings differences, but calculated before tax. Costs should include both private and social costs. In other words, three cost elements are considered: income forgone plus direct training cost borne by the trainee plus public training expenditure per student per year.

Private rates of return are usually considerably higher than social rates because of government subsidization of education and training. For individual benefits, the reason for the increase in earnings is not important. It might be linked to improved productivity, but it might not. By contrast, for the social benefits, it is important that educational investments result in improved individual and national productivity. If productivity does increase as the outcome of training, this provides a rationale for VET managers to increase public investment in certain programmes.

A sample calculation of social rate of return is provided in table 4.13. The data on graduates' wages and their expenditure on training may be collected through a tracer study (see section 4.3 above). Trainees' forgone earnings may be calculated on the basis of data for the comparison group or national/ regional averages. For computing private rates of return, the social unit costs in Column (a) are to be replaced by the private unit costs, while graduates' and comparison groups' earnings should be corrected for income tax (net of tax).

The rate-of-return ratio could be used in assessing and planning VET programmes, as it produces a gross economic measure of their comparative social and private efficiency. The role of VET administrators is to help school principals understand the concept and to assess the social and private rates of return in their investment and programming decisions. The most expensive programmes should become a prime focus for such an assessment, as they may seem to be the least cost-efficient and decisions may have to be made regarding the reallocation of public funds.

Private rates of return contribute to an understanding of private patterns of financing training. For VET managers, knowledge of the private rates of return associated with certain training programmes is an important prerequisite for offering them. If private rates of return are high, fees can be charged for some public programmes. If returns are low, individuals will not be able to earn their living after training and will need to seek work in other occupations.

Some general trends relating to the rate of return on educational and training investments have been identified. Private and social rates of return to primary education are higher than returns to secondary and vocational education. Returns to the academic/general secondary school track are higher than returns to the vocational track. The difference in social returns between the general and vocational avenues is more dramatic because of the much higher unit cost of VET. Returns on educational investments also appear to decline by level of schooling. Finally, education and training complement each other. Training appears to have an effect on earnings only after a worker has eight years of formal education. The quality of education is also very important. Education in high quality schools (e.g. those with fewer pupils per teacher) adds significantly to returns (Psacharopoulos, 1994).

A number of conceptual and technical *limitations* associated with the application of this technique for VET assessment and planning have been reported.

Table 4.13 Comparative social rates of return by programme

Training programmes	(a) Social unit cost (public+ private)	(b) Graduates' average earnings	(c) Comparison group's average earnings	(d) Difference in earnings (b)-(c)	(e) Social rates of return (b)-(c)/(a)
Computer programming	$1 900	$4 400	$4 100	$300	15.8
Welding	$1 300	$3 600	$3 500	$100	7.7
Woodworking	$1 300	$3 000	$2 950	$50	3.8

First, rate-of-return analysis can only measure the monetary returns from investment in education and training. Under this approach, there is little reason to finance public VET programmes that do not lead to increased earnings. In many industrialized countries, vocational skills are considered as part of the standard living skills that generate broad private and social benefits. Investment in VET may not, therefore, immediately result in measurable productivity and wage improvements.

Second, calculation of the social rates of return is based on the assumption that wage fluctuations follow productivity movements, but this can be observed only as a trend. Differences in social and private rates of return on education and training investments have been observed for different age groups, educational levels, social classes, regions, races and sexes. The personal characteristics of individual graduates, their educational background and learning potential will affect their labour market success and, therefore, rates of return. This means that the rate of return for individual courses needs to be estimated on a relatively large sample of graduates, which may not be possible.

Third, graduates' earnings do not always increase immediately after course completion. In addition, when private individuals choose to invest in VET, they use data on the wages that older and experienced workers earn as an estimate of what they might earn after training. This may be a misleading indicator since present wage policies may not be valid in the future. Rates of return on training investments reflect actual market conditions at the time of assessment and may change in the future. They have been found to diminish when the number of trained graduates in the same occupation increases and the market becomes saturated: the more students with the same qualification the lower the wages offered.

Fourth, the competence of industry managers is a considerable factor in rates of return. An industry's productivity and profits and, eventually, employees' wages (and corresponding rates of return) depend on the competence of managers to utilize skilled labour and capital, which is completely beyond the control of the VET system. However, rates of return also depend on managers' ability not to saturate the market with skilled graduates possessing the same qualification.

It may be concluded that rate of return analysis can provide gross signals that one type of VET programme is more cost-efficient than another. However, anticipated trends in rates of return should be used as only one factor among others for strategic planning and investment decisions. In combination with the forecast of capital investments and employment, productivity and output growth in certain economic sectors, the rate of return could be used for setting strategic priorities and for allocating funds, as well as for evaluating the cost-efficiency of large-scale educational and training investments.

FINANCING VET[1]

Module 5

Unit 1. Concept of VET financing

Learning objectives

This unit is designed to provide a better knowledge of:

1. Arguments for public and private investment in training
2. Approaches to VET financing
3. Structure of financing mechanisms
4. VET funding problems

1.1 Who should finance training?

1.1.1 Government financing

In general, VET financing mechanisms should reflect the principle that training is a service and that its *beneficiaries should bear the cost*. Skill development is expected to generate positive private and social benefits (externalities). Educated and trained workers produce and earn more than those who are less educated and trained (*private benefits*).

While education and training benefit trainees, VET can also yield *social benefits* for other members of society. The measure of the social benefits associated with skills acquisition is, however, speculative and extremely difficult to assess. Social benefits arise when:

- education and training result in increased employment and improved national productivity and income;

---

[1]This Module is based primarily on Gasskov, 1994

- abundant skilled labour attracts additional foreign investment;
- a highly skilled labour force helps transform national production towards high value-added products and greater export capacity;
- acquired knowledge and skills result in lower crime rates, better social communication, improved health and family life, etc.; and
- equal distribution of state-funded education and training among territories, industry sectors, and individuals irrespective of race, sex or income creates equal opportunities for personal development and employment, which can contribute to equalizing national income distribution.

Public funding of vocational education and training is justified when these social benefits are broad enough and affect large groups of the population. Social priorities can be established and used to guide VET budgeting. Improved productivity and employment promotion are usually regarded as the most important priorities. Thus, public financing of training is justified as long as the trained workers can be absorbed in employment or in gainful self-employment and as long as training results in the improved welfare of the population. As the social benefits of general education have been found to be greater than those of vocational training, public funding of general education often takes priority over public financing of VET programmes (Psacharopoulos and Woodhall, 1985).

In addition, labour and training markets can generate weak incentives for enterprises and individuals to invest in training, and this makes public involvement in VET financing necessary. Governments may become the prevailing source of funding in countries and areas where VET markets are rudimentary or virtually non-existent and where market imperfections distort incentives for investment in human resources. By contrast, in countries with well-developed labour and training markets that encourage private investment in VET, the financing role of the government may be less significant. There are various economic and political arguments concerning governmental, employer and individual investment in VET, some of which are listed in box 5.1. A common theme running through the various perspectives is that society, private individuals and enterprises all benefit from education and training.

Many public training systems operate under conditions of limited funding, which cover only wage-related expenditure, while other important inputs such as curricula, equipment and staff development may receive insufficient funds. At the same time, public training institutions may be denied the possibility of earning part of their budget by selling training programmes and charging fees. In many countries, demand for VET is increasing and training is becoming more and more expensive, but national training budgets are either stagnating or decreasing. Public administrators must attempt to maximize outputs with limited

Module 5. Financing VET

> **Box 5.1 Pros and cons of investment in training**
>
> **Government arguments**
>
> *Pro*
> - Training improves individual and social productivity and revenues.
> - Highly skilled labour can contribute to high value-added products and greater export capacity.
> - Abundant well-trained labour attracts additional foreign investment into the country.
> - Training contributes to more equitable income distribution.
>
> *Con*
> - VET programmes can be expensive.
>
> **Employers' arguments**
>
> *Pro*
> - Training improves enterprise competitiveness, productivity and profits.
>
> *Con*
> - Markets may not appreciate training investment because of their high volatility and low demand for high value-added products.
> - Training affects productivity only indirectly; enterprise management may not be good enough to benefit fully from a skilled workforce.
> - Trained workers can move more easily between enterprises, and employers may lose their training investment (the poaching argument).
> - Skilled workers can be made available in the labour market without additional training investment.
> - Government regulations and collective labour agreements may keep minimum wages and wage ranges too high, thus reducing the enterprise interest in improving employees skills.
> - Financial markets may not provide employer access to training capital.
>
> **Private individuals' arguments**
>
> *Pro*
> - Training can contribute to improved wages, employability, mobility and freedom in the labour market.
>
> *Con*
> - Better skills may not help as long as wage ranges are compressed and wages do not reflect individual skill levels and productivity.
> - Better skills may not help as long as jobs are not forthcoming.

or contracting resources. *Co-financing* of national VET activities by governments, employers and private individuals is increasingly necessary.

The creation of *equal opportunities* for individual development, employment and higher incomes generates important social benefits, and in this regard the government role in providing equal access to vocational training is unique. In basic education and training, equity can be achieved through the following financing mechanisms:

- free or inexpensive training courses and readily available training and labour market information for anyone willing to acquire skills at public institutions located throughout the country;
- training vouchers which entitle young people to education and training services for a guaranteed sum; and
- selective financing of fellowships for individuals on a low income who otherwise have no access to training.

In continuing training, equity can be achieved through:

- government-guaranteed training loans to private individuals;
- promotion of paid leave for continuing education and training that is co-financed by government and industry or promotion of collective agreements that guarantee employees' right to a specified number of training hours per year; and
- training vouchers or training accounts which entitle adults to education and training services for a guaranteed sum.

These approaches involve very large populations and are very expensive. Public vocational training budgets would hardly be sufficient to satisfy the ever-growing demand for equitable education and training. Therefore, in this area, priorities must be established regarding state-funded VET programmes for target groups.

1.1.2 Private financing

Because of their improved skills, graduates can expect higher earnings. Employers can also receive benefits from training in the form of higher productivity and profits. Government budgets are one major source of VET financing, but, since education and training also generate *private benefits* that accrue to trainees and employers, they are the major direct beneficiaries and should finance VET. Job-related training of employees is the most direct way to benefit from training and, therefore, trainees and employers should contribute to the cost of such training. However, the cost of individual training is often subsidized by governments on the grounds that trainees do not reap all the benefits of their training investment, as some accrue to society as a whole. Yet the government may require employers and private individuals to finance their training if enterprises and workers are clearly the direct beneficiaries of training, or if workers acquire broad skills which are transferable to other firms.

The private and social benefits of education and training as well as rates of return on investment in education and training can be calculated (see Unit 4 of Module 4; see also Psacharopoulos and Woodhall, 1985; Carnoy, 1994; Richards and Amjad, 1994). Higher wages reflecting increased individual productivity are assumed to be the principal private benefit resulting from educational investments.

Individuals finance training through:

- fees paid for courses;
- accepting reduced wages during training periods at enterprises;
- training after working hours; and
- repayment of training loans.

Tuition fees can be charged by both public and private training providers. The introduction of tuition fees results in private financing of training and has the following advantages. It mobilizes additional funds and creates training markets with the pressure on providers to improve programmes and make them demand-driven. Individuals themselves become more selective since they have to pay for their training. Less waste of resources may be expected. As a rule, tuition fees are preferable for adults and for shorter courses leading to available jobs. The application of fees is limited by the ability of individuals to pay. Families may not have enough money to pay for training, while credit markets may not be sufficiently developed to provide training loans. The limited variety of private VET courses usually reflects the commercial nature of training markets. The private sector tends to offer only low-cost programmes rather than expensive technical programmes. Since these providers tend to economize, problems of training quality can arise: less investment in equipment and insufficient maintenance of programmes may occur.

Employers can directly finance training and upgrading for their employees. They may subsidize employees' private training which fits the job requirements. They may also be required to co-finance paid educational leave through contributions to national or sectoral training funds. Enterprises may also be obliged to pay a broad payroll-based or other training tax to cover the cost of national/sectoral VET activities. In some countries, the employers' contribution outweighs that of the government.

Enterprise benefits from their training investments depend on local circumstances. For instance, training investments tend to produce more private and social benefits in conditions of growing foreign investment in the local economy, booming local and export markets for locally produced products, high market demand for value-added products and adequate availability of management skills to utilize the productive capacity of skilled labour. If there is no possibility for firms and individuals to recoup the cost of training through increased productivity and wages, they will not enter into training. Each country has its own combination of conditions which may support or hinder both public and private investment in training.

Although employers are normally expected to invest in human resources development (HRD), the training undertaken by enterprises has in many countries been considered insufficient and underfinanced. Special incentive and compulsory schemes are therefore used by governments, with different rates of success, to elicit greater enterprise investment in HRD.

1.2 Public financing schemes

1.2.1 Financing as a management technique

There are three basic management approaches to financing VET. The first views funding as traditional *funds disbursement*. Simple budgeting and disbursement procedures assume that certain standard costs for existing VET institutions (wages, and other operational and maintenance costs) are established and resources are allocated to them from year to year, irrespective of the types of programme they deliver, enrolments and outputs (budgeting and funding per institute rather than per output). When types of programme and planned enrolments are not considered in budgeting, the resources allocated determine the type of courses and training capacity. In this case, funding functions are routinely performed by ministry or agency bookkeeping and accounting offices. Many industrialized and developing countries apply this approach.

The second approach views financing as a *management technique*. Financing schemes can aim at directing providers towards certain priorities and outputs (e.g. number of graduates, their level of achievement and rate of labour market success); encouraging a reduction in training unit cost; and improving providers' flexibility. This approach would distinguish between types of programme and planned enrolments and assume that, since more sophisticated programmes are more costly than entry-level training, the institutions involved in technological courses should be better financed. Such funding schemes usually incorporate mechanisms for measuring performance and outputs/outcomes, and they link funding to the achieved outputs.

The third approach views education and training as *an investment*, emphasizing social and private rates of return. Expected measures of cost-effectiveness and rates of return can drive resource allocation, as well as organizational, management and programming decisions. A number of studies have concluded that there is no correlation between the amount of government spending on education and the amount that students learn. Therefore, as in any other activity, greater training outputs could be achieved with lower levels of funding (see, for instance, Osborne and Gaebler, 1992). For instance, the estimated cost-efficiency of an entry-level training courses may be compared with that of a vocational education programme or skill upgrading course. Applying VET financing as an investment or as a management technique calls for solid management competence from administrators (see Unit 4 in Module 4).

1.2.2 Structure of financing schemes

Diverse VET financing mechanisms exist and they all send signals to their respective beneficiaries. Each of these mechanisms has limitations and produces the best results in particular environments. VET financing mechanisms can be distinguished in terms of combinations of (1) the sources of funds and methods of redistribution; (2) the types of authority which administer funds; and (3) the formulas and conditions for allocating funds to training providers.

The first variety of financing mechanism arises from the *types of funding source and their redistribution*. VET funds can be taken from general revenues, with school budgets allocated directly from the state education budget. (Central collection and redistribution of general revenues between regions do not encourage cost-efficient use of funds at local level, but remain viable in many larger countries.) Alternatively, general revenues can be raised centrally but distributed through formula-based transfers towards lower levels of government. Or, governments at each level can tax and raise their own education funds, with training schools receiving funds from one or more government levels. Another option assumes that a special tax earmarked for VET is collected from enterprises or other entities and administered centrally or redistributed, with schools receiving their funds either directly from the national fund or as a combination of government grants and tax-based moneys.

The government levels and bodies which administer training funds are not always the same as those which generate them. The second variety of combinations arises, therefore, from distinguishing government levels and other actors from the *authority to administer the training funds*. The responsibility for managing public funds may be delegated to lower levels of government, specially created professional management bodies or national training agencies and employers' and workers' organizations.

The *allocation formula*, in its turn, establishes the link between training funds and providers. The formula may take account of national targets, if any, in order to ensure that providers are working towards them. The formula may also be linked to enrolments and school outputs. In this case, the VET financing mechanism becomes a management tool. Conditions that define how these funds can be used may also be important. Although the situation in which state-funded VET providers have little freedom to manage their funds remains widespread, in some countries training providers are free to spend money as they see fit.

1.2.3 Allocation formulas for financing schools

In practice, there are two main types of resource allocation formula. The first may be called *normative*. It assumes that each training school is equipped with a certain number of teachers and technical and administrative staff and that a certain level of wage-related expenses as well as operational and maintenance costs are covered, sometimes with no link to enrolments, performance and outputs. Certain ratios, such as the number of students per teacher, may also be established for the purpose of budgeting. The school's performance may not affect its funding. The central administration and funding model, which is normally based on standard decisions and uses a standard cost principle, is simple and often cheap to implement. However, central decisions and funding schemes, by their nature, constrain schools' initiative, lack operational flexibility and do not consider local variations in the demand for training and the corresponding need to reallocate funds. This approach also fails to respond to local and regional variations in school maintenance and operational costs. Normative models are often unable to command the best possible performance from individual schools.

Alternatively, the *performance-based* approach links funding to providers' current or planned performance and output indicators. The following schemes have been applied:

- State grants are linked to enrolment figures, so that schools which attract and retain more students are encouraged. This mechanism, however, promotes enrolment alone and has been unable to encourage providers to develop and offer complex and therefore expensive programmes. As a result, low-level and low-cost courses have been encouraged. In addition, this scheme encourages providers to enrol only the students who are most likely to remain on the course, rather than those most in need of training.
- State grants per student vary for programmes of different degrees of sophistication. Since more complex programmes are assigned higher funding rates per student, schools may be encouraged to offer the programmes that the government wishes to promote. By establishing higher rates for particular programmes, the supply of certain qualifications can be

expanded. It also allows promotion of training for particular target groups. Providers' efforts to attract and train disadvantaged populations, which are often potentially unsuccessful, could be rewarded through higher funding rates for each student enrolled and graduated from the programme.
- Additional grants to schools can be linked to the percentage of students who graduated with certificates and who graduated with higher levels of achievement.
- Grants can also be linked to the percentage of graduates who find jobs and remain employed for a certain period of time (e.g. 6–12 months). However, the availability of jobs is often beyond the control of training providers and such schemes should be applied with caution. They are primarily used to finance providers of labour market training, which should be directly linked to the labour market success of graduates.

Under a performance-related mechanism, no public funding is guaranteed to providers unless they demonstrate certain levels of performance and output. Those that are funded may have full or almost full freedom in the use of funds. Providers will find themselves close to the free market when they need to compete for enrolments and generate higher student achievements in order to earn their funds. They can even be encouraged to make a profit. Obviously, in performance-related funding schemes, audits of enrolment and assessment of graduates should be external. The introduction of such funding schemes seems to make providers' operations market-driven and ensure that better performers are rewarded.

1.3 Funding problems and solutions

A major problem faced by many countries is *under-funding* of public VET due to constrained state education budgets. Another challenge, especially in countries with limited education resources, is the need to use funds in a *cost-efficient* way. A number of solutions that have been applied to these problems are discussed below.

Decentralization of VET budgets to local authorities is the most common response. Lower levels of government may receive formula-based automatic revenue transfers from central budgets. Through the redistribution of general revenues, local governments are made responsible for more efficient use of state education resources. Local governments are in a position to produce coherent decisions which better target local economic growth, labour markets, equity issues and use of training capacity. In some countries, central governments provide only wage-related funds while local authorities are responsible for school maintenance and operational expenditure. This can improve the cost-efficiency of local services.

Decentralized funding can also mobilize local authorities' fund-raising powers. Local governments may be given the power to collect a special tax which is earmarked for education. Local authorities can then establish and pursue local, rather than national, education and training priorities. Some industrialized and transitional economies of Europe raise additional funds through training taxes imposed on enterprise payrolls and, sometimes, on the value of production contracts. Payroll taxes are a common way to secure enterprise contributions to the labour market funds used for training the unemployed and new entrants, and upgrading employees.

Professionalization of management is another method for more cost-efficient use of VET resources. This can be achieved through the creation of national training agencies administered by professional managers responsible for training operations and the efficient use of public funds. Government departments are left to concentrate on policy development. State-funded national training agencies are free to develop and pursue their own short-term plans, but these should comply with the centrally developed VET policies. An obvious trend has been to reduce agencies' government allocations and to strengthen self-financing through market operations. Some countries have incorporated training agencies, which remain under government control.

Another option has been to establish organizations registered as public corporations which are staffed by professional administrators drawn from the private sector. These organizations operate on the basis of management contracts with the government and are commissioned to administer state training funds with the aim of implementing government policies and targets. At local level, employer-led training partnerships have been encouraged and entrusted with special purpose grants.

Co-financing schemes emphasizing joint responsibility for the efficient use of labour market training funds have been developed. In some countries, employers' and workers' sectoral organizations have been given legal responsibility for administering public funds intended for upgrading employees.

Exposing public training agencies and schools to market forces and requiring them to earn funds have been seen as a means of encouraging them to achieve greater cost-efficiency. In such a model, the government is the major purchaser, rather than the major direct provider, of VET services. A certain share of public agencies' and providers' budgets may be secured by the government. Performance-related funding of training providers appears to have had a strong impact. Self-financing is a very different alternative with its own advantages and constraints. Markets were thought to be more cost efficient than direct distribution of public VET services. However, where market demand for VET has been relatively weak, this approach has not yet been successful.

1.4 Risks of decentralized and market-based financing schemes

The principal deficiency of *decentralized* schemes that involve local funding arises from the disparities in wealth between regions. If there is no special correction mechanism involving funds from other levels, some regions may be unable to fund their VET institutions adequately. In addition, if local authorities cannot raise sufficient funds or do not have a firm interest in VET, then the change from central to multi-level funding may result in a massive decline in educational funds. Some local governments may favour general education to the detriment of VET, and in these cases decentralized education budgets may not sustain vocational education and training institutions.

Decentralization of VET often results in schools being funded from several government levels. The wider resource base of multi-level funding certainly has an advantage over a single-source system, as the failure of one financial source may be compensated by others. However, the comparative solvency of public budgets at each level and their commitment to funding VET can vary. Multi-level funding involves a larger number of decision makers at several levels of power, which has its cost and may result in delays and distortions in funding decisions.

In multi-level funding schemes the important issue is to decide which components of school budgets should be secured by central government and which should be covered locally. Commonly, state budgets secure basic wages for staff, while other school expenditures are funded locally. Local governments may be free to raise staff wages from their own sources. However, if school budgets are predominately composed of wages, with insufficient funds for equipment, curriculum development and other professional work, quality programmes are unlikely.

Central funding mechanisms may have the advantage of being more straightforward and secure, but VET systems tend to lose in flexibility and outcome. By contrast, decentralized funding schemes usually generate regional disparities in education funds and tend to be more complicated. However, since local governments are normally more flexible and accountable to the local public, they are able to gain better performance from training institutions and achieve greater cost-efficiency of allocations.

The following negative implications of *market-based financing* have been reported.

- Public VET institutions may go bankrupt because of training market failure.
- People with limited savings may be pressured into buying training courses. Reliance on trainees' income may undermine equity.

- School administrations become primarily involved in preparing tenders for public funds and have much less time for other professional functions. Management tends to become less collegiate as less importance is attached to non-financing issues, such as quality and follow up of graduates.
- VET institutions may be discouraged from offering programmes that do not generate the best revenues, even though these might be the programmes that help the most disadvantaged.

Although market models are thought to be more efficient, the efficiency and equity arguments inevitably contend with this. Therefore, the question of market-based funding mechanisms should not only take account of market imperfections. The automatic sorting function of the market can easily become a barrier to equity. In order to exploit the greater cost efficiency of market-based funding schemes without undermining equal access to VET, special correction mechanisms may be indispensable.

1.5 Requirements for VET funding mechanisms

VET can be financed through alternative schemes which differ with regard to sources, organization, costs and results. Recipients, objectives to be achieved and conditions are elements of all financing schemes. Those who either provide or administer funds influence training policies and targets, providers' programming and their accountability for the use of resources. They direct systems towards certain policies and goals. VET financing mechanisms are never neutral and, intentionally or not, they send signals to which beneficiaries will react.

VET systems should:

- be goal-oriented;
- ensure trainees acquire sufficient skills to find, hold and change jobs;
- feature flexibility towards structural, technological and other changes; and
- secure equity, at least in general skills training.

Certain financing schemes appear to be better than others in responding to the above requirements. Schemes may be considered appropriate if they:

- provide incentives for meeting national and local economic, social and educational priorities and targets;
- take account of cost effectiveness and cost efficiency of expenditure;
- are sensitive to the equity argument;
- receive alternative sources of financing (e.g. government direct funding as well as government-backed loans; private financing);

- involve decentralized administration and financing, and provide for correction of regional disparities;
- expose VET providers to market forces and strengthen demand-driven programmes;
- are accountable to the contributors of funds and the general public; and
- are not unduly expensive.

Unit 2. Financing vocational education

Learning objectives

This unit is designed to provide a better knowledge of:

1. Approaches to financing vocational education
2. Funding schemes applied in vocational education

2.1 Types of funding scheme in vocational education

A variety of schemes, various combinations of sources, an array of sophisticated allocation formulas and authorities functioning at different levels can all be seen in the funding of vocational education. The normative, centrally generated and administered model of funding is still applied in many countries, especially developing countries experiencing resource shortages and attempting to plan operations and distribute money directly. Central administration of public education funds is also used in some industrialized countries which combine this model with a high level of independence for training providers funded according to performance and outputs and in competition for public training contracts.

A number of multi-level financing schemes involving several levels of government authority have emerged in larger states. In some countries, funds are generated by the central government while local governments receive formula-based transfers of education funds and allocate resources to schools. Additionally, local governments can acquire taxation power, combine central with local education sources and fund with a combination of grants. Some countries have also established national funds that receive contributions from enterprises through a payroll tax earmarked for VET; institutions are funded by a combination of grants issued by government and the VET fund.

In some countries market forces-based funding schemes have developed, linking government resources to providers' performance targets and outputs. Instead of allocating budgets directly to institutions, funds can also be offered to eligible consumers in the form of vouchers empowering them to purchase vocational guidance, education and training services from any provider in the market. Governments also promote various measures of cost recovery by requiring public providers to operate in the market and earn their budgets in full or in part.

Countries with a dual training system have specific funding schemes based on combining voluntary contributions provided by enterprises with public funds from central and local government.

2.2 Multi-level funding led by central government

Multi-level funding schemes with the central government in the leading role assume that most education funds are generated at national level. Although lower authorities receive formula-based transfers, spending conditions are established and controlled by central government.

For instance, in *France*, the major decision-making authorities are the national Ministry of Education, which is responsible for the most important elements in the education process (i.e. teaching staff, curriculum development and inspection of educational institutions), and the regions, which are strongly involved in financing VET institutions. The chief education officers, who run the 30 educational districts (académies) on behalf of the Minister of Education, are part of the regional prefects' offices and exercise full control over the funding of lycées.

Construction and maintenance of lycées and other facilities, technological equipment, teaching materials and running costs (except for staff costs) are co-financed by central and regional governments. For this purpose, the state gives each region an annual decentralization grant (*dotation générale de décentralisation*) to cover the lycées' running costs and an annual regional grant for lycée equipment (*dotation régionale d'équipement scolaire*). On average, about 60 per cent of construction costs and 95 per cent of operational and maintenance costs have been covered centrally.

Lycée staff costs are fully paid by the state. However, the number of teachers allocated to each lycée is decided by regional education authorities and depends on enrolment and various local conditions. The regions may, if they wish, allocate extra funds to lycées from their own resources, including tax revenues. Every year, each lycée receives an overall allocation of teaching posts (*dotation horaire global* – DHG). The teaching hours allocated to a lycée cover two categories: teaching posts, where one post represents about 18 hours of teaching a week, and the allocation of extra hours amounting, on average, to 10 per cent of the DHG, which allows for greater operational flexibility. The lycée is free to use this allocation as it wishes, provided that it respects the curriculum (Lafond, 1997).

2.3 Multi-level funding led by local government

Funding mechanisms controlled by local governments assume that funds sufficient to maintain VET institutions can be generated at local level. Contributions from other government levels or national training funds play a complementary role.

For instance, in the *United States*, there are three levels of government administration – federal, state and local. Educational authority rests with the states, which, in turn, delegate authority to local school districts. *Local* governments raise education funds through property taxes which are based on periodic assessment of property values; they generate considerable revenue and are the most stable form of taxation. Individual school districts, however, vary greatly in the value of their taxable property. Property, wealth and the need for education funds are not distributed evenly between school districts. Local jurisdictions can choose to tax at a higher rate if they want a higher level of local funding. These tax rates are set by public vote. State funding is used to offset local funding disparities, at least in part. States specify a minimum rate at which local jurisdictions must tax if they are to be eligible for state funds.

State financing for public education comes mainly from income taxes, which are less stable than property taxes because they are directly influenced by economic fluctuations. Most states use some type of equalization scheme to even out differences between school districts in their ability to support education. States usually allocate a given amount per full-time equivalent (FTE) student enrolment to all schools. In order to compensate for differences in taxable wealth, states provide additional funds to low revenue-generating districts. This results in a basic level regardless of community wealth. Common practice among states is to provide additional funding for VET because it is a higher cost programme. The allocation may also vary according to different categories of programme. Special VET funds are usually a percentage of regular FTE funding.

Federal funds are distributed to correct differences in wealth and to encourage certain kinds of VET programming locally. The federal government allocates funding from general tax revenues in two basic ways: matching and categorical. Local school districts, not states, are eligible for these funds. Matching funds are allocated to local school districts on the basis of an equalization formula. However, the local school district must first commit a certain amount of its own resources. In this way, the Federal Government gains influence over local programming, but its resource commitment is modest. Matching funds, however, are an unstable source of funding, since federal appropriations are subject to delay and fluctuation. They usually account for no more than 6 to 8 per cent of local schools' recurrent expenditures (Herschbach, 1994).

Local school districts provide the most funding and have the greatest control over vocational training operations. Although the overall level of state contribution to vocational schools is considerably higher than the federal level, it is largely general aid based on FTE enrolments without much policy leverage. In contrast, federal funds encourage innovations with a very limited financial investment; most states align their priorities with those of the federal government. A relatively high level of federal funding is provided to state authorities to carry out monitoring.

Through collaborative funding, each government level achieves objectives that it otherwise could not attain by funding VET alone. The three levels of funding complement one another. In this way, some of the adverse consequences of public financing are countered, and greater equity and sustainability are achieved. A collaborative relationship must be developed between the three governmental levels, with clearly defined authority and responsibility. However, multiple funding sources can cause distortion. Through financing, all three government levels translate their policy guidelines, which are not necessarily uniform, to local VET schools, which develop programmes taking each of them into account.

A three-tier system of balancing vocational education funds, like that in the United States, works in conditions of high decentralization and a very limited federal government role. (For another example of multi-level funding led by the local level in Australia, see section 3.5.3 of Unit 3, Module 4.)

2.4 Funding schemes that involve training taxes

Some countries collect taxes earmarked for VET from enterprises. In such cases, enterprise funds may become part of the overall funding mechanism. Other countries encourage enterprises to provide grants to the institutions that supply them with trained labour. Although enterprise contributions may be substantial they tend to remain sporadic and training schools need to make continuous efforts to secure them. Such funding schemes are applied, for instance, in Hungary and France (see also Unit 4 of this Module).

Vocational education in *Hungary* is financed from three sources – state subsidies, local government subsidies and the Vocational Training Fund (VTF). The state subsidies are fixed annually for vocational secondary schools and for apprenticeship schools. For the former, the sum of HUF 66,000 is allocated per student without regard to the type of vocational programmes offered. For the latter, state allocations are made separately for theoretical programmes, workshops and accommodation. Although these allocations take account of the greater cost of practical training, they too are standard and do not differentiate between the types of vocational programme. Thus, for 1995, the overall grant per student in apprenticeship schools was HUF 42,100 for theory and HUF 40,600 for workshops, totalling HUF 82,700, which is higher than the grant for secondary schools. Therefore, county authorities are expected to encourage the development and provision of more complex and more expensive vocational training programmes (Simonics, 1996).

Companies are legally required to spend 1.5 per cent of their wage bill on training. Within the compulsory training allocation, companies can make a payment to the VTF, which is administered by the tripartite National Training Council (NTC). Alternatively they can finance their own courses or provide direct assistance to vocational schools. For instance, in 1995, out of the compulsory training allocation, companies spent about 43 per cent on training their employees and 37 per cent on direct financial assistance to schools, while 20 per cent was remitted to the VTF.

The education funds of counties and big cities come from the wage tax, between 15 and 30 per cent of which is left for local budgets. County educational authorities receive and combine state grants with their own funds and make up the budgets of local training schools. School budgets are enrolment-based, but schools are free to spend them as they see fit. In addition, the tripartite County Labour Councils receive the VTF contributions, which they distribute between local schools on a competitive basis. Schools are invited to submit proposals for the development of training programmes.

The role of the three sources has been changing over time. In 1996, vocational secondary schools received funding, on average, in the following proportion: from state budgets, 27.5 per cent; from local governments, 53.5 per cent; and from the VTF, 19 per cent. While overall state allocations have remained stable in recent years, contributions from the VTF and, more significantly, from county governments have increased.

2.5 Funding schemes that involve market forces

2.5.1 Performance-related financing

Vocational training schools relying on market-based financing receive funds not as guaranteed budget allocations but as fees charged for training. The government is usually the major purchaser and therefore determines the rates and conditions of funding. Performance-related funding assumes that schools demonstrate certain performance levels or achieve prescribed outputs in order to be financed. This approach uses formulas and conditions for funding, and also for contracts between schools and those who buy their services. The most developed versions of such schemes are applied in Denmark and the United

Kingdom and are described below. In these countries, management powers have been delegated to colleges, which have acquired full freedom and responsibility for operating independently in the market. The legal status of the colleges has changed and they have emerged as non-profit companies (United Kingdom) or self-owning institutions (Denmark).

In *Denmark*, the Ministry of Education no longer administers training schools. Instead it develops vocational training policies and issues Education Orders which establish a broad framework for VET courses; independent schools wishing to obtain public funds must comply with the Education Orders. The schools are expected to earn revenues through selling courses in the market, though the Ministry of Education remains the major purchaser of authorized training courses. Training schools receive grants that are calculated on the basis of actual performance (see also box 3.6 in Module 3).

Grants are divided into expenses directly related to teaching and joint expenditures. The contribution towards *teaching expenses* is computed on the basis of the school's actual performance and programme costs. Performance is measured in student full-time equivalents (FTEs) (e.g. a designation of 40 student-weeks could be calculated as one student spending 40 weeks at school or 40 students spending one week at school). Regarding programme costs, all courses are divided into groups that are assigned certain rates ranging from DKK20,000 to DKK60,000 per student FTE (see table 5.1). The expenses that are directly related to teaching include salaries, costs of materials and teaching aids, and equipment.

The grant towards *joint expenditures* includes a basic grant per school and supplements to the basic grant which covers the cost of school administration. Its rates distinguish between commercial and technical schools. For commercial schools the grant amounts to DKK730,000 and for technical schools it totals DKK1,210,000. Supplements to the basic grant take account of school size and the number of courses offered. For each type of course a standard number of square metres is prescribed, and standard maintenance cost rates are calculated per square metre. The administration rate is DKK2,600 per student in commercial courses and DKK4,000 per student in technical courses. Joint expenditures also include grants for capital expenses involving rent, mortgage interest and taxes and other adjustment grants.

Schools receive grants four times a year on the basis of auditing reports presented to the Ministry. The grants are adjusted regularly in relation to the actual number of FTEs. If students dropout, the grant totals automatically shrink. The grants are not earmarked, and schools are free to allocate resources as they see fit. These funding arrangements promote efficiency through competition for students. Certain schools, however, have experienced funding problems and have

Module 5. Financing VET

Table 5.1 Grants for school-teaching expenses in Denmark

Courses	DKK per 40 FTEs
Basic VET course	11 000
Specialist course (commercial and clerical trades)	18 000
Market economics programme	22 400
Higher technical examination course, 2nd year	26 700
Technical vocational education course, level 1	36 000
Further technical course	39 600
Computer specialist	44 300
Workshop school	42 400
Technical vocational education and training course, level 2	43 700
Technical vocational education and training course, level 3	51 400
Further technical courses, rate 4	60 000

either had to merge with other schools or apply to the Ministry of Education for additional grants.

In the *United Kingdom*, colleges, which are independently operated corporations established by Government, are guided by and receive funds from the Further Education Funding Council (FEFC), an intermediary management body created by the Government with the status of a company limited by guarantee. The colleges are contracted by the FEFC to provide training. Colleges decide on enrolment and programmes, although contracts may stipulate particular courses and set national enrolment targets. The performance of each college is monitored against the funding agreement, and funding may be reduced if it fails to achieve specified outputs. Funding is exclusively based on enrolment and output. Colleges aim to earn "funding units", which are computed on the following basis: a student who completes a full-year programme in the lowest cost band and achieves qualification will generate 100 funding units.

A college may claim funding on the basis of entry, programme and achievement elements, as well as additional support, if necessary. The *entry* funding element covers all activities leading to the enrolment of a student. The *programme* element includes all activities of learning, assessment and student support. Programmes are defined in terms of qualification aims. Their cost is reflected by their length and by the tariff value of each on-programme unit. The length of each programme is defined in terms of "guided learning hours" (the actual time spent incurring expenses in support of a student programme). The costs of some programmes are individually identified in a tariff; other programmes attract tariff values in one of six bands according to the number of guided learning hours they require. The cost of programmes aimed at National Diploma level is much greater than that of programmes leading to National Certificate level; this difference is reflected in the value of their basic on-programme units and of their corresponding cost-weighting factors. The *achievement* element of funding is offered only for eligible qualifications and achievements, such as the qualifications externally accredited by validating bodies. College certificates without external validation are normally not eligible for this type of funding. *Additional support* funding is defined as any support over and above standard programme activities provided to a student. It may include the extra costs of teaching to remedy difficulties with literacy or the costs associated with accommodating students with disabilities.

The total number of units generated by each student varies according to the type of programme followed, the student's progress through the programme and success at the end of it. If a student dropped out during the second term, the institution would be able to claim on-programme units for the first term only. Each institution receives a guaranteed percentage of the funds received from the FEFC in the previous year (about 90 per cent). In return, institutions are expected to deliver a given percentage of the previous year's activity expressed as *a core number of funding units*. Colleges receive recurrent funds in monthly instalments in accordance with the agreed funding profile for the whole financial year.

Funding schemes also aim to meet *national training targets*. For example, the main priority for 1994-95 was to achieve a 7 per cent increase in student numbers. Institutions were invited to apply for additional funds to achieve this target. However, the availability of additional (growth) funding is linked to the degree to which colleges achieved the previous year's performance targets. Applications for additional funding from those meeting targets were given priority, while the balance of growth funding was applied to those who had not met them. The funding model seeks to ensure *efficiency gains*; therefore, institutions are required to produce more outputs with less recurrent funding. The amount of funding made available to secure the 7 per cent increase in student enrolments in 1994-95 was only 5.2 per cent. Allowing for price inflation at 4 per cent, achieving the target increase in enrolments required an average efficiency saving of between 5 and 6 per cent. From 1994-95 to 1996-97, the FEFC's recurrent funding was scheduled to rise by 9 per cent against an increase in student numbers of 11 per cent (FEFC, 1994a, 1994b).

In 1993-94, 9 per cent of full-time enrolments and 36 per cent of part-time enrolments in colleges were funded by sources other than the FEFC, including cost-recovery courses. For 1996-97, the increase in full-time enrolments funded from other sources was projected to increase. Colleges can also borrow money provided that total borrowing at any time does not exceed 5 per cent of the college's annual revenue. Institutions are free to set their own tuition fee policies, subject to certain conditions in the funding agreements. Many colleges identified the need to invest in property and equipment as central to their plans for student growth. Together they decided to invest some £1.2 billion from 1994-95 to 1996-97 to achieve these plans. Of this, colleges planned to contribute over £400 million from their own revenues and to raise a further £175 million in loans.

2.5.2 Financing through vouchers

Vouchers are government-financed entitlements to certain services for a given amount of money. States establish eligibility requirements, issue vouchers and monitor quality and compliance. Both private individuals and schools may be eligible for vouchers to buy public services. Funding schemes involving vouchers have several objectives. First, they attempt to improve the efficiency of training systems by enhancing individual choice. Second, they expose providers to market forces. Providers have to compete for trainees' vouchers, from which they obtain part of their budget. With vouchers for education and training services, individuals can select programmes and providers. Individuals can use vouchers as cash to pay for tuition. In some countries, funds for vocational guidance have been redirected to schools instead of to suppliers of guidance. As a result the markets for counselling services have strengthened (Hövels and Meijers, 1994). Examples of the application of education and training vouchers in the United States and the United Kingdom are given below.

As a response to the perceived inadequacy of local schools, *Minnesota (United States)* began experimenting with a system allowing students to use vouchers and choose public schools. Starting in the mid-1980s, junior-, senior- and college-level students were allowed to take their education dollars to schools in any district. In other words, public funds followed students across district lines. Parents were responsible for transporting students to their school district boundary, unless the family income was low, in which case the state paid for transportation. Three thousand students participated in the first two years after legislation was introduced allowing students aged 12 to 21 who were not succeeding in one school to attend another. Half of them were drop-outs returning to school. In other words, simply by allowing choice, drop-outs were brought back to school. Minnesota subsequently opened the programme to adult drop-outs. In 1990-91, more than 6,000 students applied to leave their district for schools in other districts. Another 6,000 chose the college option, while 8,000 enrolled in Area Learning Centres, 3,000 chose public Alternative Programmes and 750 chose private Alternative Programmes that contracted with school districts. In all, nearly 24,000 of Minnesota's 720,000 students exercised the new option (Osborne and Gaebler, 1992).

The competition introduced among schools and other education and training providers also resulted in dramatic changes in the schools' administrative behaviour. One district reopened a school it had closed, because so many students left the district in response to the closure. Another district which initially tried to stop its students from taking the college route, finally turned around and developed an education, training and placement package. In a suburban district where 200 students signed up to leave, the superintendent personally interviewed all 200 families, and voters passed a tax increase by 70 per cent. The district developed a strategy to compete with its neighbours through the use of technology in classrooms. Finally, a bill was passed allowing groups of teachers to create new public schools. The reason was that even in competitive conditions, some district administrations' ability and willingness to respond to the demand for education and training appeared to be limited. The answer was found in a system that allows teachers, parents or private organizations to create schools and have them approved by the local administration. Schools accepting vouchers are allowed to charge tuition beyond the amount of the voucher. Parents are given information about the quality of each school so that they can make informed decisions (Osborne and Gaebler, 1992).

In the early 1990s, the *United Kingdom* also adopted a voucher system in an attempt to create a genuine training market. On the supply side, the network of government skill centres was privatized. In 1993, the Colleges of Further Education (FE) were moved out of local authority control and incorporated as independent organizations. On the demand side, the Training Credits Initiative was introduced in an attempt to radically increase the number of training purchasers. Training Credits (vouchers) with explicit cash values entitled mainly 16- and 17-year-old school leavers to training. Credits could also be allocated selectively to young people finding or seeking employment in certain skill areas. It was planned to give every 16- and 17-year-old leaving full-time education the offer of a training credit (Fairley, 1994).

The cash value of credits varies from less than £500 to over £5,000 to reflect local labour market conditions and the cost of training for different occupations. Training Enterprise Councils (TECs) determine the value of credits allocated to trainees on the basis of the individuals' action plans and the actual local cost of the required training. Potential trainees consult with approved training providers to prepare the training plans which the TECs examine. Approved training might include apprenticeship programmes, short general and specific courses, or more academic, college-based courses. Credits are released by the TECs in stages, via the Careers Service, according to the nature of the approved training programme.

The Training Credit Initiative increased competition between colleges for trainees with credit entitlements. The need to attract trainees has led colleges to adopt marketing strategies of a kind traditionally used in the private sector. College capacity to manage training programmes under the new market conditions has improved. Reform of college management, featuring increased autonomy and employer participation in the newly-established management boards, has contributed to genuine market development. However, this voucher scheme seems to be expensive because young people need access to information and advice and because staff skilled in assessing providers and monitoring performance are required, as well as effective controls on expenditure. Major outcomes outweighing this additional public cost are the increased enrolment of young people, improved efficiency of providers and higher quality of training. Young persons have the right to make their own decision on how to spend public training credits. At the same time, the scheme depends upon employers' willingness to collaborate, because only training approved by an employer is eligible for credit-based financing.

2.5.3 Cost recovery

Cost-recovery schemes rely on vocational schools' ability to charge fees, trainees' ability to pay for services and institutions being authorized to retain all or some of their earnings. The involvement of public institutions in market activities may create problems for private providers, since state institutions usually enjoy guaranteed public grants and revenue serves only a complementary role, while for the latter revenue is the only source of funding. Experience with cost-recovery funding in the United States is described below.

Two-year community colleges are the most rapidly expanding technical training institutions in the *United States*. The strongest programme area in many colleges is now continuing education (CE). These are short-term, specialized courses set up to retrain displaced workers, upgrade employees, provide community services or offer highly customized training. In some community colleges full-time equivalent (FTE) enrolments relating to CE currently approach 50 per cent or more of regular enrolment.

Traditionally, the regular curriculum (technical and academic) has been financed through a combination of state support, local taxes and student tuition. State funds are allocated on the basis of FTEs. While tuition fees can affect the quality and substance of instruction by compelling institutions to be more responsive to students' financial leverage, when charges are too high (e.g. 30 per cent or more) of total programme costs, there is usually a drop in enrolment. Excessive demand can be controlled by increasing tuition fees, but this affects lower income groups disproportionately.

By contrast, CE programmes are primarily financed through fees paid by the clients. These may be local firms wanting to upgrade adult workers, large corporations interested in literacy or remedial skill development, or government projects for retraining the unemployed. More commonly, the client requests a customized course designed to address a specific work requirement. A price is negotiated to cover planning and development and instructional costs. Facilities, equipment and personnel may be complemented by those of a local firm. Local firms can also train college instructors.

CE programmes usually generate surplus income which is used to support other college functions. They have low operating costs and generate large enrolments, which count towards basic state funding through their typically high FTE counts. Some states also provide a modest start-up grant of $3,000 to $5,000 to encourage training initiatives, pay the training costs of new companies or completely fund high-priority programmes such as those for displaced workers. These state subsidies, in whatever form, provide an incentive for joint training ventures between two-year colleges and private industry, labour and government. In this way, full use is made of the facilities, equipment and personnel of the community college (Herschbach, 1994).

The balance between regular and CE programmes is important. Regular programmes provide the financial foundation for community colleges; CE courses have more income-generating capacity, but the level of income is less constant from year to year. It is prudent for CE programming to remain under 50 per cent of FTE. In general, there are no restrictions on the pricing of CE programmes or on how college income can be used.

In *New Zealand*, funding of tertiary institutions, which provide education and training beyond secondary schooling, is based on tuition fees. The Government requires public and private training providers to set tuition fees and they become eligible for partial tuition subsidy. Students under 22 years of age attract a tuition subsidy of 95 per cent of the course-related funding category; students who are not eligible attract only 75 per cent. Institutions are publicly funded on the basis of student full-time equivalents (FTEs) that cover 80 per cent of the cost, while students pay on average 20 per cent of the cost of their courses. The student contribution will rise to 25 per cent by the year 2000. To cover the cost of administration each institution is given a government grant of $1000 per student FTE up to a maximum of $250,000, assuming 250 students enroll and that small institutions have a greater proportion of administrative cost. Institutions recover the balance from tuition fees. Tertiary providers are legally required to specify the objectives and outputs that they are funded to deliver; they are held accountable for those outputs before the Ministry of Education, which signs purchase arrangements with them. Failure to deliver normally results in recovery funding in a subsequent year. Courses are funded on the basis of *standard grants*, so that similar courses delivered by any provider receive the same amont of funding (Preddey, 1996).

2.6 Financing the dual system

Austria, Denmark, Germany and Switzerland apply dual training systems which combine practical on-the-job training with part-time, school-based education. Financing the dual system combines employer contributions covering the entire cost of practical instruction with the public funds that governments provide to the training schools. Trainees' contributions normally come from their productive work. The funding mechanism that is applied in Germany, and largely replicated in other countries that have adopted a dual training system, is described below.

The German dual system is financed by the federal and Länder (State) governments, employers and trainees; the employers' share is the largest. The federal contribution consists of providing budgets for the Federal Ministry of Education and Science and the Federal Institute for Vocational Training. In addition, the Government provides rebates to employers, whose training expenditures are deductible from taxable profits. The Länder provide grants to local authorities for the construction and maintenance of training schools, purchase of equipment and instructors' wages.

The cost of the dual system to employers is enormous. Apprentice allowances form the major component. Employers pay fees to the vocational training schools which train their apprentices. High expenditures are required in order to pay instructors' salaries and maintain facilities in accordance with the legislated guidelines. In most firms, but by no means all, apprentices are productive enough to reduce the burden of employer expenditures. Recent estimates suggest that the ratio of expenditure to benefits differs widely among various types of firms. The largest enterprises tend to receive fewer productive benefits from their expenditure; small firms benefit considerably more and spend somewhat less. In 1991, the average expenditure of an employer reached DM31,800 per apprentice per year; the average productive benefit from apprentices was DM11,300. In other words, employer average net costs exceeded DM20,000 per apprentice per year. This figure was very high, considering that only half the apprentice graduates remain with the firms that provided their training. In 1991, in addition to the overall government expenditure of about DM12.2 billion, employers spent roughly DM24.5 billion on the dual system. Thus, the total annual national cost of apprenticeship – roughly DM36.7 billion – was divided among governments (33 per cent), employers (44 per cent) and trainees (23 per cent) (Thiele, 1994).

Given the advantages of instruction under the dual system and the need to encourage the beneficiary funding of training, this financing mechanism seems to be one of the most promising. On the other hand, many attempts to introduce the dual system in other countries have failed because of disagreements on the financing mechanism, which requires a firm, voluntary commitment from enterprises.

Unit 3. Financing labour market training

Learning objectives

This unit is designed to provide a better knowledge of:

1. Approaches to financing labour market training
2. Funding schemes applied in labour market training

3.1 Types of funding scheme in labour market training

Labour market training involves entry-level courses, employee upgrading programmes and retraining for the unemployed, which may be conducted by general education and vocational education institutions, by specialist labour market training agencies, by enterprises or by private institutions. The financing schemes for public vocational education institutions are discussed in Unit 2 of this Module; this Unit discusses funding through labour market employment and training agencies and other financing schemes. Unlike vocational education, labour market training relies on employment funds established within government-funded unemployment assistance systems. In some countries, separate funds have been established to finance labour market training. Although unemployment insurance funds are more commonly used for distributing benefits, they often provide funding for training courses. Funding schemes for labour market training have developed rapidly in industrialized and most transitional economies (World Bank, 1997).

Such schemes can be organized in many ways. Employment assistance is commonly sourced from general revenues, while unemployment insurance funds are raised through taxes on payrolls and (insured persons') wages; governments can also be important contributors. In certain countries, employment insurance systems are national and compulsory and involve taxes which are earmarked for training (e.g. Japan). In other countries, they are voluntary and only participating enterprises and workers are entitled to benefits such as training grants or reimbursement of their training expenditures (e.g. Denmark, Sweden). In certain countries, employment insurance and government-funded unemployment assistance have been combined into so-called dual insurance and unemployment assistance systems which finance a broad range of services and benefits. These countries include France, Finland and the Netherlands (United States Social Security Administration, 1995).

National labour market funds are commonly administered by labour ministries. Compulsory employment insurance funds are managed by the national social security administration, while voluntary insurance funds are sometimes managed by bipartite management-labour bodies or unions. Training moneys can be allocated either to a national labour market training agency that administers training operations or to the procurers of training services who can contract out courses. Among the eligible procurers could be local labour market training councils or social partners' training bodies. In the countries that have not established labour market training agencies, the corresponding funds can be administered by specialist management bodies created and guided by governments. These bodies contract out public training courses to both public and private providers. Various incentives have been developed to make providers meet the market demand and to secure trainee placement. Government-guaranteed training loans are also used in some countries, mostly to finance adult training and upgrading.

3.2 Funding national training agencies

3.2.1 Direct funding

National labour market training agencies have been instituted in almost all industrialized countries. They aim to train young people, mostly school dropouts, retrain the unemployed and, sometimes, to offer upgrading programmes for workers. The agencies have become very large with thousands of instructors and hundreds of training centres. They take care of people on an individual basis, train them for available or forthcoming jobs and try to remain flexible. The experience of Japan, where the national training agency enjoys guaranteed financing from the unemployment insurance fund, is described below.

Japan's Employment Insurance system consists of four services: one service providing unemployment benefits and three special services aimed at the development of vocational abilities, stabilization of employment and improvement of workers' welfare. The general purpose of these special services is to sustain employment. The Employment Insurance budget is divided into two accounts, one of which is for unemployment benefits. Employers and workers pay an equal contribution of 0.55 per cent of individual wages into the unemployment benefits account. The government contributes one-third of the total cost of unemployment benefits and covers administrative costs. However, only employers contribute to the other account which covers the three special services: vocational abilities development, employment stabilization and improvement of workers' welfare. Their current contribution is 0.35 per cent of the company payroll. The three special service budgets are roughly equal. The scheme is administered by the Ministry of Labour (MOL). Major decisions on policy, concerning revisions to the Employment Insurance Law, changes in the financial contribution ratio, qualifications of trainees and period during which benefits are paid, require the approval of the tripartite Employment Insurance Council (Hamada, 1994).

Japan has two VET financing streams: the Employment Promotion Corporation (EPC) and the prefectural governments. The EPC is administered by the MOL and financed entirely from the employment insurance tax. It is decentralized and the catchment areas of the regional offices do not coincide with the prefectures. The EPC has its own colleges and training centres, which operate in parallel with those administered by prefectural governments. However, EPC training centres are primarily for the unemployed and older workers and they offer a much greater variety of courses. Centres receive grants based largely but not exclusively on enrolment.

At the prefectural level, the Department of Labour is in charge of locally provided VET. It monitors and finances both higher technical colleges (university colleges), vocational skills development promotion centres and training subsidies to enterprises. One-quarter of the overall allocation for these institutions also comes from the employment insurance tax; local revenues, such as residence taxes, supply the other three-quarters. Budgets for these institutions are provided on the basis of their training capacity alone and, when they fail to ensure full enrolment, pressure is exerted on them to succeed. Prefectural governments finance public training institutions offering pre-employment training to regular school graduates and provide financial assistance to authorized training programmes for the private sector, particularly small firms.

There are subsidy and grant training programmes under which funds can be offered to private firms. Subsidies for authorized training are applied only to small firms and their training cooperatives. Grants, on the other hand, cover both large and small firms, for which entitlements vary. For in-house group training, small firms are reimbursed by one-third, while large companies receive one-quarter, of the costs of instructors and teaching materials. The same proportions apply to entrance fees and tuition at outside institutions, as well as for reimbursing employers for wages paid to workers while they are in training. Employers' applications for subsidies are submitted to the governors of prefectures after completion of the authorized training programmes or at the end of a fiscal year.

3.2.2 Contract funding

Contract funding of labour market training assumes that national employment and training agencies do not receive guaranteed budgets in full.

They are expected to earn a portion of their funding in the market through bidding for public training contracts or offering services to enterprises or other customers. In some countries, labour market training agencies have been fully incorporated and are required to operate with no guaranteed public funding at all. Experience with this system in Denmark and France is discussed below.

In *Denmark*, labour market training is financed by the subsidized voluntary insurance system. Funding sources include the membership contribution for the unemployment fund paid by insured persons. Employers also contribute to this fund. The government cost is partially refunded from the labour market contribution paid by workers and the self-employed (United States Social Security Administration, 1995). This contribution was scheduled to equal 8 per cent of total wages in 1998. This fund provides grants for training to both employees and the unemployed, although employees have first priority. In 1990-91, for example, employees constituted 65 per cent of participants in training programmes; the remaining 35 per cent were unemployed.

The overall labour market training allocation is channelled towards three major groups of institution. First, the National Labour Market Training Agency (AMU) receives a central allocation amounting to one-third of its budget, which is to cover its basic operational costs as well as the cost of training programmes for disadvantaged groups. Second, the Minister of Labour has formed bipartite Labour Market Training Committees for four major economic areas (industry, construction, commerce and services, and the public sector) and appoints a chairperson for each. These Committees are fully responsible for programming training and financing courses in their economic sector. They decide on and claim government funds for adult training. The Committees contract out training to providers, including the AMU. Therefore, another one-third of the AMU budget comes from orders made by Labour Market Training Committees. Third, the Regional Labour Market Councils, which are responsible for procuring initial training courses and programmes for the unemployed, also receive allocations and purchase training from AMU centres and colleges; these services bring in the residual one-third of AMU resources (Nielsen, 1995).

In *France*, the National Association for Adult Vocational Training (AFPA) is the leading training agency with tripartite administration. It targets young people, the long-term unemployed, and those at risk of redundancy. It has 22 regional agencies and 130 training centres which are staffed by 10,000 employees. From 1947 to 1995 AFPA was fully financed by the Government; however, in 1995 it received only 70 per cent of its budget and was required to make up the balance by selling training services to Employment Services, Regional Councils, and private firms. From being the administering and funding agent for AFPA, the State is becoming, rather, a client negotiating the training services it buys from this agency. AFPA's regional agencies have to operate directly in the training markets and their regional training centres are becoming profit centres (Willems, 1994).

3.3 Funding through national programmes

In some countries, labour market training operations are organized and funded through national programmes and national training agencies are non-existent. In the *United States*, for example, labour market training is organized as federally funded programmes which channel funds to the state governments and local providers. When federal programmes are terminated, or changed, funding arrangements follow suit. The Job Training Partnership Act (JTPA) of 1982 is the largest training and employment programme administered by the Federal Department of Labor. The JTPA provides grants to support programmes for specific categories of disadvantaged people, youth and adults, and training for older workers. Federal regulations establish eligibility for funding under this programme, the services that can be provided, and performance standards. These standards are applied to contractors, as well as to programme completers and to training placements. Allocations given to the states under the JTPA are based on a formula which attempts to balance need with population size, effort, and financial capacity. However, funding is available for only 6 per cent of the eligible population (Herschbach, 1995).

Labour market training operations are contracted out to providers in the market. Training providers are paid according to programme completions and job placements. Typically, the contractor is paid $700 for each trainee enrolled, an additional $300 for each trainee completing one-half or more of the course, and $800 more for each graduate placed in a job. If the trainee is paid a wage of more than $4 per hour, the contractor is paid an additional $600, and if the trainee remains employed for a year or longer, another $400 is paid. The purpose is to emphasize job placement. Financing mechanisms which link contract fees to programme completion and job placement result in what is called "creaming" when contractors select those who can progress rapidly and show the most promise because payment is based on the success of trainees. This leads to better training results, but it also leads to the exclusion of the most disadvantaged individuals. When funding is based on performance, the programme output is monitored through test scores, completion rates or job placements.

Another financing scheme links public money to enrolment, which results in less tendency to cream. The incentive is to maximize enrolment regardless of the quality or background of students. If the programme objective is to extend training opportunities to the most disadvantaged, then there is no floor to the selection criteria; however, there is usually an upper cut-off level for admission. Individuals may be excluded because of the level of school completed, income, ability, or other factors. Only the most disadvantaged are selected. This practice is justified on the basis of equity. United States government policy has fluctuated between training the most capable among disadvantaged groups, and training the least capable. Under conditions of limited resources, the tendency is to cream. Demand is so high that there is a large pool of likely candidates (see also box 3.12 in Module 3.)

3.4 Funding through management intermediaries

Some governments, instead of administering and financing public services directly, rely on intermediate management bodies which they create and staff with professional administrators drawn from the private sector. For instance, in the *United Kingdom*, labour market training is guided by the Department of Education but operationally administered and funded by 82 Training and Enterprise Councils (TECs) in England and Wales. These are non-profit making companies established by the Government with a board of directors dominated by local private employers. The TECs' task is to contract with, supervise and monitor training organizations commissioned to carry out state-funded training schemes. Providers could be ordinary firms in production, sectoral organizations, firms established mainly to provide training or colleges (Russell, 1995).

Each TEC is given a designated territory and has sole responsibility for its area. Inside each area is a population varying from about 200,000 to about two million. The staff of a TEC numbers between 50 and 140 but the internal organization varies, because they are all independent companies. The TECs decide which private firms to place contracts with, and which industrial sectors to develop training for. As any other company, TECs operate outside civil service rules, but under the rigorous financial discipline and obligations of the market and of Company Law. They must contract with the Government, or any other purchaser of services, to provide training and they must operate without a loss, in the market place. Their directors are under the same obligations as all company directors and have to file annual reports at the Companies Registration Office.

Three major programmes are funded through TECs – Youth Training, Modern Apprenticeships and Training for Work – with funds provided on a per trainee basis. The overall national budget is basically determined by the government department and then allocated to individual TECs, with some negotiation. They in turn select training providers likely to achieve the targets on their behalf. Individual trainees have to apply to the TEC for funding and have to agree, with the training organization, a target qualification for their training. The TEC funds this if it is confident that the trainee and the trainer can reasonably be expected to achieve this outcome. The TEC-based organization and funding of labour market training is perhaps a cheaper option than financing a national training agency (see also box 3.16 in Module 3).

3.5 Sources of funding in countries in transition

Almost all the European countries in transition have set up national labour market funds which receive allocations from *privatization revenues* as well as unemployment insurance and state budget allocations. Privatization revenues are most often raised from new owners of industrial property who did not retain the previously employed labour force. These employers are required to pay a flat charge for each laid-off worker. In addition, part of the money received from the sale of public property may be used to finance retraining programmes. The countries not implementing any broad privatization programme have apparently been unable to activate this major source for financing training. In countries with a decentralized government structure, regional tripartite labour councils receive and administer the combined labour market allocation, which is used to pay unemployment benefits as well as to fund training courses. However, in relative terms, the training portion of labour market funds is commonly very small, amounting to 1–2 per cent.

For instance, in *Hungary*, labour market training was financed from the Employment Fund, which received state budget allocations as well as privatization revenues from public companies which were sold off. By contrast, the Social Fund, which handled unemployment benefits, was financed by taxes of 4.5 per cent on company payrolls and 0.5 per cent on individual wages. The sources of the Employment Fund were less secure and, in 1994, the Social Fund accumulated a large surplus, while the Employment Fund was in deficit with a number of training programmes suspended. To redress this situation, the two Funds, plus the Vocational Training Fund and certain other funds, have been amalgamated into the new Labour Market Fund (LMF). Use of the LMF training allocation is recommended by the National Training Council and decided by the Minister of Labour. The National Labour Market Council has been set up to advise on disbursement of the LMF component dealing with unemployment benefits. The tripartite County Labour Councils have set up vocational training boards which make recommendations for decentralized vocational training allocations. County Labour Councils support job creation and manage funds through their County Labour Centres, which commission training centres and private providers to carry out courses. Local training programmes are conducted by regional labour market training centres (LMDTCs), each of which serves to two to four counties. The development of LMDTCs was financed by contributions from the state, a county and a World Bank loan. A county provided premises for the LMDTC, the state covered the cost of upgrading buildings, while equipment and instructor training were financed from the loan. Currently, 40 per cent of LMDTC annual budgets comes from the state and the balance comes from selling services to County Labour Centres (Benedek, 1997; Gasskov, 1996).

3.6 Career development loans

In some countries, such as the United Kingdom, private investment in training is encouraged through government-backed training loans. This public investment has been found to be more cost-efficient than public expenditure on direct training provision. Career Development Loans (CDLs) are part of the United Kingdom's strategy to "empower" individuals in the training market and to motivate them to take the lead in their own training and development. CDLs are unsecured, deferred-repayment bank loans for educational and training courses which are offered by four of the main retail banks. The Government pays the interest during the course and for the first month afterwards. If the trainee is unemployed after the course, repayment may be deferred for five months. Individuals on CDLs must pay at least 20 per cent of their course fees and are responsible for loan repayments after completing training. By the end of 1991-92, some 26,500 loans valued at £66.5 million had been approved. Throughout the 1988-96 period, the rate of applications for CDLs rose rapidly. Between 1988 and April 1996 some 78,000 loans were taken out throughout the United Kingdom. These varied in size from £200 to £8000. It is not yet clear how far demand for CDLs may rise, or at what point it may become saturated and level off. Preference for full-time CDL-supported study grew (to 55 per cent of the total in 1992), as did the distance learning mode (to 14 per cent). Part-time study declined in popularity. Completion rates are high, reflecting trainee motivation: in the period October 1991 to September 1992, the national rate averaged 79 per cent (Fairley, 1994; Fairley and McArthur, 1999).

Almost two-thirds of CDL-supported courses started in 1991-92 were in commercial and professional areas, computer skills, driving, management, health, training and welfare. About 80 per cent of trainees are under 40 years of age and two-thirds are male. CDLs are probably most popular in areas perceived to have stronger labour market demand and greater mobility. At the time of review, roughly 35 per cent of CDL applicants were in full-time employment when they started training, 31 per cent were unemployed or not working, 17 per cent were students, 9 per cent were self-employed and 7 per cent were in part-time employment. These figures suggest that this type of programme is capable of wide popularity.

The cost of this undertaking to the Government lies in the interest-free period, which makes CDLs attractive to students, and in providing the banks with a default guarantee. In 1991-92, CDLs were estimated to cost the Government £12.36 per training week, making CDL the lowest public cost of all government programmes. The Government estimated that public expenditure of £9 million in 1993–94 would generate loans to the value of £59 million. In 1991–92, the average loan was about £2,600. Of this, an average of £1,700 was spent on course fees. The remainder went to meet full-time students' living costs. In 1995/96 the 13,000 approved loans had an average value of £3,555.

Unit 4. Financing enterprise training

Learning objectives

This unit is designed to provide a better knowledge of:

1. Government policies on financing enterprise training
2. Voluntary and compulsory funding schemes, their advantages and disadvantages

4.1 Government-employer financing arrangements

The principal types of government-employer financing arrangement regarding training are listed in box 5.2. They vary from fiscal incentives for enterprises, to almost absolute freedom of enterprises to train, and from strict regulations imposed on levels of enterprise training expenditure, to the supervisory involvement of national tax authorities in their implementation.

Several types of voluntary national training arrangement have emerged. First, in some countries, governments do not regulate enterprise training expenditure. In countries with well-developed employer commitment to human resources development, there is no need for such regulation; the employers' responsibility for training of workers is legally recognized. However, in other countries, the neutral role of governments commonly results in employer under-investment in training and in chronic shortages of skilled labour. Second, governments can offer direct financial incentives to training enterprises in the form of reimbursed training expenditures or grants. Governments can also attempt to legally secure employer training investments. Regulations may specify that employees will have to refund part of the training cost if they leave the enterprise before a given time after completion of training. Third, in many industrialized countries, collective labour agreements have become an instrument for voluntary industry

> **Box 5.2 Principal types of government-employer financing arrangement**
>
> The multiplicity of arrangements between government and employers include the following major types:
>
> - Enterprises have no legal obligations regarding training and its financing (e.g. Canada, the Netherlands, Sweden, the United Kingdom and the United States).
> - Employers voluntarily take significant responsibility for legally recognized financing of employee training (e.g. Germany, Japan and Switzerland).
> - Employers and unions set up training development funds under the training clauses of collective labour agreements (e.g. Belgium, Denmark and the Netherlands).
> - Governments offer training incentives to enterprises (e.g. Chile, Germany, the Republic of Korea, Pakistan and the United Kingdom).
> - Governments introduce compulsory training schemes (e.g. Denmark, France, India, Ireland, the Republic of Korea, Pakistan, Malaysia, Nigeria, Singapore and various Latin American countries).
> - Governments and enterprises co-finance paid educational and training leave for workers (e.g. Belgium and France).
>
> The arrangements are not discrete. Governments may refrain from using compulsory measures, but still influence enterprise training activities by extending incentives (as in the United Kingdom, for instance).

financing of training. The agreements often include training clauses which specify industry training schemes and minimum levels of resource allocation. Governments may intervene to promote training clauses and to co-finance industry training. Fourth, industry and government may agree to co-finance paid educational leave for employees. Such national arrangements normally assume payroll-based financial contributions from enterprises while the government acts as regulator, co-funder and supervisor.

It appears that employers in most countries perceive the conditions for their investment in training as unfavourable. There may be many reasons for the unwillingness of enterprise to pay for training. One possibility is that weak or over-regulated markets are unable to send adequate signals to employers. This has created the impression that employers are often short-sighted, have little capacity to understand future trends and show insufficient social concern. Given the short-term employer training behaviour and the social desirability of certain levels of national training investment, many governments have introduced compulsory financing schemes. These are most often based on training taxes. Through compulsory schemes governments attempt to raise the level of training beyond that which is provided by the free market and to encourage a move towards lifelong training.

Among the tax-based interventions, the following funding schemes can be distinguished: revenue-generating levies, levy exemptions, levy-grants and training cost reimbursement. Through revenue generating levies assessed on company payrolls, governments collect moneys for funding national VET institutions. Tax-exemption schemes also establish minimum levels of employer investment in training as a percentage of a company payroll. However, they offer a possibility for employers to gain exemption from or a reduction in their levy obligations by providing training for employees. A minimum level of enterprise training expenditure can also be fixed as a proportion of employees to be trained each year. Levy-grant schemes assume that enterprise levy contributions are collected and distributed between national/sectoral priority programmes. These funding mechanisms and their features are discussed below.

4.2 Sectoral training development funds

Some industrialized countries of Europe have succeeded in applying the concept of joint responsibility for VET between government, employers and workers. Pressure to expand training has evolved in the course of collective bargaining at company, sector and state levels, and has resulted in the development of special training-related clauses in collective agreements. Following the introduction of these clauses, a number of sectoral and territorial training funds have been established. These are financed by employers' and sometimes by workers' contributions and they also receive state allocations. Collective training arrangements usually cover only part of the total national workforce and channel relatively small employer and worker contributions, thereby allowing essential freedom of training behaviour to the individual employer. Through sectoral funds, strong employer-government cooperation in training has been achieved. Governments encourage the funds and help to finance training. States make voluntary contributions with the aim of supporting the development of particular training paths, such as apprenticeships and training for disadvantaged groups. The success of the European sectoral funds demonstrates that the expansion of enterprise training can be achieved with limited government intervention. The features of sectoral training development funds are summarized in box 5.3.

For instance, in *Denmark*, there are 15 sectoral funds which have been agreed through collective bargaining and cover a significant portion of the workforce. Training funds have been established by special clauses in collective agreements

Module 5. Financing VET

> **Box 5.3 Features of sectoral training development funds**
> - Funds are set up under sectoral labour agreements and administered by bipartite boards.
> - Funds finance the development of sectoral training policies and course curricula, rather than the actual provision of training.
> - The major part of fund budgets come from levies, with the remainder made up of government subsidies.
> - Levies vary across sectors and are most often paid by employers. In some sectors, employees also contribute.
> - Training remains the firms' responsibility, as the average rate of sectoral levies is low.

for the metal and plastic industries, transport, retail and other sectors. Employers are required to contribute an amount that varies across sectors from DKK0.03 to DKK0.13 per working hour to these funds, which annually collect at least DKK 60 million. These sectoral funds do not finance training courses directly but provide funding for the development of courses, qualification analyses and pilot projects. Nevertheless, the Government provides a substantial contribution to the cost. The sectoral collective agreements cover between 700,000 and 1 million of Denmark's 2.9 million workers. In addition, all employers are required to pay a flat rate levy of DKK1,500 per employee per year into the so-called AER Fund, which is guided by the social partners. Employers who enter into apprenticeship contracts are entitled to have 90 per cent of their apprentices' allowance paid during the school-based training periods and 80 per cent of their travel expenses reimbursed from this Fund (Nielsen, 1995).

In the *Netherlands*, employers' organizations and unions have established Industrial Social Funds (ISFs) that are involved in the development of training. Of the 7 million people in the Dutch labour force, nearly 3.3 million are covered by sectoral collective labour agreements, which are the framework for establishing and administering the ISFs. Of the 120 collective labour agreements concluded in 1998 some 100 contain clauses regarding training of employees and apprenticeships and provide for enterprises to pay training levies and maintain the ISFs. The ISFs are voluntary rather than statutory; they are established by employers and unions with no intervention from or obligation to the Government.

The operations of ISFs follow the policy agreed by the Government and industry which aims at improving skills, increasing employment and reducing the cost of the social security system. Due to this, the State supports ISFs through encouraging the levy-based financing of training. The Minister of Social Affairs and Employment has the power to make the freely concluded collective labour agreements obligatory for all firms in an industrial branch, thus confirming the articles regarding levies for the ISFs. The Government also provides grants to the ISFs for training the unemployed. On average, 80 per cent of ISF training budgets are generated through levies, while 7 per cent are made up of government subsidies from the European Social Fund.

The average rate of the training levy is 0.7 per cent of the wage bill. Some sectors train more and raise higher levies, others less. The rate of the levy is negotiated between employers' organizations and unions. ISFs usually offer one to-three day training courses which are kept brief in order to reduce losses caused by the absence of trainees. Subsidies from the ISFs cover direct training costs and part of the loss from trainees' absence. Reimbursement may also be given for training activities organized by the ISF itself, as well as for certain training activities approved by the ISF which are purchased on the market. Of the overall annual budget of 600 million Guilders, ISFs allocate 22 per cent to apprenticeships, 60 per cent to training of employees, 3 per cent to employment projects, and 15 per cent to child care.

As the government intervention is financially quite small it has resulted in considerable leverage of industry financing of training. Approximately 14 per cent of overall industry training operations are financed from levy-based money and public grants through the ISFs. The total volume of training in companies is increasing as reflected by the increase in individual employers' training budgets. It was estimated that in 1998 enterprises spent 3.5 billion Guilders on training, which equals 1.7 per cent of their total annual labour costs. One of the major advantages of ISF is that its levy-financed training has weakened the grounds for "poaching" skilled labour, which had been popular with employers.

For instance, the Training Fund of the Road Transport Branch covers 8,400 enterprises which have an average of 12 employees each. In 1998, the Training Fund collected a levy of 1.39 per cent of the wage bill, of which 1.13 per cent and 0.26 per cent are paid by employers and workers, respectively. From the total amount collected, half (30 million Guilders) was allocated to training. The remainder was used to finance medical care. The Fund financed more than 2,500 apprenticeships and supported skill upgrading courses for employees with the number of participants growing from 600 in 1985 to about 18,000 in 1998. Employers are entitled to a flat rate trainee wage compensation of 150 Guilders per employee per training day. Participating firms pay only 25 per cent of the direct training costs.

The following problems related to ISFs have been reported. First, small firms benefit less from ISF-funded training than larger firms. One reason is that the latter can replace workers on training days more easily and are more prepared to comply with ISF procedures. Second, participation in training is inequitable. Employees do not have the right to a specified number of training hours. As a result, the participation of unskilled workers, women and minority groups is low. This problem has been addressed in some industrial branches through establishing a special right of employees to ISF-financed training. The entitlement to training can accumulate, enabling employees to attend longer courses (Veeken, 1999).

4.3 Government incentives for enterprise training

Some governments opt for various incentive schemes in order to promote enterprise training. Examples of training incentives are listed in box 5.4. They commonly exempt enterprises from various taxes and provide low-cost government loans. The most prominent example of government incentives is the scheme developed in Chile which is described below.

Chile offers rebates to industrial, service and agricultural firms for their expenditure on training. Firms can reduce their income-tax bill up to an equivalent of 1 per cent of their payroll. The incentive was intended to encourage firms' training demand in order to strengthen their competitiveness, and, secondly, to establish a competitive training market. The mechanism is administered and audited by the National Service for Training and Employment (SENCE), which is part of the Ministry of Labour. Six hundred public and private institutions are authorized to provide training to enterprises under the incentive scheme. The Government has established a training unit cost ceiling to be met by enterprises claiming tax exemption. Within this cost limit, enterprises have the right to employ training firms or to organize training themselves. Training programmes must be directly linked to current or related jobs within the company and must be approved by the SENCE in order to qualify for the tax rebate. Deductible training expenditures include the direct costs of contracted-out training, the administrative cost of the firm's training departments up to the equivalent of 15 per cent of direct training costs, the cost of training needs assessment up to a maximum of 10 per cent of direct training cost, the cost of trainees' transportation and per diem up to 15 per cent of direct training cost and apprentice allowances up to a maximum of 60 per cent of the legal minimum wages. Enterprise training expenditure in excess of the tax deduction ceiling are treated as ordinary costs to the firm. However, if deductible training expenditures exceed the firm's tax liability (applicable, in fact, to low-profit firms) the Treasury pays the balance in cash to the firm.

Since its inception, this incentive scheme has increased the amount of public funds available for training. State investment in employer-based training grew from US$1.4 million in 1977 to US$29.4 million in 1991. Accordingly, the number of employees whose training was subsidized increased from 22,600 in 1977 to almost 291,000 in 1991. In 1992 more than 12,000 firms benefited from

> **Box 5.4 Government incentives for enterprise training**
>
> Among the incentives offered by governments for enterprise training are the following:
>
> - Up to a certain level, enterprise training expenditure is deductible from taxable profits or from other taxes. Thus, within established limits, governments bear the cost of training conducted by employers (as in Chile, Malaysia, and the Republic of Korea).
> - Enterprises are exempt from import taxes on training equipment (as in Pakistan and the Republic of Korea).
> - When enterprises build training centres they are offered low-interest government loans and they are exempt from appropriation, property and land taxes (as in the Republic of Korea).
> - State subsidies are offered to enterprises for training and upgrading employees, or cost-sharing is applied (as in the United Kingdom and Belgium).

this incentive. In addition, the scheme has enlarged the market and made training more demand-driven. The tax rebate scheme has become the major mechanism, accounting for about 95 per cent of government training investment. On average, the training rebate for large firms constitutes about 6.5 per cent of their income tax bill. Many employers provide training which is entirely subsidized. Less profitable firms, however, receive only minimal training entitlements which cannot be put to significant use. This mechanism is sensitive to wage and skill levels. Since reimbursable training expenditure is linked to the payroll, the higher a firm's labour costs, the greater the subsidy it can, in theory, receive. Since wages tend to match skill levels, skill-intensive firms seem to benefit most from the subsidized training (Corvalán-Vásquez, 1994; Espinoza, 1994).

4.4 Revenue-generating levies

4.4.1 Payroll taxes

Revenue-generating levies are commonly assessed as a percentage of enterprises payrolls, as a fixed rate per working hour or as a fixed rate per employee. Less frequently, training taxes are assessed on company production or export value or the value of work contracts. Training taxes can also be assessed as a percentage of expatriate wages and collected from local employers. Revenue-

Module 5. Financing VET

generating schemes aim at funding national or sectoral vocational training agencies and are mainly administered by governments. Such schemes have been the most reliable source of funds for VET systems in countries facing persistent shortages of public education funds and where other sources of revenue are limited. The classic revenue-generating levy mechanism is widespread in Latin America and the Caribbean region; it is used in most industrialized countries to finance training for the unemployed.

Revenue-generating levies require only a sufficient number of firms and a functioning tax-collection apparatus. Even these few basic preconditions may not be available in some countries. The tax collection mechanism may not be operational where employers have a negative attitude towards the levy and resist paying. In small, low-income countries, the number of formal-sector enterprises may be insufficient. Only a few low-income developing countries have so far been able to utilize payroll levies to finance training.

Under such schemes, employers may have little influence or control over the tax money collected by governments (see box 5.5). As a result, funds may be used in ways that do not benefit the levy-paying employers. The major deficiency of revenue-generating funding mechanisms has been their inability to provide incentives for employer training. However, some ways of utilizing levies more cost-effectively have been suggested. For instance, regularly reviewing the levy rate can help prevent the accumulation of surpluses and increase training authority flexibility. Levy-financed institutions must respond to employer needs and pursue appropriate financial policies. Employers should manage these training institutions or, at least, be represented on institutional boards.

In *Brazil*, for instance, the problems related to revenue-generating levies have recently been addressed by partially exempting enterprises that finance their own training courses from the levy. Venezuela and Honduras have also introduced partial exemptions from the levy payment for those employers who provide in-company training of acceptable quality. In Peru, the payroll tax has been lowered and supplemented through agreements with businesses (Ducci, 1991). This is a move towards the advantages of a less rigid levy schemes.

The four major sector-based training corporations in *Brazil* – SENAI, SENAC, SENAR and SENAT – are privately managed and are financed from the payroll levy (see also section 4.2 in Unit 4 of Module 3). Established under the Brazilian civil code, they are administered by the private National Federations of Employers (Industry, Commerce, Agriculture and Transport). The SENAR is exceptional in that it has a tripartite board involving employees' representatives. These vocational training institutions (VTIs) have a particular status and are formally supervised by the Ministry of Labour's Secretariat of Vocational Education (SFDP). The SENAI's funds are obtained from a payroll contribution of 1 per cent (known as

> **Box 5.5 Features of revenue-generating levies**
>
> *Mechanism*: Payroll levies are collected as a percentage of company payrolls by the national social security institutions and remitted to the government budget or directly to training agencies.
>
> *Advantage*: Levies constitute a reliable source of funding for national training systems.
>
> *Disadvantages*:
>
> - Levies do not provide incentives for enterprise training.
> - Levies are collected by governments and can easily be isolated from employer influence.
> - Levy-based funds can be misused; training services may not be received by employers in proportion to their payments.
> - Levy-financed agencies are subject to bureaucracy and often accumulate unspent surpluses.

the "ordinary contribution") from industries. Industrial corporations with over 500 employees have to pay an "additional contribution" of 0.2 per cent directly to SENAI. This is used for scholarship programmes for technicians, managers and teachers from SENAI and contributing corporations. In SENAC, however, levy-based funds make up 70 per cent of its revenues; the remainder of its budget is generated by selling services. By contrast, SENAR is funded by the 2.5 per cent levy imposed on companies' production value. SENAT is financed by a levy of 1 per cent. Both SENAI and SENAC have exemption tax schemes or agreements which allow enterprises to finance their own training institutions or programmes (Leite, 1995).

Ordinary levy contributions, along with other social security contributions, are collected by the National Institute of Social Security (INSS). The INSS collects the tax and, after withholding 1 per cent to recover its operating expenses, transfers the funds to the national headquarters of SENAI and SENAC, which, in turn, redistribute them to the regional offices. The Brazilian civil code requires that VTI financial audits be approved by the Federal Account Court. The VTI Fiscal Councils are mainly responsible for detailed auditing of the Regional and National Departments.

Enterprises do not buy training services from VTIs; in return for their contributions, they receive free training courses from them. In order to expand enterprise training activities, in contrast to the centrally developed and provided VTI courses, co-financing agreements have been introduced. These are private contracts between

VTIs and enterprises. Instead of paying the levy in full and obtaining training from VTIs, employers establish direct relationships with VTIs for some proportion of a levy to be spent on enterprise-based training. There are two types of agreement. The first, the "exemption agreement" (EXA), exempts enterprises from the ordinary levy contribution (and part of the additional contribution). It usually allows firms to spend between 40 and 60 per cent of their payroll levy bill which would otherwise be destined for SENAI. This money could cover the costs of enterprise-based training, primarily the recurrent costs of their own training schools. EXAs are not therefore a common practice and are applied primarily by leading foreign corporations and major public transport, energy and water supply companies with their own training schools. The second kind of agreement, the "technical and financial cooperation agreement" (TFC), allows firms to pay 90 per cent of the levy to VTIs and to retain 10 per cent for on-the-job training. TFCs are more appropriate for on-the-job and short training courses, and can be applied by smaller firms which lack their own training facilities (Leite, 1995).

4.4.2 Taxes on the value of work contracts and exports

In some countries or areas, training funds are generated through taxes on enterprise turnover of particular goods or services. Ecuador, for example, collects a 0.2 per cent import tax on industrial machinery; Hong Kong, China, has imposed levies of 0.25 per cent of value on construction projects and 0.3 per cent of value on clothing exports. In Kenya, employers in the construction and civil engineering industries have to pay a certain percentage of their total quarterly turnover into the sectoral Training Levy Fund. This approach is also taken in some industrialized countries. For example, in Queensland, Australia, the purchasers of construction services are obliged to pay levies which are calculated as a percentage of the cost of building work. In the United Kingdom, purchasers of construction services are also liable to pay the training levy.

Production-based levies are applied in certain sectors of Latin American countries. For instance, under Mexican federal labour law it is mandatory for employers to offer training to their employees. Employer contributions are paid to the sectoral industrial training institutions. In Mexico, public and private sector construction enterprises have to pay 0.2 per cent of the value of their business contracts to the Construction Industry Training Institute (ICIC) (Ducci, 1991). The ICIC renders its services to enterprises without linking its training activities to each firm's contribution; this implies a redistribution towards those firms that actually receive training from ICIC. Another financing mechanism, the Training Institute of the Sugar Industry (ICIA), emerged from collective bargaining within the industry and is based on the annual production of each sugar mill in the country. Each firm contributes the equivalent of $0.0125 per kilo of standard base sugar produced.

4.4.3 Taxes on expatriates

Training taxes on expatriates are applied in Indonesia, the Marshall Islands and Hong Kong, China. For instance, in *Hong Kong, China*, economic restructuring resulted in a massive transfer of workers from industry to the service sector. However, a sizeable number of displaced workers experienced difficulty in adjusting their skills to the new job requirements. A statutory Employees Retraining Board was appointed in 1992 and empowered by the Employees Retraining Ordinance to impose a levy on employers importing workers into Hong Kong, China (Man Tak, 1996). Since 1990, enterprises have been allowed to import labour at craft and technician levels to ease skill shortages in certain critical areas. The law requires enterprises to pay a levy of $HK 400 per week for each foreign worker imported under the special scheme. The money is collected and used to finance the operations of the Employees Retraining Board. The government co-finances these training operations. Because they involve public funds, the Retraining Board has to submit its programme and budget to the Secretary for Education and Manpower for approval. Its accounts are subject to government audit. However, since its budget estimates do not form part of the government budget, it is not subject to the Legislative Council's annual considerations.

4.5 Levy-exemption schemes

A levy-exemption mechanism allows firms to eliminate or reduce their levy obligations by the amount of training they provide or purchase. This funding scheme assumes that firms are most likely to know what their training needs are, so that they are likely to spend their money on appropriate training programmes. This mechanism eliminates the burden of employers having to pay a levy at the beginning of a financial year. Funds that have been earmarked for training remain with the employer, who can then establish a plan for spending them effectively. The levy-exemption mechanism operates through employers' individual actions and is normally supervised either by the Ministries of Labour or by the national general revenue service. Therefore, a levy-exemption mechanism does not require special and costly organizations. On the other hand, exemptions deal with each employer individually and provide less opportunity to develop national or sectoral training policies and activities. Such funding schemes have strong advantages over other schemes in terms of employer satisfaction with their relative freedom in training and funding operations, low

Module 5. Financing VET

cost of administrations and true impact on industry training (see box 5.6). Examples of the levy-exemption mechanism in France and in the Republic of Korea are given below.

French firms are assessed on two payroll levies: the "apprenticeship tax" which promotes and finances apprenticeships and the "training tax" which finances training of employees. Both taxes operate as levy-exemption schemes. They are not collected at the beginning of the fiscal year, nor are employers' training expenditures subject to reimbursement at the end of the fiscal year. Payment is due at the end of each year unless an employer can present evidence that an amount equal to the tax due has been spent on authorized training. Employers fully utilize the allocations: only 4 per cent of the total 1989 apprenticeship tax (FF6,000 million) was not spent by employers and paid to the state.

The apprenticeship tax is unique in that it legally allows employers to give grants to training schools. In 1989, almost FF4,000 million was granted to public and private schools. The apprenticeship tax obligation (and supplements to it) is divided into two parts: 0.5 per cent of the payroll is to be spent on apprentice training expenditures and wages, or granted to training centres, and 0.1 per cent of the payroll is to be spent on training young people seeking their first employment. Authorized training expenditure includes instructors' wages (with the limit established as one supervisor per ten apprentices) as well as the cost of fellowships and tools for apprentices. Compulsory contributions of enterprises to the Chambers of Commerce and Industry and to the National Compensation Fund, which promotes apprenticeship in small firms, are also made from this tax (see box 5.7) (Bas, 1994; Willems, 1994).

The rate of the training tax has increased from 0.8 per cent to 1.5 per cent of payroll. Its focus has also shifted from general educational and cultural development of personnel towards continuous education and training for employment. At present, within the framework of the training tax, 0.4 per cent of the payroll is destined for government training programmes for youth seeking first employment, 0.2 per cent is allocated to paid training leave, and 0.9 per cent is spent on employee training. Employers can deduct FF50-60 per training hour per young trainee. Small firms with small levy allocations prefer to make payments to approved training agencies instead of providing training themselves.

To expand employer involvement in training and to raise VET funds, in 1976 the *Republic of Korea* made it compulsory for all private companies to provide skills training to a certain percentage of their workforce. Firms which do not comply with this requirement must pay the training levy. The scope of application for this system has changed several times with a mixed response from companies. In 1989, for instance, these regulations applied to companies with 200 employees or more, but since 1995 when the employment insurance system was introduced,

Box 5.6 Features of levy-exemption schemes

Mechanism:

- The government fixes the percentage of a payroll to be spent by employers on training or granted to any training institution.
- Employers manage their compulsory training allocations in compliance with regulations.
- Enterprise training expenditures relating to the compulsory allocation are reported to the tax commissioner; unspent allocations are transferred to a government-established account or fund

Advantages:

- Financial allocations remain with enterprises; employers are free to plan and manage their funds and to administer training.
- For this levy scheme central administration is not required; the national cost of administration is low.

Disadvantages:

- The compulsory allocation may be spent ineffectively by both employersand employees.
- Sectoral training activities lack enterprise contributions.

Box 5.7 The levy-exemption scheme in France

To finance apprenticeships from the apprenticeship tax of 0.5 per cent, employers must allocate: 0.1 per cent to apprentice wages or make payments to apprenticeship centres or grants to training institutions; 0.05 per cent to the Compensation Fund, which reimburses the cost of apprenticeships to employers with low levy allocations; and 0.35 per cent to agencies that provide preliminary technological training to apprentices.

To finance youth training schemes, employers allocate: a 0.1 per cent supplementary (to the apprenticeship tax) levy; and 0.4 per cent (within the training tax) to be spent by the employer or transferred to special training funds.

To finance continuing training from the training tax of 1.5 per cent the employer must allocate: 0.2 per cent to special training funds which finance individual training leave; and 0.9 per cent to training under the employee training plan.

Any unspent allocation is paid to the Treasury.

it has been confined to firms with 1,000 or more employees. Currently, this system regulates training operations in 359 companies in six industrial sectors. The company training obligation is calculated as a percentage of payroll which varies according to industrial sector and company size. Larger companies are assessed to higher training obligations. This percentage varies from 0.03 to 1.72 per cent (the average for 1998 was 0.614 per cent). However, larger firms provide training instead of paying the levy, not only because their compulsory training obligations are set higher but also because they actually need more training. A greater proportion of smaller companies pay a training levy rather than provide training for the following reasons: (a) many companies with 1,000 to 2,999 employees do not have their own training facilities; (b) the compulsory training obligation is low and paying the levy costs less than providing training. For instance, in 1994, out of a total of 3,753 companies obliged to conduct in-plant training, only 843 companies or 22.5 per cent actually did so, while the remaining 2,910 companies or 77.5 per cent chose to pay the levy. After the removal of certain government regulations regarding company training programmes in 1995, there was a sharp increase in the number of companies choosing to conduct training instead of paying the levy.

The training levy paid by companies helped to establish the Vocational Training Promotion Fund which was administered by the Ministry of Labour. The Fund strongly contributed to the promotion of national training activities, and its 1998 budget amounted to US$108 million. It covered the cost of training subsidies granted to companies and authorized training institutes, developing and publishing textbooks, instructor training, etc. However, the levy-based system appeared to be rigid and failed to respond flexibly to the changing needs of companies. For instance, training courses financed from the compulsory training allocation required advance approval of the Ministry of Labour, which encouraged companies to emphasize specialist training tailored to their needs to the detriment of general training. A more flexible system for human resource development is needed with greater autonomy of the private sector. As a result the training levy is gradually being replaced by the employment insurance system which includes a vocational ability development programme. The Vocational Training Promotion Fund was discontinued at the end of 1998, with the balance being absorbed by the Employment Insurance Fund.

Under the employment insurance system, all employers have to pay an insurance premium for vocational ability development to the Employment Insurance Fund. The rate varies with company size and total payroll. Firms with 150 or fewer employees have to pay 0.1 per cent of payroll. Companies with 150–999 employees are assessed at 0.3 per cent (preferential group) and 0.5 per cent (non-preferential group). Larger firms employing 1,000 or more employees are assessed at 0.7 per cent. "Preferential group" refers to companies with 150–500 employees in manufacturing, and companies with 150–300 employees in construction, mining, transport and warehousing and communications. Efforts are also made to secure financial resources by allocating a larger part of the government budget to vocational ability development projects. The revenue generated amounted to more than US$274 million in 1998.

Companies which provide training are subsidized by the Fund. In the case of in-plant training, the entire cost is covered. Therefore, companies can train freely and not worry about training costs. The situation changes when firms outsource training courses. In this case, the subsidy depends on training cost, company size and training pattern, and ranges from 40 to 90 per cent of the cost. The upper limit for the subsidy amounts to 120 per cent of the insurance premium paid by ordinary companies and 180 per cent for companies in the preferential group. This limit can be raised to 240 per cent for ordinary companies and 360 per cent for the preferential group, if a company provides mass entry-level training. The former levy-exemption scheme is therefore being converted into a levy-grant scheme (Park, 1999).

4.6 Levy-grant schemes

Levy-grant funding schemes use payroll contributions collected from enterprises and distributed between firms as grants. The administration of levy-grant schemes requires that certain bodies be established. Grants do not usually reflect firms' levy payments closely and can be destined to priority training programmes, strengthening training facilities in individual enterprises as well as developing sectoral training curricula, advisory services, etc. A levy-grant scheme therefore allows a much greater redistribution of levy-based funds to firms which train. Some levy-paying firms may receive no grants at all if they do not offer training or if their activities do not follow training priorities. The administration of levy-grant schemes requires many case-by-case decisions and management competence, and involves some cost. The features of levy-grant schemes are summarized in box 5.8.

Levy-based reimbursement schemes reimburse training costs to firms. Firms' individual training expenditures are closely linked to their levy contributions. In this arrangement, firms send their training bills to the funds which administer levies and have at least part of their expenditure reimbursed, provided that their training programmes comply with the rules and regulations. Reimbursement schemes have certain weaknesses: they are costly; they emphasize routine training instead of new programmes; they involve a lot of paper work, which discourages many firms; and they are usually slow to approve company claims.

> **Box 5.8 Features of levy-grant mechanisms**
>
> *Mechanisms*:
>
> - Levies are collected and administered by special training funds.
> - Grants are offered to firms on a case-by-case basis according to certain criteria.
>
> *Advantages*:
>
> - Schemes promote the most promising training programmes.
> - Levies may support industry-wide training initiatives.
>
> *Disadvantages*:
>
> - Administration of schemes is costly.
> - Schemes require solid management skills that may not be available.
> - Many levy-paying firms may not benefit if they do not meet the established criteria.

A levy-grant scheme, the Skills Development Fund (SDF), was established in *Singapore* to provide incentives for the development of higher-level skills to support economic restructuring. The SDF is guided by the National Productivity Board under the Ministry of Trade and Industry. Its primary role is to develop employer-based training. This goal is pursued through the collection of a levy and the provision of financial incentives and assistance to employers. Grants are awarded on a cost-sharing basis, which ensures that firms are financially committed to the proper selection and implementation of subsidized upgrading programmes.

The Skills Development Levy Act of 1979 empowered collection of the levy from all employers at the rate of 2 per cent of the remuneration of low-wage, low-skill employees earning S$750 per month or less. In 1986 the rate of the levy was reduced. Currently it is collected at 1 per cent of the remuneration of employees earning S$750 and below. The scheme emphasizes upgrading workers' skills and wages. Under the SDF scheme, firms could claim partial reimbursement of their training expenditures in accordance with the following flat rate: S$2 per trainee per hour for in-house training programmes; S$80 per trainee per day for overseas training programmes subject to a maximum subsidized period of 12 weeks; course fee support at 30 per cent, 50 per cent and 70 per cent subject to a maximum grant of S$10 per trainee per hour.

In recent years the SDF has expanded its role in the development of national training programmes. It has launched and financed two national programmes aimed at building up a training infrastructure: the Core Skills for Effectiveness and Change (COSEC) programme and the Information Technology (IT) programme for office workers. The SDF has been effective in making continuous efforts to develop a training culture in small firms. The Training Needs Analysis Grant Scheme was launched to address the problem of skill shortages and resources for the planning of training in firms. SDF grants are extended to firms which engage external consultants to conduct a training needs assessment. Firms can qualify for grants amounting to 70 per cent of the cost of consultancy fees, subject to a maximum of S$70 per hour.

4.7 Paid education and training leave

Several industrialized countries in Europe (e.g. Belgium, France and Italy) have introduced, through national collective labour agreements, paid education and training leave for employees. Leave is funded through a combination of contributions raised from enterprise payrolls and from general revenues. Legal arrangements specify the amount to be contributed, the type and duration of education and training programmes, workers' eligibility for paid leave and the administration of the scheme.

Paid educational leave (PEL) in *Belgium* entitles full-time workers in the private sector to be absent from work for a certain number of hours in order to attend recognized training and education courses. Civil servants and teaching personnel are excluded. The employer can neither oblige employees to attend, nor prevent them from attending courses recognized by the law. Since 1995, employees have been entitled to an annual maximum of 120 hours of PEL for vocational training and to a maximum of 80 hours for education courses. Employers have to pay wages while workers are on PEL. Trainee wages and social security contributions are reimbursed to the employer by the Federal Ministry of Labour and Employment (FMLE), to a maximum of BEF 68,000 per month. The State pays the full cost of PEL-related general education programmes but only half the cost of vocational courses. The state contribution is directly allocated to the FMLE. The other half of the cost of vocational courses is covered from a payroll training levy of 0.04 per cent, which is collected from employers by the State and transferred to the FMLE. Employers with workers on PEL claim reimbursement of the related expenditure. They have to declare the number of workers on PEL, the number of training hours effectively taken up and related salaries (including social security contributions). They also have to provide certificates of subscription to courses as well as certificates of course attendance.

Because of a budget deficit, the state contribution to PEL has been reduced. As a result, the Commission for Recognition of PEL has abolished a number of recognized courses, and employers have been required to raise their contribution to PEL. Therefore, another payroll levy, which normally aims at financing training for labour market risk groups, has been increased by 0.05 per cent. The duration of PEL has been cut by almost half due to increasing demand. The number of PEL beneficiaries increased from under 30,000 workers in 1986 to more than 52,000 in 1991. One of the reported weakness of the system is that it can easily be abused. Reimbursement may be claimed by enterprises without employees actually attending courses. Since reimbursement is authorized on the basis of course attendance, this requires a costly control system to audit both enterprises and education and training providers. Regulations limit the number of employees on PEL at the same time. PEL entitlements for trainees who do not pass exams or are found to be absent from courses can be reduced or withdrawn. Although the number of beneficiaries of the PEL system increased rapidly from less than 30,000 workers in 1986 to more than 50,000 in 1991/1992, they decreased to 39,000 in 1995/96. It appears that government funds allocated to PEL are insufficient to respond fully to demand, while some industry sectors benefited from this entitlement more than others. Only 8–9 per cent of workers in small and medium enterprises participated in PEL as compared to approximately 20 per cent in larger firms (Geers, 1999).

In *France*, private-sector employees with indefinite-term contracts have the right to individual training leave, which is financed by the 0.2 per cent contribution (within the training tax) paid by employers to joint management-union bodies set up for the administration of individual training leave (OPACIFs) (see also section 4.5 of this Unit). Training insurance funds (FAFs) may also be accredited by the state to collect the levy-based amounts from employers. Alternatively, a fund may be set up specifically to administer training leave. For the first year, the amount subsidized is 80–90 per cent of the employee's remuneration; if the training is to last for a period of more than a year or 1,200 hours, in the second year the employee's remuneration will be subsidized by only 60 per cent. Employers are reimbursed for the wages they pay. A fund may refuse an application for paid leave if it cannot cover the cost. Control of financial operations is conducted by the government authorities. Any application for a level V qualification gives the worker the right to a 50 per cent state contribution to the cost of funding, which is paid to an OPACIF. In 1990 about 75 per cent of applicants were at that level. OPACIFs accept some 20,000 applications a year, which is only 70 per cent of those submitted. The number of applications rises more rapidly than acceptances. On average individual training leave lasts 850 hours at a cost of some $20,000. Training usually consists of long courses leading to qualifications. Any employee who has worked for five years is also entitled to absence for a skills audit in an audit centre. The absence should not exceed 24 working hours and the cost of the skills audit and payment of remuneration is also covered by OPACIFs (Willems, 1994).

4.8 Advantages and disadvantages of levy-based schemes

The major advantage of levy-based schemes is their ability to raise national training funds or to ensure a certain measure of enterprise training through self-financing. To a certain extent, such schemes also control the training offered by employers through the establishment of conditions for a given programme to become eligible for financing from levy-based funds. On the other hand, serious liabilities have also become apparent. Levy-based funding schemes may not have enough power to mobilize additional training. As a result, they may be subsidizing programmes that would have been provided by firms in any case. Debate continues over whether levy rates should be uniform or differ across sectors. The need for training and training costs vary among industries, as do skill levels. Levy rates that do not reflect these differences seem counterproductive.

Under levy-based funding schemes, many firms tend to implement programmes that accomplish little beyond meeting the compulsory training level, failing to bring about any real change. In addition, employers never recover their levy contributions in full. Large enterprises tend to benefit disproportionately from tax-based funding schemes. Many smaller firms pay levies but fail to participate, thus losing their money. The same scheme can never work equally well for all firms, large or small, well-established or vulnerable. Those firms and sectors showing little sensitivity to a particular funding mechanism should be assisted by the introduction of other, potentially more attractive schemes. Special efforts should be made to administer incentive schemes at a lower cost and with higher flexibility. Sharing decision-making power between employers and employees would do much to improve the quality of levy-financed training.

Most incentive schemes impose rather strict conditions for eligibility and they govern factors such as training content, course duration, unit cost and even the age of trainees. Such conditions are a management tool and cannot be avoided. Through them, governments try to reconcile the preferences of individual employers with society's training needs. However, if the right balance is not found, incentive schemes will prove ineffective. Although a time frame for reasonable and sustainable growth of employer-based training is hard to predict, monitoring should take place and management should act in accordance with the progress achieved. If employer-based training expenditure consistently increases, and the training market shows evidence of strength, it might prove useful to revise levy rates and conditions.

Some developing countries (DCs) have succeeded in applying levy-based incentive schemes in imperfect or limited markets. In less technologically advanced DCs, low demand for better skills combined with economic systems that do not reward achievement may call into question the need to encourage

Module 5. Financing VET

employer training through levy-based schemes. Some DCs may not have enough enterprises to make a levy system feasible. The tax collecting apparatus may be unreliable or non-existent, and management skills may be lacking. Some general conclusions regarding financing schemes are summarized in box 5.9.

Box 5.9 Conclusions on levy-based funding schemes

There are several options for financing mechanisms, all of which serve *different targets*, such as:

- financing national VET institutions;
- ensuring a guaranteed level of national investment in human resources;
- equalizing training expenditure among enterprises; and
- expanding national/sectoral priority programmes.

The basic conditions for the viability of levy schemes are:

- a sufficient number of levy-paying enterprises;
- solid tax-collecting machinery; and
- government-employer cooperation.

A single levy-based funding scheme can never suit all firms. Alternative mechanisms are required to influence training activities in both large and small, profitable and low-income enterprises.

The introduction of training levies usually results in an expansion of the demand for training and in the development of national training markets.

Training levies tend to increase the cost of labour to enterprises, which may adversely affect employment.

Levy schemes should be administered with the close involvement of employers and unions.

GUIDING TRAINING PROVIDERS

Module
6

Unit 1. Government administration of training providers

Learning objectives

This unit is designed to provide a better knowledge of:

1. The principles of direct administration of training providers
2. Conditions for operating public providers, supervision and technical support

1.1 Direct administration versus independent operators

Considerable variation exists between the national context which determines the legal status, autonomy, organizational structure, etc. of training providers around the world. National political and social circumstances reflect traditions of government and public service, the roles and responsibilities of the government and of the social partners. Because of this variation, there are a number of differences between countries regarding the structure and operation of their training providers. One of the important patterns is that in many countries, public training providers' organizational structures, budgets, programming, enrolments, staffing and operational procedures are directly determined by government departments. The common legal status of training institutions is that they are government-owned organizations with all or part of the staff being civil servants, who usually enjoy guaranteed employment. Training institution budgets are part of the government budget and deal with the mechanics of expenditure rather than the achievement of outputs. In such settings, vocational training institutions have few incentives and little freedom for self-development and innovation. Many state-owned institutions have become known for inefficiency due to overcentralization, mismanagement, protectionism, weak operational and financial flexibility, low staff commitment, and high operational and management costs. Efforts have been made to improve the situation by strengthening school self-management, introducing performance measurement and partial decentralization.

Another pattern of guidance that is becoming popular can be called *market guidance*. This approach views public training providers as market operators who are expected to set targets and plan operations close to market demand and to earn their funds by selling services. The government provides guidance through national strategic planning, and VET providers are expected to operate in line with government financing conditions. Eligibility for public funds is linked to performance and outputs, particularly those that reflect the implementation of national VET strategic targets.

A large variety of guidance schemes fall between the two extremes. Organizational and management structures; staffing and pay systems; labour market analysis and planning of activities; budgeting, use of budgets and revenues, and borrowing; course development and curriculum changes; teaching methods; reporting on activities; and institution and programme evaluation are all affected by the pattern of guidance used. The two patterns are compared along these lines in table 6.1. (Market guidance is discussed in more detail in Unit 2.)

1.2 Government guidance and control

1.2.1 School management structure

VET providers that are directly administered by a government usually have a very similar structural, centrally determined configuration. Training institution structures often make use of the traditional, specialized departments. They also have functional units providing technical support to management, teachers and students; these include financing and bookkeeping, personnel, examination officers, budgeting and planning, purchasing and storing, registry, data processing, equipment maintenance, relations with employers and placement of graduates, and curriculum development. Centrally developed job descriptions for the institutions' management and teaching staff, as well as institutional rules of procedure, are very common and leave little room for change (see section 1.3 below).

In centrally administered VET systems, little real power is given to school councils. However, teaching staff are often able to maintain a great deal of autonomy within their classrooms, even though they are bound by a strict curriculum. Managers experience more difficulty, as they are severely restricted by central guidelines and by voluminous paperwork.

Module 6. Guiding training providers

Table 6.1 Comparative features of guidance patterns

Areas of intervention	Central administration	Market guidance
Style of guidance	Guidance by rules and procedures.	Guidance by objectives.
Organizational and management structures	Centrally determined and uniform to all providers.	Designed and changed by institutions themselves.
Staffing and pay system	Staff are civil servants. Principals have little power over staff careers. Pay is determined centrally and is not linked to performance.	Staff are employed by the institution and do not enjoy job security. Institution pay scales and performance-related pay are being introduced.
Labour market analysis and planning of activities	Institutions may sometimes be required to conduct training needs analysis. Providers' programme offers are decided mostly by the government.	Market analysis is a pre-condition for receiving public contracts and funds. Institutions have to provide evidence that programming responds to market needs.
Budgeting, use of budgets and revenues, borrowing	Budgets emphasize expenditure. Some use of revenues is allowed. No borrowing is authorized. Budgets emphasize expenditure. Some use of revenues is allowed. No borrowing is authorized.	Budgets allocate funds against planned outputs and activities. Revenues are strongly encouraged and freely used. Borrowing is authorized and regulated.
Financing	Funds are allocated to an institution with no direct link to performance and outputs.	Funds are allocated per performance target and are to be earned through selling services; no public funds are guaranteed.
Course and curriculum development and change	Only national curricula are taught. New courses cannot be developed and offered at the discretion of institutions.	Each institution can develop its own programmes and curricula leading to national qualifications.
Reporting and evaluation	Annual comprehensive reports emphasize compliance with rules and regulations.	Quarterly reports on enrolment and throughput. Annual reports on achievement of targets. Comprehensive evaluation once in several years.

1.2.2 Management by rules

Many aspects of school life are legally formulated, including the rights and duties of teaching staff and parents, curricula and teaching targets. As a result, the role of centrally established operational rules and procedures is very strong. Compliance with rules and procedures has been regarded as a means to control the quality of education and training provision. An extensive inspectorate is needed to ensure that numerous central guidelines are carried out.

The main subjects of control are compliance with rules and regulations and the use of staff, facilities and other resources. Rules determine the standard faculty workload by prescribing the number of students per teacher, the number of working days a year and the number of teaching hours per week. Ratios of the number of working hours to the time spent preparing new programmes can also be applied. Teacher workload may be reduced in some countries so that they can take a second job in order to increase their earnings. Managers' teaching load is usually only 60 per cent of the standard to allow time for management and coordination. National standards can be set for school buildings, equipment levels and resources (Gordon and Parkes, 1993). A reporting system on the use of school premises and equipment may be applied, while the students' average school marks may be published.

1.2.3 Central curriculum

A national curriculum is drafted by education ministries, leaving no freedom to schools. Under such a system, all schools have the same timetable and curricula (Standaert, 1993). New approaches to centrally determined curricula have attempted to extend more freedom to schools. For instance, in British general education schools, a central education curriculum is applied which leaves 15 per cent of the timetable to the discretion of schools. In the Netherlands, too, a core curriculum has been introduced in all general education and vocational streams at the lower-secondary level. Each school is required to devote 25 teaching hours a week to the 15 compulsory subjects, which amounts to 80 per cent of total teaching time.

1.2.4 Instructor development

Although most countries draw vocational teachers from industry rather than formal teacher training colleges, centrally administered VET systems tend to regulate instructor development. For instance, in France, skill upgrading of trainers is regulated through levy-based funding of their training. The national collective agreement concluded by public training organizations determines that they must earmark 2.5 per cent of their payroll for staff training, using at least half of this allocation for instructors. The training of trainers is one of the criteria set up by the Homologation Commission of France when considering applications for training for national vocational awards. Governments can also intervene in vocational instructor development through the promotion of national competence standards and licensing of instructors.

1.2.5 Planning, budgeting and financing

Centrally administered VET providers are not usually expected to respond directly to labour market needs. Training needs analysis is commonly conducted by institutions associated with central government. The student demand-driven programming model is favoured, allowing anyone wishing to acquire a qualification from the list of state-financed and/or provided programmes to do so.

In such systems, budgets allocate resources for salaries, equipment, transport, etc. Budgets emphasize cost control rather than performance and output. The institutions' fixed budgets are calculated according to the number of trainees enrolled and the number of teachers employed, usually with no link to market demand for VET services. Some flexibility allowing providers to react to market signals can, nevertheless, be introduced. This can be achieved through allocations (10-15 per cent of their budget) permitting institutions to launch flexible courses and recruit external teachers. In directly administered VET systems, the normative approach to funding is applied (see section 1.2.3 in Unit 1 of Module 5).

1.3 Administering lycées in France[1]

1.3.1 The role of central government

The *lycées professionnelles* (LPs) and *lycées technologiques* (LTs) are the major state vocational training institutions in France. Public lycées are relatively small, with an average of 480 students in LPs and 815 in LTs. They provide vocational education and training programmes at the upper secondary level and are guided by two levels of government administration, each of which has its own scope of guidance and control. Everything to do with the organization of teaching is run by the state government. The relevant ministries (e.g. education or agriculture) decide on curricula and define national diplomas. Teachers are

---

[1] Based on Lafond, 1997

hired, trained, appointed to specific posts, evaluated and paid by the central government in accordance with strictly graded national pay scales.

The state controls the education system as a whole and each individual lycée through the education ministry inspectorates. Their evaluations form the basis of an annual national report. The education ministry Evaluation and Futures Department (DEP) evaluates the lycées through statistical inquiries and the compilation of indicators.

The central government studies labour markets and evaluates training needs. Training needs assessment involves observing major labour market trends and drawing pragmatic guidelines from them. Using tracer studies, the Centre for Studies and Research on Qualifications (CEREQ) collects original data on the relationship between training and employment. Seven months after the end of each lycée year, the DEP conducts inquiries on lycée graduates and former apprentices who have just completed training. It supplies CEREQ with the results of its research.

1.3.2 The role of the regions

Responsibility for VET has been partly decentralized to regional governments, which include 30 regional education authorities headed by their chief officers, and to regional advisory councils (see section 2.2 in Unit 2 of Module 5). Regions are required to devise plans for proposed training courses spanning several years, designed to reflect the region's quantitative and qualitative training needs; they also draw up investment plans setting out, in order of priority, the number and type of lycées to be built, rebuilt or extended. The state representative then uses the region's proposals to draw up an annual list of the major work that will actually take place.

Regional autonomy in vocational education planning has produced a great diversity of methods, degrees of success and training quality. Training activities are driven by national VET policies and priorities, which cover areas such as enhancing the value of vocational education, revamping apprenticeships and helping young people find employment. Each region is expected to tailor these policies to local circumstances. Each region has a Regional Observatory for Employment and Training (OREF) responsible for analysing regional employment and economic circumstances (see box 4.2 in Module 4). There is no uniform model for reports, which vary widely from region to region. Regional VET planning focuses on coordinating existing programmes and financial incentives are used to persuade various providers to fulfil regional priorities. Rather than listing training courses or creating schedules, OREFs evaluate local conditions to determine priorities: state-region planning contracts are also used. These agreements establish joint projects and determine their financing over five-year periods. Projects could range from schemes to help young people find work to the building of a university – anything that is at the same time a national priority and a regional goal.

Regional inspectors, who report to the chief education officers, monitor the day-to-day running of lycées as well as the quality of teaching. Their role is to take part in an overall evaluation of lycées for which the general inspectorate is responsible; to ensure that timetables are respected; and to inspect staff by sitting in on actual classes. In addition to the general education inspectors, there are 590 regional inspectors for initial vocational training.

1.3.3 Self-management of lycées

The Law of 22 July 1983 decentralized the administration of lycées, which have acquired the status of local state teaching institutions (*établissements publics locaux d'enseignement* – EPLE) with national and regional authorities sharing control of them. A lycée is headed by a principal appointed by the ministry and run by a management board with 24 to 30 members, depending on the size of the school. The board is made up of representatives of teaching and other staff, parents, students, local elected representatives (such as the mayor and regional councillor) and lycée executives. The principal chairs the board, which every year decides on the lycée's internal regulations; approves the accounts of the previous year; adopts the proposed budget drawn up by the principal on the basis of the grant made by the region and, where appropriate, other expected resources; approves the timetables drawn up by the principal in accordance with the teaching resources allocated by the chief education officer of the region; and adopts the lycée's draft educational and teaching plan.

In administering the lycée, the principal is assisted by one or two deputies, a manager in charge of administrative issues, and a chief of vocational education (*chef de travaux*) and several educational advisers. The teaching staff are divided into those responsible for general education and those specializing in vocational education. The *chefs de travaux* are commonly experienced former teachers who organize vocational training and manage workshops. They liaise with companies to organize training. They also play an active part in choosing teaching materials, following technological and professional developments and devising training programmes for the lycée staff.

1.3.4 Staffing and financing

Regional authorities decide the allocation of state staffing resources to the lycée. The grant is calculated on the basis of several factors including the number of students, surface area of buildings, type of vocational programmes and other local conditions. If they wish, regions may allocate extra funds to lycées from their own resources.

Each lycée receives an annual allocation of teaching posts (*dotation horaire global* – DHG), with one post representing about 18 hours of teaching a week; and an allocation of supplementary teaching hours which amounts, on average, to 10 per cent of the overall number of teaching hours. A supplementary allocation is utilized at the discretion of the principal in order to increase flexibility and better respond to demand. The DHG is the product of the following calculation:

DHG = S(e) x H/S(a)

where:

H = the total number of teaching hours needed to implement the curriculum;
S(a) = the total number of students in the education district; and
S(e) = the number of students enrolled in the particular lycée.

The ratio H/S(a) is therefore an average characteristic for each district and equals 2 for the LPs. For example, for a lycée with 400 students and for an education district with H/S(a) equalling 2, the DHG would be 800 hours. This would result in the allocation of 40 teacher positions (18 x 40 = 720 hours) plus 80 supplementary hours to be used at the discretion of the principal. This ratio may be higher in economically and socially disadvantaged areas, and in rural areas, where the population is scattered and it is considered appropriate to retain training facilities despite the low number of students.

The number and type of teaching posts allocated to a lycée are revised each year according to student numbers. This reappraisal, carried out several months ahead of the next academic year, takes into account the principal's projections, collated with the statistical work of the DEP. If new training courses are considered necessary, a new section is opened. This involves converting premises, buying technical equipment and allocating new teachers. However, the staffing issue becomes more sensitive when it is a question of abolishing a course that is no longer considered useful. It is then necessary to move the teachers to another lycée or retrain them so that they can teach another subject. The question of retraining also comes up when the content of a training course alters. In the regional chief education officer's department, a service for the training of national education staff (MAFPEN) organizes continuing training of teachers. The courses are either optional and organized according to teachers' needs and schedules or compulsory if they are intended to help teachers adapt to new curricula and diplomas. The evaluation of staff, carried out by inspectors or by lycée principals, may bring certain career benefits, such as faster promotion or extra pay. No attempt is made, however, to relate career promotion or pay to lycée outputs or other performance indicators.

Lycées enjoy a certain measure of financial and educational autonomy, being free to decide how to use the resources allocated by regions. They do not have to fulfil any particular conditions in order to receive the grant. They may use it as they wish provided that they put aside sufficient funds to cover heating, electricity, telephones and cleaning. In addition, lycées can explore their own sources of revenue (e.g. grants from companies and sale of goods or services by students under the supervision of teachers). In some cases the revenues reach 30 per cent of the school's basic budget. These additional resources do not affect salaries.

The lycées are not asked to assess training needs or to design their training offers. Their role is to provide the programmes determined by the ministry and the regions. The decision to introduce or develop a particular type of vocational education is taken jointly by the region and the regional representatives of the education ministry. Once a training programme is in place, the lycée has to respect national directives about programme content. Lycées are encouraged to maintain close relations with companies and to follow the career of their students to determine whether graduates find work quickly and companies are satisfied with the training that their recruits have undergone.

As a result, the lycées' educational autonomy is limited to devising a teaching plan that deals with teaching methods, implementing educational projects and arranging compulsory periods of practical training in firms. The teaching staff are responsible for entering into training partnerships with local companies, finding company training places and arranging joint work of teachers and monitors in following and assessing students during their time with a company.

1.3.5 GRETAs as a solution for lycée flexibility

The lycées and other establishments are linked in GRETAs, voluntary associations for the provision of continuing training. The reason for instituting this association is said to be to pool lycée resources in order to ensure more varied and effective offers on the continuing training market. However, another important reason seems to be to overcome various regulations driving the lycée. Each GRETA, which groups at least ten lycées, has its own inter-lycée advisory board. Therefore, the teachers and facilities for continuing training in the GRETAs are spread among several lycées. The continuing training advisers are civil servants. Everything is planned so that the GRETA's work will not interfere in any way with the initial training provided at the lycées. Initial and continuing training operate independently, even though they use the same facilities and some of the same teachers. Such independence is necessary because the lycées must follow a curriculum imposed from outside, whereas the GRETA can adapt its courses according to demand. The GRETAs adjust the level of training they provide depending on the qualifications of their staff. If better-qualified teachers are required for a particular course, temporary staff are hired. Supervisory staff, such as the principal and manager, receive a remuneration that is proportional to turnover (with a ceiling of FF65,000 per person per year) and is fixed by complex regulations. Teachers are paid on the basis of national pay scales according to the level of training they provide. As long as turnover allows, the scales may be from 25 to 50 per cent higher in certain circumstances, such as with specific types of training, courses taught in the evening or on Saturday or at a company in a remote location.

1.3.6 Steering institutions

Lycée performance is steered, externally and internally, through the measurement of a set of indicators. External indicators enable the state inspectors to judge each lycée's performance. Their findings are published in the national and local press and allow for students' families and the public at large to have a better knowledge of lycées. Three performance indicators are taken into consideration for the external evaluation: the proportion of students who passed the exam compared to the number enrolled; the number of students who began their first year of upper secondary education three years beforehand; and the number of students who left the lycée before taking the exam.

The indicators for internal evaluation are known as the IPES (indicators for steering secondary institutions). Each lycée is provided with about 20 indicators calculated on the basis of data gathered by national information and management bodies. Lycées are given software that enables them to calculate, monitor and record the indicators of their choice. These indicators, which may be specific to a particular lycée, are combined with national and regional points of references so that a school can measure itself against other institutions' performance. If a lycée's results are far below the average, an audit is carried out by a team of inspectors. One of three major explanations usually emerges: (1) socially disadvantaged and hard-to-teach students dominate, in which case the lycée will be given extra resources to handle the problems; (2) a poor educational programme and inadequately motivated staff, in which case educational advisers will help the teachers draw up a new educational programme and some teachers may be offered retraining; or (3) mismanagement, which will result in a new principal being appointed.

Some of the external and internal evaluation indicators are given in table 6.2.

Table 6.2 Evaluation indicators in French lycées

Indicators	Internal or external
Population indicators:	
• Characteristics of all students at the start of the academic year	External
• Former schools of students entering class at the start of the school year	External
• Knowledge acquired by students in the vocational fifth form	Internal
• Attractiveness of the lycée	Internal
Resource indicators:	
• Timetable resources	Internal
• Characteristics of teachers	External
Results indicators:	
• Pass rates in the *baccalauréat professionnel**	External
• Access rates to the *baccalauréat professionnel*	External
• Pass rates in the BEP* and 2-year CAP*	Internal
• Access rates to the BEP and 2-year CAP	Internal
• Destination of students after leaving the lycée	Internal
• Circumstances of students leaving the lycée	External and internal
Operational indicators:	
• Proportion of teaching hours provided per student	Internal
• Teaching staff turnover	External
• Accidents at the lycée	Internal
Environmental indicators:	
• Relations with the economic environment	Internal
• Data by employment area	External

**Baccalauréat professionnel*, BEP and CAP are vocational education qualifications in France.

Unit 2. Providers as independent operators

Learning objectives

This unit is designed to provide a better knowledge of:
1. VET management involving a market scheme
2. The supervision and control of independent training providers

2.1 Self-management of providers

Market guidance has emerged in countries which have introduced market principles and managerial flexibility in the public services. Service providers are free to determine their organizational structures, programming and delivery, budgeting, staffing and even pay policies. This involves the deregulation of public services and allows for market competition between public and private providers of vocational education and training. In most industrialized countries, autonomy in educational institutions is increasing. Issues such as the organization and development of lessons, teaching techniques and internal assessment of trainees are regulated not by governments but by principals and institutional management boards. Where public service providers are guided by market forces, direct government intervention is limited and guidance is provided indirectly, most notably through strategic planning and financing instruments. The administrative and operational autonomy delegated to training institution boards enables them to maintain close links with local business, to open and close courses, change curricula, sell services and follow up placement of their graduates. This means that schools are able to respond more effectively to regional and local needs (see section 2.7 below).

Sometimes deregulation involves a change in the legal status of training providers. The legal pattern most frequently applied in such countries is a public corporation (company limited by guarantee as in the United Kingdom; see box 2.7 in Module 2) or a self-owning institution (as in Denmark; see box 3.6 in Module 3). Public service providers are not privatized but become independent public operators with operational and fiscal responsibilities limited by the government guarantee. They are usually non-profit organizations. Their staff are no longer civil servants; they become contract employees instead. Funding is not guaranteed; rather, institutions' services are contracted out by the government. As a corporation or a self-owned school, a VET institution may have reasons for merging with another institution (a change that needs to be authorized by the government). However, a change in legal status should not be regarded as a pre-condition for improved operational flexibility and employee commitment. Greater freedom and flexibility to operate in the market could be achieved through decentralizing school administration and strengthening its self-management without major legal innovations. This is the situation in the Netherlands (see box 3.7 in Module 3).

2.2 Organizational structures and staffing

In market-driven systems, governments have less direct influence over the programming, operations, management and organizational structures of independent training institutions. Under the pressure of competition, most institutions become multi-purpose entities offering a broad range of services and programmes. Government influence over the providers' internal organization is exerted through the determination of: (1) the composition and codes of conduct of their governing bodies; (2) the positions that are legally required, such as bookkeeper and auditor; and (3) compulsory tasks, such as strategic planning and placement, which could be conditions for contracting out public services to them and which therefore have to be assigned to certain staff positions. In any case, providers' internal structures vary considerably as they try to comply with these requirements in the most economical way.

Governments, however, can exert a powerful indirect influence on providers' targets and operations indirectly through creating incentives, changing funding rates, setting conditions for providers' eligibility to public funds including technical guidelines for courses and qualifications, setting conditions for treating and managing capital buildings devolved to training institutions, as well as improving managers' accountability through external and internal audit.

Where staff are employed directly by VET institutions and are not civil servants, there are no legal restrictions on who can teach or train. Most vocational and technical teachers are recruited from industrial, commercial and service occupations, preferably with ten or more years of work experience behind them. Independent institutions tend to increase the part-time faculty of VET institutions in order to have staffing and operational flexibility and to maintain close links with sectoral practice. The role of teachers employed on hourly contracts tends to increase in conditions of financial insecurity. In some countries, instructors' wages are regulated by national/sectoral pay scales established by collective labour agreements. For instance, in the Netherlands providers decide, within their limits, what wages to establish, while maximum salaries for certain positions are determined by the Government (Netherlands Ministry of Education and Science, 1993). In other countries only minimum wages are determined centrally and lower authorities can offer more. In the United States, since 1980, 24 states have introduced minimum salaries for teachers as well as "master teacher" programmes to give the best teachers extra pay (Perry, 1989).

The management of independent training providers requires qualified administrators skilled in strategic management and planning and with a focus on results. They also need to work well with client groups and to manage equitable access to training, apply the productivity concept, compete with other providers and demonstrate accountability. School principals should be trained in educational management and possibly accredited for this work. Some countries have introduced a qualification in educational management. For instance, in the further education sector of the United Kingdom, supervised distance-learning programmes are offered that lead to recognized awards in the management of further education.

2.3 Programming and planning

Independent providers must have highly developed programming and planning as their courses have to match market demand and employers' need for skills. It is increasingly recognized that only independent training providers can react to market signals with a sufficient degree of flexibility. However, it would be unrealistic to think that VET programmes could be entirely determined by sectoral needs. The demand for courses always far exceeds the immediate needs of economic sectors. Therefore, young people's training priorities also matter. Hence, institutional planning should balance the needs of the local labour market with the education and training needs of private individuals. Enterprise demand and individual demand can be identified through different signals and must be handled differently. Due to the high uncertainty of labour markets, assessment of training demand must become a regular process. Labour market information should be supplied to private individuals and job seekers enabling them to make informed decisions. (For planning concepts and techniques, see Module 4).

To ensure long-term steering of labour markets, demographic and other changes, VET providers in some countries have been required to introduce strategic management techniques. Institutions' strategic plans are required to take account of national and local economic and demographic forecasts, to comply with national and local economic and strategic development objectives, and to cater to national priority target groups. Strategic planning focuses on new training needs or new clients; it recognizes forthcoming changes in population, industry and technology; and envisages long-term development of training facilities, staff, and information systems. Although local development needs have commonly been the major basis for providers' strategic planning, national VET policies and targets also guide the overall process of priority setting, public funding and programming. Institutions should be encouraged to produce internal development plans, which differ from plans for training delivery. Clear targets should be set regarding institutional development, resources and activities. Indicators measuring the achievement of set targets also need to be established. In countries that use a market-type mechanism, setting government priority performance indicators as part of performance agreements between providers and government authorities has been introduced. National enrolment targets, for example, can be translated into institutions' quantifiable annual targets. Training equity may also be targeted by establishing specific planning and reporting indicators covering the identified target groups. Supervisors' certainty about and employees' understanding of performance targets are important conditions for the success of training institutions.

Institutional managers need to be trained in strategic management techniques. The mission statement needs to be reviewed and institutional structures and performance need to be internally audited on a regular basis, while strategies should be adjusted correspondingly. Teams may be established to collect and share with other staff information about the institution's environment and trends in local demand for courses. Strategic management may be promoted or made compulsory by making public financing dependent on regularly confirmed attainment of goals.

In contrast to strategic plans, operational plans direct programming and enrolment targets, allocate resources (including staff) and establish work loads for defined periods. In operational planning, short-term, inexpensive courses leading to low-skill qualifications should be distinguished from long-term, expensive, technical courses with long lead times. Short-term initiation courses may be planned on the basis of student demand since their role is vocational guidance rather than the provision of skilled labour. Long-term programmes need to anticipate the market situation. Institutional capacity to collect and interpret market reactions to the supply of skilled labour should be developed in order to feed resources efficiently to individual programmes. The cost-effectiveness and -efficiency of programmes need to be compared in order to provide additional analytical inputs to programming. In some countries, providers' delivery plans must be cleared and agreed by local employers' bodies or by tripartite councils; this is a condition for public funding. (For planning based on labour market signals see Module 4).

2.4 Budgeting and financing

In market-based systems, providers are often required to allocate resources according to the institution's objectives, related training and other activities (e.g. engineering programmes, construction programmes, administration, research). This approach to budgeting must be preceded by well-structured planning which emphasizes activities and outputs. An objective budget allows the allocation of resources in line with priorities and facilitates the evaluation of performance and outputs. A national VET system's planning, financing, information and reporting procedures should encourage objective budgets. This technique ensures that institutional target setting and planning drive budget formulation and not the other way around.

Using objective budgeting methods, market-based training systems usually link funding to outputs. In such schemes, no public funding is guaranteed unless specified levels of performance are met. At the same time, providers usually have full or almost full freedom in the use of funds. (Sometimes a certain share of providers' budgets may be secured by the government.) The application of output-based schemes assumes that government retains the role of major purchaser of training services. (Performance-related funding schemes are discussed in Units 1 and 2 of Module 5.)

2.5 Technical guidance and quality control

Central or even local governments often establish technical guidelines for independent VET providers that can be used to determine training quality and secure consumer rights. Technical guidance usually covers programme content and training paths, curriculum and assessment of trainees. A combination of central guidance with the delegation of curriculum development to schools is becoming increasingly common. For instance, in Denmark, the Ministry of Education issues Education Orders which specify the layers of national curriculum (i.e. basic subjects, area subjects and specialist subjects; student attainment targets for various subjects; and provision for skill assessments). Basic subjects comprise general and vocational topics, aimed at enhancing the personal development of students, preparing them for further studies and socializing them. Area subjects comprise practical and theoretical instruction relevant to a broad field of the trade and are normally shared by several streams. Specialist subjects comprise theoretical and practical instruction which is specific for an individual trade. All course curricula are required to include basic (one-third), area (one-third), specialized (one-sixth) and optional (one-sixth) subjects. Syllabi are drawn up by the independent schools themselves on the basis of Education Orders to ensure general uniformity of training qualifications as well as of skills assessment. However, the specific content of curricula vary from school to school (see box 3.20, Module 3).

Local, rather than central, guidance on curriculum is provided in the United States, where most states do not attempt to standardize vocational education curricula, except in a general sense, and local school districts have full responsibility. State departments of education generally provide technical guidelines on curriculum development. Additionally, there are a number of state, regional and national sources of curriculum guidelines. Typically, education district curriculum committees are formed comprising instructors from individual schools. Vocational schools and community colleges carry out most of the technical support functions themselves or contract them out to specialist firms.

Testing of graduates can be partly assigned to training providers. As long as national skill standards and VET qualifications are well-established and trainees are rigorously assessed, the testing of theoretical knowledge can be delegated to the schools themselves, provided that teachers are qualified. However, the delegation of skill testing to schools has been criticized as an unreliable mechanism. Competence-based qualifications and assessement schemes have become a new mechanism for quality control in VET systems where training providers are fully autonomous. For instance, in the United Kingdom, the function of assessing skills and making awards is separated from training and assigned to *autonomous specialist bodies*. The assessment (testing) and awarding (certification) system for VET is conducted by, or on behalf of, Awarding Bodies which are independent of the training institutions and the Government. The National Council for Vocational Qualifications (NCVQ) requires that any Award scheme submitted should make no reference to any course of instruction or institution, the length of training, entry qualifications, or on-site assessment. Only the outcomes, expressed in terms of competencies and their performance criteria, can be referred to. The description of specific occupational standards (competencies) is developed by an Industry Lead Body. Candidates must present evidence of competence to the assessors. Some evidence will be of direct performance at work that can only be assessed by immediate observation. Other evidence relies on simulations. In both cases, in order to guarantee future performance, the underlying knowledge must be tested. Much evidence is documentary and consists of records of performance authenticated as having been produced by the candidate. Assessors must have demonstrated competence in occupational skills and evaluation techniques.

2.6 Controlling and reporting

The basic method of operational control is to compare the actual course with what was planned. In countries with market-based guidance, annual control and reporting are linked primarily to planned performance and output. School targets and corresponding funds are measured against records of output and accounting. Quarterly audits of enrolment and throughput and annual reviews of graduates' labour market performance and client satisfaction have become established practice. The focus of control should be on activities which failed to meet the targets. The procedures should require that managers responsible for areas which deviated from the targets report immediately on the reasons for failure and on corrective decisions made.

Public service providers are usually subject to a major review every few years in reaction to the reports of external inspectors. This mechanism of control is exercised through evaluations focusing on institutional goals, outputs and their quality, the use of capacity and resources, the organization of teaching and programmes, management, staffing, planning and funding. Schools may also be required to practise self-assessment following government-provided guidelines as in the United Kingdom.

Control procedures can involve the creation of performance and expenditure measures and regular data collection to evaluate providers' performance, outputs and expenditure against established plans, targets and unit cost standards. Other procedures include carrying out obligatory school plans; accrediting training providers and instructors and appraising teaching staff and school managers; controlling the quality of training premises and other inputs; and conducting external examination and assessment of educational and learning outcomes. A great number of indicators have been used to evaluate training institutions. Some, but not all, of the evaluation indicators are directly linked to planning indicators (see Unit 3 of Module 2, section 3.2.2).

In the United States, a new model of state and local school governance is evolving that has three major components: a primary emphasis on measured student performance as the basis for school accountability; a system of standards by which data on student performance can be compared by school and by locality; and a system of rewards, penalties and intervention strategies to introduce incentives for improvement. Focusing on student performance should move states away from input regulations (e.g. judging the proportion of certified staff and inspecting syllabi) to steering schools by results. In other words, less focus is placed on compliance with rules and more on learning achievements. The unit of accountability can be a whole school district involving dozens of schools (as in Mississippi) or a single school (as in Kentucky). In the former case, districts are ranked on five levels, based on a combination of performance and process variables. School districts placed at level 3 are considered to be successful. To reach levels 4 and 5, districts are held accountable for additional variables, such as a 75 per cent or higher graduation rate, national test scores and graduate follow-up data. By contrast, the Kentucky system focuses on holding schools accountable for specified performance standards in eight domains (e.g. general education and vocational subjects, retention rates, etc.). The difference between a school's actual average performance results in each domain at a baseline period (1991-92) and a standard representing all students scoring at the "proficient" level (in contrast to the "novice" level) was determined. This difference was then divided by ten and each school was evaluated on whether it achieved one-tenth of the difference between its baseline performance and the standard every two years over a 20-year period. In other words, each school is expected to achieve, through continuing annual improvements, a full proficiency level in 20 years. Each biennium, schools are judged on the degree of performance improvement. Schools scoring at least a one-point improvement over the threshold receive substantial financial awards for exceeding their performance targets, while low-performing schools are required to develop improvement plans (Ladd, 1996).

2.7 Guiding British Colleges of Further Education[2]

Colleges of Further Education (FE) in the United Kingdom are independent, self-governing, non-profit organizations which are answerable to the same regulations as regular companies. They are independent providers of training services and they enter contracts with the Government. (On the legal status of these colleges, see box 2.7 in Module 2.)

Although they are independent, the FE colleges are subject to government guidance and control in three ways. First, the colleges are funded and closely controlled by the FE Funding Council (FEFC). The FEFC secures and equips facilities for education for people over the compulsory school age; makes grants, loans or other payments to FE colleges; and ensures that there is a system for assessing and maintaining the quality of educational provision. FEFC contracts with colleges include targets for enrolment with penalty clauses.

Second, while there are no nationally established vocational curricula and no VET awards issued by central or local governments, the FE colleges are licensed to deliver vocational qualifications by the operationally and financially independent Awarding Bodies. These bodies develop, assess and award vocational qualifications and therefore colleges have to satisfy the quality requirements which they impose. The Awarding Bodies have a good deal of independence from the central Government, but the Government does direct national training qualifications through guidance provided to the Awarding Bodies.

Third, Training and Enterprise Councils (TECs), representing private industry and commerce, promote employment and develop local training schemes. TECs respond to directives and procedures issued by the Department for Education and Employment (DFEE). Their purpose is to involve local industry and commerce in the management and implementation of national government policy at local level. Colleges are required to have their draft strategic plans cleared and endorsed by local TECs.

---

[2] Based on Russell, 1997

2.7.1 Organizational and management structure of colleges

FE colleges vary considerably in size. Over two decades most of the once-separate specialized colleges of art and design and building have merged with general colleges and become multi-discipline entities. (Thirty-four agricultural colleges have remained separate entities.) Most colleges have more than half a dozen vocational areas. The title of any particular college is decided by its governors. The names have no legal significance; some are primarily geographic, some are named after famous engineers or scientists, some after local politicians. Some colleges use words like "community" or "technical" to give an emphasis to their purpose. Only the terms "University" or "University College" require permission from central government.

Given the variety of size, discipline and level, and the degree of legal independence, it is no surprise that the variety of internal organizational forms is also very large. Staff are commonly attached to college departments which fall into two main types: curriculum departments or support departments. Most colleges have five to 12 curriculum departments; each department offers a portfolio of programmes leading to specific awards. Most teachers are members of two or three teams within each curriculum department, dealing with curriculum and course development, auditing and monitoring students and ensuring a high level of quality control. Typically, each curriculum department employs the equivalent of 25 to 50 full-time teaching staff and five to ten clerical, administrative or technician support. There is a modest transfer of support between departments. For example, a Social Department may receive some support from a Business Studies Department on the law relating to the management of residential care facilities. Students from any department may receive extra tuition in English language, mathematics or word-processing from a central support unit or department.

Historically, the curriculum departments conducted themselves quite separately and did not make significant use of central staff for marketing or publicity or for curriculum and quality control. That has largely changed over the last decade and all colleges make extensive use of central departments. College principals have created their own internal support structures which resemble the divisions used in other companies. Common functional support departments include: building support, maintenance and cleaning; central student registry; clerical administration; financial services and control; marketing and public relations; management; personnel, staffing and staff development; student services, recruiting, counselling and careers guidance; library, information centres and information technology.

Management boards. FE colleges all have very similar management boards. At the time of initial incorporation, a circular letter of guidance was issued on the drafting of new Articles and Instruments of Government for the colleges. Once established, if the corporation requires any amendment to the legal documents, it must seek approval. Management boards are quite small, usually having between 15 and 20 members. Each board has, in its Articles and Instruments of Association, some indication of the overall structure. Boards typically include ten representatives of employers, two representatives of nearby receiving or supplying educational institutions, two representatives of the local community or local government, the managing director (principal), an elected staff representative and a representative of the local TEC. College principals have almost full operational responsibility and are subject to inspection, audit and quality control. They are controlled in their product-volume and product-range to a very large extent by the purchasers and the financial codes that purchasers construct and use to direct, shape and influence the system. They have financial accountability.

Colleges are operationally controlled by: a senior management team and a college management team, both composed exclusively of appointed managers. In broad terms, a senior management team comprises the top four to six managers, with no head of curriculum department included, and a college management team will be the senior team plus the heads of the curriculum departments (or heads of faculty). Most colleges also have an academic board with some supervisory functions, particularly in curriculum and quality assurance matters. This board is usually fairly large with a broad membership including some elected or representative members numbering from 24 to 40.

The colleges' legal status and procedures have been criticized for detaching colleges from local (as well as national) political control and for their lack of accountability. While there is some justification for these criticisms, there is a code of conduct, issued by the FEFC, for the conduct of management boards. They are still subject to audit by public bodies, and, like all companies, they must file their annual accounts at the Companies Registration Office, where they are available for public inspection.

Staffing and wages. Colleges, as employers, determine how many staff members to hire, the grades and salaries. They are responsible for staff dismissals, redundancies and discipline. Some of these matters are dealt with by collective bargaining. Staff members are either in academic grade posts or support grades. Teachers are graded as lecturers, as senior lecturers or as managers. The support grades are numerous, reflecting the variety of skills employed. Some colleges have experimented with new "instructor grade" staff, who work in direct support of learning but are not as well-qualified or as well-paid as those in teaching grades. Rarely is there any possibility of extra, bonus or performance-related pay. There has been a shift away from full-time permanent to part-time permanent, and from part-time permanent to hourly paid staff. About half the colleges now hire their hourly paid part-time staff through agencies to avoid the accumulation of employment rights. When services in law, building management, payroll management, graphics and so on are required, colleges hire experts from specialist firms, as most commercial enterprises do.

2.7.2 Management of operations

Planning. Little is done at national level to analyse the demand for training services. VET is treated as only one of many alternative routes for young people into the workforce and providers are allowed to compete in the market for clients. Additionally, little is done at national level to analyse vocational areas. FE colleges supply the FEFC with massive quantities of statistical data, but these do not steer FEFC policy in any significant way. Instead, planning is encouraged only for colleges. Only at this level, it is thought, can FE colleges respond in any significant way to market forces in education and training. Industrial and commercial firms will respond to their own needs by training, recruiting and informing public colleges and training agencies of their needs. Colleges will fill the gaps, or, to be more precise, their students will do this if they receive the right market information.

Each college is required by the FEFC to develop a strategic plan covering the next three years and an operational business plan covering one year. These plans are based on a review of the local labour, education and training markets. Each vocational programme area should gather exit and progression data to keep all concerned aware of the destination of trainees. This information can be used in careers guidance as well as in the production of college strategic plans.

The college planning cycle is influenced by the planning framework of the FEFC. The FEFC has reserved its right to earmark funding or otherwise attach conditions to secure particular objectives. The major planning indicators are overall student numbers, students per programme and the funds required to implement those programmes (see box 4.4 in Module 4).

The Government has established a National Advisory Council for Education and Training Targets. This is a small group of industrialists and educationalists with a small secretariat. Its main task is to set and update training targets, looking ahead over the period of college strategic plans (see box 4.11 in Module 4). The targets do not relate directly to specific vocational qualifications. The genuine desire for competition is reflected in the fact that all types of qualification are recognized as valuable. Because the Government believes that the market must operate at local level, the achievement of these national targets is difficult to monitor. Nevertheless, local TECs are asked to gather as much data as they can

Module 6. Guiding training providers

on these issues and report to the Government on the extent of local success in moving towards the targets. Moreover, schools and colleges are required to report to the Government on examination results and this information is readily available to all in the market place.

Funding. Colleges decide how much revenue they think they can successfully acquire for the coming year and how to spend it. They cannot fall back on public authorities if they experience financial difficulty; they are subject to bankruptcy like other corporations. (There are some important funding differences between FE colleges and other private companies, however; see box 2.7 in Module 2.) They must either meet FEFC requirements for management and operational procedures or risk losing public funding. The FEFC funding mechanisms thus influence college planning. Colleges bid for funding for their proposed number of students within courses or categories of courses. Annual bids are set against tariffs which establish the number of funding units available for each course or type of course. The tariffs reflect the different cost of various programmes. Though colleges are free to undertake any work they can finance, regardless of the source, the FEFC remains the dominant source of finance for most colleges, supplying between 50 and 80 per cent or all income. The relative importance of other sources varies enormously from college to college, as do fees paid by students (or their employers).

2.7.3 Monitoring systems

Assessment framework. The colleges are closely monitored and inspected by the FEFC inspectorate. They are now also required to have an internal self-assessment (quality control) system. In the FE sector three levels of quality control are recognized: (1) mechanisms within colleges for maintaining and enhancing quality of provision; (2) examinations and validation implemented by external bodies such as the National Council for Vocational Qualifications; and (3) independent external assessments of the quality of teaching and the standards achieved by students. For external assessments the FEFC relies on performance indicators and inspections. Each of the nine regions has a team of between five and nine trained, full-time inspectors and a senior inspector who oversees their work. Part-time inspectors are also engaged. Most senior inspectors have national responsibility for at least one major curriculum area. A full-time inspector is assigned to each college (FEFC, 1993).

The following principles are used:
- All inspections are planned in consultation with the college and reflect the college pattern of provision.

- College objectives and criteria for success set the context for inspection.
- Inspections involve direct observation of curriculum delivery, monitoring of college performance against the commitments in the national charter for FE and the college individual charter, and evaluation of college strategies for enhancing the quality of provision.
- The inspection cycle for each college covers four years, during which three types of inspection are executed: (1) by the college inspector assigned; (2) by specialist inspectors concentrating on particular areas of curriculum; and (3) by teams who clarify and update information on a quarterly basis. The third type of inspection leads to published reports.

Four types of documentary evidence set the context for inspection:

- the college charter and mission statement, its strategic plans and annual operating plans;
- the college's standard set of performance indicators as agreed between the FEFC and the sector, together with any internal performance indicators used by college staff to help assess the extent to which they are achieving the targets which they set for themselves;
- reports from examining, validating and accrediting bodies and the college response to those reports; and
- the findings of the college's own quality assurance procedures.

Assessment guidelines. Colleges are assessed according to a five-point scale, grade 1 indicating the highest level of training. Assessment grades are assigned to each major curriculum area which is inspected. In addition, in the quarterly published reports, grades are assigned for responsiveness and range of provision, governance and management, student recruitment, guidance and support, quality assurance, and resource utilization. Grades of responsiveness and range of provision reflect college activities in relation to FEFC targets, the interaction between schools and the community, and between schools and industry, the variety of programmes offered in response to potential client demand, and equity of access. Management grades measure the institutions' own internal targets and success criteria; communication and accountability; planning, monitoring and support procedures; resource allocation and deployment; retention rates; and trainee destinations on graduation.

Performance indicators. The following college performance indicators have been set (FEFC, 1994b):

- *Achievement of funding targets* – indications of college effectiveness in achieving strategic plans. This ratio is calculated as the number of FEFC-

Module 6. Guiding training providers

funded units earned by a college during the college year as a percentage of its target funding units for that year.
- *Student enrolment trends* – indications of responsiveness. This is calculated as a percentage change in enrolments compared with the previous college year (broken down by full-time and part-time enrolments).
- *Student continuation* – indications of programme responsiveness. This measure is calculated as a percentage of those students who, having enrolled on a learning programme of at least one year's duration, continue to attend in the third trimester of the college year (broken down by full-time and part-time enrolments).
- *Learning goals and qualifications* – indications of student achievement. This measure is calculated as: (1) a percentage of the number of students completing their learning programmes (achieving primary learning goals, as specified in student learning agreements with colleges); and (2) a percentage of the total number of qualification aims for which students have completed their learning programme (the number of qualification aims achieved is equated with the number of training credits or modules achieved).
- *Attainment of National Vocational Qualifications (NVQs) or equivalent* – indications of a college's contribution to national education and training targets. This measure is calculated as a percentage change from the previous year.
- *Average level of funding* – indications of cost efficiency as measured by the average funding per unit. This measure is calculated as the amount of recurrent funding from the FEFC for the college year divided by the total number of units earned by the college in FEFC-funded activity.

Self-assessment. The FEFC's plans for developing the system include expanding college responsibility for assessing and ensuring the quality of training. A self-assessment system has the advantage of being permanently in place; assessment can be ongoing rather than an event that occurs every four years. College self-assessments are to be subject to validation by the external inspectors; periodic inspections will continue, but they will be guided by the self-assessment report. Inspectors are also being asked to construct national sample reports on aspects of curriculum development, management and other procedures, as well as transnational studies. The categories for self-assessment have been expanded and increased. They now cover the college mission, teaching and learning, student achievements, curriculum content, organization and management, support for students, resources, and quality assurance. Each of these main categories has been given more precise targets and, most importantly, the types of "indicative evidence" are clearly spelled out. The whole process is a very demanding addition to college quality assurance systems. The inspectors assigned to a college monitor the response to the issues raised in assessment reports.

Evaluation by Awarding Bodies. Colleges are licensed to award qualifications by the national Awarding Bodies, which also require good systems of internal quality control of teaching and training. Virtually all the Awarding Bodies make regular visits to colleges. They expect to see that each curriculum, course and programme area is managed by small groups of teachers acting as a team. They themselves usually expect to see, inspect and approve: samples of students' work; records of all work undertaken by students and assessed in the college, of internal verification of the assessment of student work, of team meetings to manage the courses, and of qualifications of staff involved in assessment; and basic data on entry, leaving and student progression.

BIBLIOGRAPHY

Adams, J.D. 1986. *Transforming leadership: From vision to results* (Alexandria, Virginia, Miles River).

Australian National Training Authority. 1994. *Towards a skilled Australia: A national strategy for vocational education and training* (Brisbane, Australian National Training Authority).

—. 1995a. *Directions and resource allocations for 1996*, Report to the Ministerial Council (Brisbane, Australian National Training Authority).

—. 1995b. *Guidelines for the development of 1996 state training profiles* (Brisbane, Australian National Training Authority).

—. 1995c. *Guide to training priorities of national industry training bodies, 1995-1997* (Brisbane, Australian National Training Authority).

Banner, D.K.; Gagné, T.E. 1995. *Designing effective organization* (London, Sage Publications).

Bas, D. 1994. "The French system", in Gasskov, 1994.

Benedek, A. 1997. *The Labour Market Fund. Ministry of Labour, Hungary*, International Conference on Employment and Training Funds (Antalya, Turkey, World Bank).

Bennell, P. 1994. *Improving the performance of the public sector in LDCs: New approaches to human resource planning and management*, Occasional Paper No. 25 (Geneva, ILO).

Blanpain, R.; Engels, C.; Pellegrini, C. (eds.). 1994. *Contractual policies concerning continued vocational training in the European Community Member States* (Leuven, Peeters Press).

Boediono, W.; McMahon, W.; Adams, D. (eds.). 1992. *Education, economic and social development: Second 25-Year Development Plan and Sixth 5-Year Development Plan Background Papers and Goals* (Jakarta, Indonesia, Ministry of Education and Culture).

Bulgarelli, A.; Giovine, M. 1994. *Decentralization of vocational training in Italy*, Training Policy Study No.10 (Geneva, ILO).

Burgess, P. (ed.). 1993. *Training and development: European management guides* (London, Incomes Data Services and Institute of Personnel Management).

Carnoy, M. 1993. *Methodological guidelines for measuring the equity effects of training policies and programmes*, Paper for the Workshop on New Trends in Training Policy (Geneva, ILO).

—. 1994. "Rates of return to education", in Husén and Postlethwaite, 1994.

Chandler, A.D., Jr. 1962. *Strategy and structure* (Cambridge, Massachusetts, Massachusetts Institute of Technology Press).

Commonwealth Roundtable. 1992. *Administrative structures and reforms*, Proceedings of a Commonwealth Roundtable held in Sydney, Australia, February (London, Commonwealth Secretariat).

Cope, G.H. 1989. "Budgeting methods for public programmes", in Perry, 1989.

Corvalán-Vásquez, O. 1994. "Income tax rebate incentive in Chile", in Gasskov, 1994.

de Moura Castro, C.; Alfthan, T. 1992. *Five training models.* Occasional Paper No. 9 (Geneva, ILO).

Danish Ministry of Education. 1994. *Danish youth education: Problems and achievements*, Report to the OECD (Copenhagen, Ministry of Education).

Department for Education and Employment (DFEE). 1995a. *Labour market information for Further Education Colleges: A handbook for practitioners* (London, DFEE).

—. 1995b. *Competitiveness White Paper* (London, DFEE), 22 May.

Dougherty, C. 1988. "Occupational training maps: What are they and why are they indispensable?", in *International Review of Education*, Vol. 34.

—. 1990. *Education and skill development: Planning issues*, Regional seminar on technical and vocational education and training (Manila, Asian Development Bank and World Bank).

Ducci, M.A. 1991. *Financing of vocational training in Latin America*, Discussion Paper No. 73 (Geneva, ILO).

Elliot, R.F. 1996. *Pay reform in the public service: Initial impact on pay dispersion in Australia, Sweden and the United Kingdom*, Public Management Occasional Paper No. 10 (Paris, OECD).

Espinoza, E.M. 1994. *Vocational training in Chile: A decentralized and market oriented system*, Training Policy Studies Paper No. 8 (Geneva, ILO).

Fairley, J. 1994. "Market forces in publicly-funded training in the United Kingdom", in Gasskov, 1994.

Fairley J.; McArthur A. 1999. *Government intervention into the private financing of education and training in Scotland*, unpublished background paper (Geneva, ILO).

Ferrari, S.; Lankaster, D.F. 1992. *Management of training institutions* (Turin, International Centre for Advanced Technical and Vocational Training/ILO).

Fluitman, F. 1997. *Training policy analysis. A methodology: A set of training modules* (Geneva, ILO).

Fortin, Y. 1996. "Autonomy, responsibility and control: The case of central government agencies in Sweden", in OECD, 1996.

Further Education Funding Council (FEFC). 1993. *Assessing achievement*, Circular 93/28 (London, FEFC).

—. 1994a. *College strategic plans*, Circular 94/30 (London, FEFC).

—. 1994b. *Measuring achievement*, Circular 94/31 (London, FEFC).

—. 1995. *College strategic plans 1995-96 and beyond*, Circular 95/02 (London, FEFC).

Further Education Unit. 1992. *Vocational education and training in Europe: A four-country study in four employment sectors* (London, Further Education Unit).

Bibliography

Galbraith, J. 1976. "Environmental and technological determinants of organizational design", in Lorsch and Lawrence, 1976.

Gasskov, V. (ed.). 1994. *Alternative schemes of financing training* (Geneva, ILO).

—. 1996. *Financing vocational education and training*, Report for the European Training Foundation (Turin, ILO).

Geers, F. 1996. *VET management in Belgium*, unpublished background paper (Geneva, ILO).

—. 1999. *Government intervention into private financing of training*, unpublished background paper (Geneva, ILO).

Godfrey M. 1993. *Training and equity: A minimalist approach to training*, Workshop on new trends in training policy (Geneva, ILO).

—. 1994. "Planning for vocational education, training and employment: A minimalist approach", in Richards and Amjad, 1994.

—. 1996. *New approaches to employment planning*, Employment Paper No. 5 (Geneva, ILO).

Goodman, P.S.; Penning, J.M. 1977. *New perspectives on organizational effectiveness* (San Francisco, California, Jossey-Bass).

Gordon, J.; Parkes, D. 1993. *Strategies for VET in Europe—The project report: A feasibility study* (Paris, European Institute of Education and Social Policy).

Groszyk, W. 1996. "Implementation of the Government Performance and Results Act of 1993", in OECD, 1996.

Grubb W.N.; Ryan P. 1999. *Plain talk on the field of dreams. The roles of evaluation in vocational education and training* (Geneva, ILO).

Hamada, M. 1994. "Employment insurance-based financing of TVET in Japan", in Gasskov, 1994.

Herschbach, D. 1994. "Decentralized public funding of vocational education in the United States", in Gasskov, 1994.

—. 1995. *VET management in the United States*, unpublished background paper (Geneva, ILO).

Hövels, B.; Meijer, K. 1994. *Structures of vocational education and training (VET) and the match between education and work: An international comparison* (Tilburg University, Netherlands, Tilburg Institute for Social Security Research, TISSER-OSA).

Hunn, D.K. 1994. "Measuring performance and policy advice: A New Zealand perspective", in OECD, 1994b.

Hunting, G.; Godfrey, M. 1996. *System-wide evaluation of TVET: Report on evaluation* (Manila, TESDA).

Husén, T.; Postlethwaite, T.N. (eds.). 1994. *The international encyclopaedia of education* (Oxford, Pergamon, 2nd ed.).

ILO. 1996. *Combating unemployment and exclusion: Issues and policy options*, Contribution to the G7 Employment Conference, Lille (Geneva, ILO).

Irwin, T. 1996. "An analysis of New Zealand's new system of public-sector management", in OECD, 1996.

Kakabadse, A.P.; Brovetto, P.R.; Holzer, R. (eds.). 1988. *Management development and the public sector* (Avebury, United Kingdom, Gower Publishing Co.).

Khandwalla, P.N. 1977. *The design of organizations* (New York, Harcourt Brace Jovanovich).

King, K. 1994. "Technical and vocational education and training", in Husén and Postlethwaite, 1994.

Kirsch, J-L. 1994. *Structures of vocational education and training and the match between education and work: An international comparison* (Paris, National Report/OSA publication).

Kubr, M. 1982. *Managing a management development institution*, Management Development Series No. 18 (Geneva, ILO).

Ladd, H.F. (ed.). 1996. *Holding schools accountable: Performance-based reform in education* (Washington, DC, Brookings Institution).

Lafond, A. 1997. *Management of the French lycée*, unpublished background paper (Geneva, ILO).

Leite, E.M. 1995. *VET management in Brazil*, unpublished background paper (Geneva, ILO).

Lorsch, J.; Lawrence, P. (eds.). 1976. *Studies in organization design* (Homewood, Ill., Richard Irwin).

Madigan, K. 1998. "A kink in the profits pipeline", in *Business Week*, 2 March.

Man Tak Au-yeung. 1996. *Financing training in Hong Kong*, Paper for the APSED/ILO/Japan Regional Seminar, Chiba, Japan.

McCaffery, J.L. 1989. "Strategies for achieving budgetary goals", in Perry, 1989.

Merriden, T. 1997. "Vacancies in the skills department", in *Management Today*, May.

Middleton, J.; Ziderman, A.; Van Adams, A. 1993. *Skills for productivity: Vocational education and training in developing countries* (Oxford, Oxford University Press).

Mintzberg, H. 1979. *The structuring of organizations* (Englewood Cliffs, New Jersey, Prentice Hall).

Mitchell, A. 1998. *Strategic planning partnerships between the state and enterprises*, Employment and Training Papers. No. 19. (Geneva, ILO)

Monash University; Syntec Economic Services. 1995. *Guide to growth: Australia's 112 industries ranked and projected* (Melbourne, Monash University and Syntec Economic Services).

Muneer, M. 1995. *VET management in Pakistan*, unpublished background paper (Geneva, ILO).

Naschold, F. 1995. *The modernization of the public sector in Europe: A comparative perspective on the Scandinavian experience* (Helsinki, Finnish Ministry of Labour).

Netherlands Ministry of Education and Science. 1993. *Changing role of vocational and technical education and training*, Report to the OECD on the VOTEC project (The Hague, Netherlands).

Nielsen, S.P. 1995. *VET management in Denmark*, unpublished background paper (Geneva, ILO).

Noonan, R.; Söderberg, C. 1994. "From public training agency to corporation in Sweden", in Gasskov, 1994.

Organisation for Economic Co-operation and Development (OECD). 1989. *Measuring performance and allocating resources*, Public Management Studies No. 5 (Paris, OECD).

—. 1993. *Managing with market-type mechanisms* (Paris, OECD).

—. 1994a. *Performance measurement and results-oriented management*, Public Management Occasional Papers No. 3. (Paris, OECD).

—. 1994b. *Performance measurement in government: Issues and illustrations*, Public Management Occasional Papers No. 5 (Paris, OECD).

—. 1995. *Budgeting for results*. Perspectives on public expenditure management (Paris, PUMA, OECD).

—. 1996. *Performance management in government: Contemporary illustration*, Public Management Occasional Papers No. 9 (Paris, OECD).

Office of Training and Further Education. 1996. *OTFE mission* (Melbourne, Victoria)

Oman, R.C.; Damours, S.L.; Smith,T.A.; Uscher, A.R. 1992. *Management analysis in public organizations: History, concepts and techniques* (New York, Quorum Books).

Osborne, D.; Gaebler, T. 1992. *Reinventing government: How the entrepreneurial spirit is transforming the public sector* (New York, Penguin Books).

Pack, H. 1987. *Productivity, technology and industrial development: A case study in textiles* (New York, Oxford University Press for World Bank).

Park, Y. 1999. *Government interventions into private financing of training*, unpublished background paper (Geneva, ILO).

Perry, J.L. (ed.). 1989. *Handbook of public administration* (San Francisco, California, Jossey-Bass).

Peters, T.J.; Waterman, R.H., Jr. 1982. *In search of excellence: Lessons from America's best-run companies* (New York, Harper and Row).

Pfeffer, J.; Salancik, G. 1978. *The external control of organizations* (New York, Harper and Row).

Preddey, G. 1996. "Report: Comprehensive reform: The case of New Zealand", in *Human Resource Sector Professional Development* (Washington, DC, World Bank), January.

Preddey G.; Doyle, J. 1998. *Performance management and budgeting for results in the VET sector of New Zealand*, unpublished background paper (Geneva, ILO).

Psacharopoulos, G. 1994. "Returns to investment in education: A global update", in *World Development* (Elmsford, New York), Vol. 22, No. 9.

—; Woodhall, M. 1985. *Education for development: An analysis of investment choices* (Oxford, Oxford University Press and World Bank).

Richards, P.; Amjad, R. (eds.). 1994. *New approaches to manpower planning and analysis* (Geneva, ILO).

Richter, L. 1986. *Training needs: Assessment and monitoring* (Geneva, ILO).

Robbins, S.P. 1987. *Organization theory: Structure, design and applications* (Englewood Cliffs, New Jersey, Prentice Hall, 2nd ed.).

Russell, R. 1995. *VET management in Britain*, unpublished background paper (Geneva, ILO).

—. 1997. *Management of the provision for vocational education and training in England*, unpublished background paper (Geneva, ILO).

Shin, M.H. 1995. *VET management in the Republic of Korea*, unpublished background paper (Geneva, ILO).

Simonics, I. 1996. *Financing VET in Hungary*, unpublished background paper (Geneva, ILO).

Standaert, R. 1993. "Technical rationality in education management: A survey covering England, France and Germany", in *European Journal of Education*, Vol. 28, No. 2.

State Training Board of Victoria. 1995. *Trends in vocational education and training, Supplement to Strategic directions for vocational education and training* (Melbourne, Australia, State Training Board of Victoria).

Technical Education and Skills Authority (TESDA). 1995. *TVET Sector Study Series*, No. 8 (Manila, TESDA).

Thiele, P. 1994. "Financing the German dual system", in Gasskov, 1994.

Thompson, J.D. 1967. *Organization in action* (New York, McGraw-Hill).

United Nations Department for Development Support and Management Services. 1993. *Improving public policy analysis: Study material for top executives* (New York, UN).

United Nations Educational, Scientific and Cultural Organization (UNESCO). 1970. *Administrative problems of education planning* (Paris, UNESCO).

United States Social Security Administration. 1995. *Social security programs throughout the world – 1995*, Publication No. 13-11805, Research Report No. 64 (Washington, DC, SSA).

Veeken, N. 1999. *Industrial social funds in the Netherlands*, unpublished background paper (Geneva, ILO).

Willems, J-P. 1994. *Vocational education and training in France* (Berlin, CEDEFOP).

—. 1995. *VET management in France*, unpublished background paper (Geneva, ILO).

Wilson, D. 1996. *VET management in Canada*, unpublished background paper (Geneva, ILO).

Woodward, J. 1958. *Management and technology* (London, Her Majesty's Stationery Office).

World Bank. 1996. "Philippines" in *Education financing and social equity: A reform agenda* (Washington, DC, World Bank).

—. 1997. *International Conference on Employment and Training Funds* (Antalya, Turkey, World Bank).

Key Indicators of the Labour Market 1999 (KILM)

This valuable, wide-ranging reference tool meets the ever-increasing demand for timely, accurate and accessible information on the rapidly changing world of work. *Key Indicators of the Labour Market* (KILM) provides the general reader, as well as the expert, with concise explanations and analysis of the data on the world`s labour markets.

Harvesting vast information from international data repositories as well as regional and national statistical sources, this important reference offers data on a broad range of countries for the years 1980 and 1990, and all available subsequent years. The volume employs an expanded, up-to-date range of 18 key labour market indicators allowing researchers to compare and contrast between countries and within regions across time. Using statistical data on the labour force, employment, unemployment, underemployment, educational attainment of the workforce, wages and compensation, productivity and labour costs, and poverty and income distribution as market indicators, the volume enables readers to access the most current information available.

In the process, KILM includes rich and varied overviews of topics such as employment to population ratios, hours of work, youth unemployment, wages in manufacturing, and labour productivity and costs. By highlighting multiple labour market indicators, this comprehensive resource sheds light on equity and other job concerns as well.

KILM is available in two formats – standard print version and CD-ROM. The CD-ROM's interactive design allows users to customize their searches by any combination of indicator, country, year, data inputs, and more. Its easy-to-use format makes searching for relevant information quick and simple.

The CD-ROM version includes the *Key Indicators of the Labour Market, Country Profiles, 1999 Edition*, a quick reference for users.

ISBN 92-2-110834-1 CD-ROM   92-2-110833-1 book

1999   600 pp, A4, softcover
Price for either the CD-ROM or the book: Sw.fr 140, US$99.95, £59.95
Price for the set (CD-ROM + book): Sw.fr. 250, US$180, £110

The roles of evaluation for vocational education and training : Plain talk on the field of dreams

W. Norton Grubb and Paul Ryan

The authors of this book work from the premise that some plain talk is needed about the subject of evaluation in vocational education and training. After providing substantive background on the conceptual issues, the book focuses on the why and how of evaluation before presenting and judging the results of available evaluations. The discussion takes in the use and abuse of available evaluation results in policy-making and the implications for evaluation of recent trends and issues in VET such as decentralization, the declining role for the State, the shift towards work-based learning and the continued concern for meeting equity concerns through vocational education and training.

ISBN 92-2-110855-4

1999   179 pp., softcover
30 Swiss francs, US$18.95, £12.95

World Employment Report 1998–99
Employability in the global economy : How training matters

The *World Employment Report 1998–99* reviews the global employment situation and examines how countries in different circumstances and stages of development can develop the best training strategy and flexible and responsive training systems to address these far-reaching changes. The report presents a close analysis of training systems worldwide and an examination of training strategies for increasing national competitiveness, improving the efficiency of enterprises and promoting employment growth. It critically examines policies and targeted programmes for improving women's employment opportunities and enhancing the skills and employablility of Informal sector workers and members of vunerable groups (especially at-risk youth, long-term unemployed, older displaced workers and workers with disabilities). The report suggests specific policy reforms for making training more efficient and effective. Given the rapid and continuous pace of change in the demand for new skill, the report concludes that training and lifelong learning need to be given the higher priority. The best results from enhancing the education and skill levels of the workforce are achieved in an overall growth-promoting environment and when trainng decisions are taken in close consultations between government, employers and workers.

The *World Employment Report 1998–99* is the third in a series of ILO reports which offer an international perspective on current employment issues.

ISBN 92-2-110827-9

1998   271 pp., softcover
45 Sw.frs; US$34.95; £19.95